# The J. Frank Norris I Have Known For 34 years

by

Dr. Louis Entzminger

www.solidchristianbooks.com

2015

# Contents

- ABOUT THE AUTHOR... ........ 7
- FOREWORD ............ 8
- INTRODUCTION ............ 9
- PREFACE ............ 11
- From the Most Despised and Defeated Preacher to the Pastor of the World's Largest Membership............ 19
- PROLOGUE ............ 21
- SECTION I ............ 34
  - CHAPTER I............ 34
  - CHAPTER II............ 40
  - CHAPTER III............ 43
  - CHAPTER IV............ 48
  - CHAPTER V............ 55
  - CHAPTER VI............ 57
  - CHAPTER VII............ 61
  - CHAPTER VIII............ 63
- SECTION II ............ 67
  - CHAPTER I............ 67
  - CHAPTER II............ 94
  - CHAPTER III............ 98
  - CHAPTER IV............ 101
  - CHAPTER V............ 104
  - CHAPTER VI............ 106
  - CHAPTER VII............ 108
  - CHAPTER VIII............ 112
  - CHAPTER IX............ 116
  - CHAPTER X............ 118
  - CHAPTER XI............ 126
  - CHAPTER XII............ 135
  - CHAPTER XIII............ 137

- CHAPTER XIV .................................................................. 142
- CHAPTER XV ................................................................... 150
- CHAPTER XVI .................................................................. 152
- SECTION III ...................................................................... 158
  - CHAPTER I ...................................................................... 158
  - CHAPTER II ..................................................................... 166
  - CHAPTER III .................................................................... 170
  - CHAPTER IV .................................................................... 176
  - CHAPTER V ..................................................................... 180
  - CHAPTER VI .................................................................... 186
  - CHAPTER VII ................................................................... 190
  - CHAPTER VIII .................................................................. 196
  - CHAPTER IX .................................................................... 199
  - CHAPTER X ..................................................................... 201
  - CHAPTER XI .................................................................... 205
  - CHAPTER XII ................................................................... 231
  - CHAPTER XIII .................................................................. 233
  - CHAPTER XIV .................................................................. 241
  - CHAPTER XV ................................................................... 243
- SECTION IV ...................................................................... 247
  - CHAPTER I ...................................................................... 247
  - CHAPTER II ..................................................................... 251
  - CHAPTER III .................................................................... 255
  - CHAPTER IV .................................................................... 261
  - CHAPTER V ..................................................................... 271
  - CHAPTER VI .................................................................... 273
  - CHAPTER VII ................................................................... 277
  - CHAPTER VIII .................................................................. 298
  - CHAPTER IX .................................................................... 304
  - CHAPTER X ..................................................................... 317

CHAPTER XI ........................................................................ 325
CHAPTER XII ....................................................................... 337
Dr. Norris' Letter To President Truman ............................... 348

"What is needed is a school that teaches the whole English Bible. What is needed is a school that will take men from the engine cab, from between the plowshares and teach them the Bible. What is needed is a school that is free from modernism. What is needed is a school that will teach a man how to go out with the Bible under his arms, faith in his heart, and in the power of the Holy Spirit begin in a vacant lot and build a church to the glory of God."

— J. Frank Norris

*THIS BOOK IS IN FOUR GENERAL DIVISIONS:*

I

Personal Early Life, Education and Family

II

Tragic Experiences —

Conflicts With Mayors, Governors, Courts

III

Denominational Controversies On Evolution,

Ecclesiasticism, Modernism and Communism

IV

Scriptural Methods Used In Building The World's

Two Greatest Sunday Schools and Churches

# ABOUT THE AUTHOR...

Dr. Louis Entzminger was a giant among Giants... He excelled in many areas and many of his contemporaries considered him to be the best in building aggressive, soulwinning Sunday Schools and in Teaching God's Word.

In 1949 a careful survey of the 25 largest Sunday Schools on the North American continent revealed that 23 of them had Dr. Louis Entzminger to come and conduct an enlargement campaign and establish his Sunday School system in them. Among those churches and pastors were – 1st Baptist Church, Fort Worth, Dr. J. Frank Norris; Temple Baptist Church, Detroit, G. W. Vick; 1st Baptist Church of Minneapolis, Dr. W. B. Riley; Moody Church of Chicago, W. P. Philpot; Jarvis Street Baptist Church, Toronto, Canada, T. T. Shields; Broadway Baptist of Knoxville, Tennessee, Herschel Ford.

Dr. Entzminger was Dean of the Bible Baptist Seminary of Fort Worth, Texas and was considered by many to be the greatest Bible teacher of his day. The simple style which he had in bringing to the surface the rich nuggets from God's Holy Word still can be enjoyed today in the many books which Dr. Entzminger left behind.

# FOREWORD

by Dr. Raymond Barber Pastor of Worth Baptist Church, Fort Worth, Texas President of Independent Baptist Fellowship International

This "man among men" did as much for Baptists as any man in his generation, and paved the way for thousands of Bible-believing Baptists to identify themselves as a spiritual entity to be reckoned with, known as independent, fundamental Baptists.

His personal contacts included interviews with such notables as priests, prime ministers, popes, and presidents. He spoke the language of the commoner and the king, feeling equally at ease with both. In the archives are autographed pictures of Norris and Churchill together with letters from Truman and Speaker Rayburn. Whether he was in the office of the Grand Mufti of Jerusalem, the Pope in Rome, or the Prime Minister in London, he was capable of leading the conversation in political and religious topics of international interest. Whether he was preaching in an open air meeting in Detroit or the spacious Spurgeon's Tabernacle in London, he spoke with the same clarion voice, and preached the same glorious gospel. Whether he stood in a courtroom or a state legislation hall, he was listened to as a man who knew his subject and sensed the needs of his audience.

# INTRODUCTION

## By Bruce Cummins, Pastor Massillon Baptist Temple, Massillon, OH

My first few days in Fort Worth, Texas, the first time I met Dr. J. Frank Norris, and the first time I heard him preach, all made a lasting impression upon my life to say the least.

With great anticipation I looked forward to that first service in the First Baptist Church, and to hearing Dr. Norris preach.

The morning service – thousands of people – great music by the choir, and a congregation that could make the rafters ring with their singing.

Then, that tall, slim Texan stepped to the pulpit to preach. He wore a steel grey suit that matched his steel grey eyes—he opened his Bible, read the text, and PREACHED! Dr. J. Frank Norris was an imposing figure, and a great pulpiteer.

He thrilled and challenged our hearts as he spoke in College Chapel services, and as he expounded the Word in his Sunday sermons from the pulpit of the First Baptist Church.

We left that school with the words of Dr. J. Frank Norris ringing in our ears: "You can go anywhere in these United States, or the world, with nothing but faith in God, and this old Bible under your arm, and build a Church for the glory of God!" We had no better sense than to believe it!

Dr. Norris challenged our hearts to stand for God and right, no matter what! He told of his fight against modernism in the pulpits and in the schools of the Southern Baptist Convention – even in his own alma mater, Baylor University. He challenged them doctrinally, and on their questioning the Word of God. One of his great battles was concerning the (false) Theory of Evolution.

This preacher, who started out in life as an invalid, then weak, sickly, and frail; sometimes in his early ministry only able to speak for fifteen or twenty minutes at a time, is surely an evidence of God's Grace and enabling power!

Dr. J. Frank Norris was, to state it quite mildly, an unusual man.

He was a man with strong will, and great energy and drive. He was a man of great and unusual preaching ability. He was a diligent personal soulwinner. He was a great friend to young preachers.

Dr. J. Frank Norris was a man marvelously blessed and greatly used of God! I am so glad I knew him personally, and was permitted to sit at his feet, and hear him preach the Word.

Few men have so impressed my life and helped form my ministry as has Dr. J. Frank Norris.

I thank God for his influence and his memory.

# PREFACE

## To Be Read

In writing this biographical sketch of Dr. Norris, I am not trying to write from the commonly accepted point of a real biography.

If I were writing about the average great man it would be an easy matter to trace his life from his ancestry and birth to its end.

But I doubt if there ever was a man in the Christian world since the apostolic days where there is such diversity and variety of experiences and of service.

Then, too, his life necessarily must be presented from many angles, so instead of following the usual lines in writing this biographical sketch; I have used materials from different sources.

For instance, I quoted several chapters from one of Dr. Norris' former publications, "Inside the Cup." These former chapters in the new setting make a very vital part of his life's ministry.

In the next place, I use several of his sermons and a number of conclusions from sermons formerly stenographically reported and many of them published in his paper, or from former publications of his. These sermons and portions of sermons seep to me to present an angle of his ministry that could not otherwise be presented.

I have also asked Mr. G. B. Vick for the use of several articles he has written about Dr. Norris at different times, which I consider valuable for the purposes of this work. It is certainly not my purpose to flatter when I say that Mr. Vick is the greatest layman in Christian service I have ever known. His life's work is a greater testimony to that fact than any poor words of mine. He became associated with Dr. Norris when a mere lad and his intimate association with him enables him to speak about these things that will give the reader an important angle to the diversity of Dr. Norris' character and work.

I have had to get Dr. Norris' assistance on many things presented to confirm things that I knew and yet not in every detail as I wanted to present them. There are some of the stories about incidents and experiences in his life, which I take the privilege of presenting, that might be open to criticism, but when you are writing about a man who has been hounded by the bloodhounds of hell; who has been maligned and slandered, and in many instances by good men whose minds were prejudiced against him, and unjustly so; when the great denominational leaders, many of them truly good men, sought for some reason or other to destroy his life's work; when the lowest dives and gangsters of the underworld have been used to malign his character and wreck his ministry, I feel that the readers of this volume are entitled to know some of these really tragic things that took place in connection with his long and varied ministry.

There is necessarily some repetition but not without purpose. In certain great addresses made by Dr. Norris, which I have used, he uses, in some instances, the same incidents and experiences. To cut these out in the connection in which they are used would mutilate the address and the reader would thereby lose the true perspective or the purpose of the address itself.

I may be criticized for some things I say about some great and good men who have contacted Dr. Norris' life from different angles. Far be it from me to reflect on anybody's good name but these different men are so interwoven with Dr. Norris' experiences and ministry that it would be almost impossible to present to the reader many of the things vital to a true presentation of this story without these personal references.

As to the facts recorded in this work, many of them I did not personally observe but the facts, as I present them, have been confirmed by those who did and in some instances by those who, in former years, were greatly prejudiced against Dr. Norris.

Most of these great addresses and sermons I heard. Most of these experiences related in this book were occurrences in his life while I was personally associated with him the major part of the last 34 years.

My prayer is that in presenting this work God will use it for the encouragement of multiplied thousands of faithful ministers who know the difficulties, the hardships, the sufferings of a minister of the gospel who is true to the Word of God, and I believe the name of our Lord and Saviour Jesus Christ will be honored and glorified through the influence of these facts in the life of the most unusual man of all my acquaintance and of all my knowledge in Christian history.

The Author and Editor,

LOUIS ENTZMINGER

LaGuardia Field, New York, Aug. 19, 1947 – Reading from left to right, Messrs. G.B. Vick, Temple Baptist Church, Detroit; J. Frank Norris, Frist Baptist Church, Fort Worth, and Temple Baptist Church, Detroit, Luther C. Peak, Central Baptist Church, Dallas; and Wendell Zemmerman, Kansas City Baptist Temple, Kansas City, as the boarded American Overseas Airlines Flagship "Norway" for Europe and the Middle East. They will visit London, Rome, Jerusalem, Palestine, Egypt, Babylon and Greece.

Dr. Louis Entzminger, the author of this book. Founder of the Bible Baptist Seminary, and a member of the faculty – Professor of Old Testament Interpretation and New Testament Church.

Mr. G.B. Vick, Superintendent of the Temple Baptist Church, Detroit, Michigan, and President of the World Fundamental Baptist Missionary Fellowship.

Mr. Vick started his religious work in the First Baptist Church, Fort Worth, Texas 23 years ago.

Dr. J. Frank Norris, pastor First Baptist Church, Fort Worth and Temple Baptist Church, Detroit, President of the Bible Baptist Seminary and editor of The Fundamentalist.

40.000 listening to Dr. J. Frank Norris in Great Revival in Detroit

# From the Most Despised and Defeated Preacher to the Pastor of the World's Largest Membership

What is the secret of this, the most remarkable success in the history of modern times?

**Dr. J. Frank Norris, Pastor of First Baptist Church, Fort Worth, and Temple Baptist Church, Detroit... Following Report of 13 Years' Joint Pastorate:**

Over 25,000 additions to both churches.

Over three million, one hundred fifty thousand dollars raised for all purposes.

Three million three hundred thousand dollars of real estate and buildings of both churches.

Eighteen million, six hundred seventy thousand copies of Fundamentalist, weekly paper, has carried the gospel to the uttermost parts of the earth.

During the time, 38 years Fort Worth, 13 years Detroit, the pastor has traveled 904,000 miles.

Two largest Sunday Schools in the world judged by the average attendance.

Both Sunday Schools use Bible only as textbook in all classes instead of hop-skip International lesson series.

Both Churches support New Testament World Fundamental Baptist Missionary Fellowship, and have no part or lot in any ecclesiastical machine.

## Dr. NORRIS' FAVORITE POEM WHICH HE OFTEN REPEATS
## *FROM MEMORY*

*If you can keep your head when all about you*
    *Are losing theirs and blaming it on you;*
*If you can trust yourself when all men doubt you,*
    *But make allowance for their doubting too:*
*If you can wait and not be tired by waiting,*
    *Or being lied about, don't deal in lies;*
*Or being hated, don't give way to hating,*
    *And yet don't look too good, nor talk too wise.*
*If you can dream – and not make dreams your master;*
    *If you can think – and not make thoughts your aim,*
*If you can meet with Triumph and Disaster*
    *And treat those two impostors just the same:*
*If you can bear to hear the truth you've spoken*
    *Twisted by knaves to make a trap for fools,*
*Or watch the things you gave your life to, broken,*
    *And stoop and build 'em up with worn-out tools;*
*If you can make one heap of all your winnings*
    *And risk it on one turn of pitch-and-toss,*
*And lose, and start again at your beginnings*
    *And never breathe a word about your loss:*
*If you can force your heart and nerve and sinew*
    *To serve your turn long after they are gone,*
*And so hold on when there is nothing in you*
    *Except the will which says to them: 'Hold on.'*
*If you can talk with crowds and keep your virtue*
    *Or walk with Kings – nor lose the common touch,*
*If neither foes nor loving friends can hurt you,*
    *If all men count with you, but none too much:*
*If you can fill the unforgiving minute*
    *With sixty seconds' worth of distance run.*
*Yours is the Earth and everything that's in it,*
    *And – which is more – you'll be a Man, my son!"*

– "IF" – Kipling.

# PROLOGUE

## By Louis Entzminger

I am writing this inside story for several reasons.

First, during the 34 years that I have known and been associated with J. Frank Norris I have been asked questions concerning him from coast to coast. And I am going to put down, over my own signature, the answers to many of these questions. It will be no eulogy, it will be a blunt, straightforward, honest review of this remarkable man whose name has received more publicity, pro and con, than any living minister.

Second, what is the secret, the mainspring of a minister's life who is pastor of the largest membership in the world? He has been pastor of the First Baptist Church for 38 years and of Temple Baptist Church for 13 years, making a total of more than 50 years in these two churches. There's not another similar pastorate on the face of the whole earth in this generation.

Third, no man since the Apostle Paul has been so maligned and all manner of evil said against him as J. Frank Norris. And when I say all manner of evil, I mean, literally, that has been true.

Fourth, how has he sustained great crowds, the greatest that I know of, in the same two churches, and having increasing results in multitudes saved and baptized?

Fifth, how did he build and maintain what has been, for many years, the two largest Sunday Schools in the world?

Sixth, how did he build from the ground up, without any rich people but from the gifts of poor people, more than two million dollars of most practical church properties?

Seventh, how from broken health 35 years ago, and financial bankruptcy, he struggled on to the finest of robust health, which he has enjoyed for many years.

Eighth, how he won the friendship and admiration of a great city where once he was despised with only a little handful of poor people for him, and all of the business, political and ecclesiastical organizations combined against him – how he not only survived it but how they turned out to be his strongest friends and supporters

July 9, 1913, while secretary of the Sunday School work for the General Association of Baptists in Kentucky I received the following telegram:

"Would you consider coming as superintendent of First Baptist Sunday School, Fort Worth, to build the largest Sunday School in the world at same salary you are receiving there? If so will you come to Fort Worth my expense for conference?

(Signed) J FRANK NORRIS

I replied immediately I would come.

I came to Fort Worth, arriving Friday morning about two weeks later.

The storms were raging around this man at that time and, using Dr. Norris' own words, "razor blades were flying a thousand feet high."

I confess that I came with much trepidation and I wondered what kind of man was this that the newspapers were headlining and maligning, but I came.

The church had been destroyed by fire; the membership was scattered. He had a small group under a flat-opped tabernacle at the corner of Seventh and Burnett.

When I walked up to the platform I saw a long, tall, lean, gaunt young fellow and I knew he wasn't the J. Frank Norris I was looking for, and I asked him:

"Can you tell me where I can find Dr. Norris?"

In a soft-spoken voice he said, "I am he."

I could not believe my eyes. There we sat and talked thought was, "is this quiet-looking, soft-spoken young fellow the one that has been the storm center of the political and church life of Fort Worth and Texas?"

But as I talked on – he said very little – he gave one of his characteristic quick turns of his head and looked me squarely in the eye and I said to myself, "Oh, there is somebody at home" for I could feel his piercing steel-grey eyes going through me.

At the close of our first interview he said:

"Now, Entzminger, you can hear all manner of evil things about me, and I want you to hear them all to start with. Therefore, you take your time, talk to everybody and anybody, especially my enemies."

I went to Dallas and I talked to several of the denominational leaders and found many very sharp criticisms, but I also found a very strong friend in the person of the greatest statesman Southern Baptists ever produced – Dr. James B. Gambrell!

I went out to Southwestern Baptist Theological Seminary and talked to some members of the faculty and students and then I went incognito and interviewed many business men and newspaper men, and I found everybody in Fort Worth was either ready to hang him or deify him – nobody was neutral.

Sunday morning he asked me to speak. I suppose there were approximately 250 to 300 under the tabernacle. But there must have been at least ten thousand people in and around the Tabernacle at night.

On the opposite side of the street there was a Methodist church and a Methodist preacher trying to conduct a service. But part of Norris' audience was actually sitting on the steps of the Methodist church and leaning up against the wall and filling all vacant space between the church and the street.

He had advertised that he would give the record of ten of the biggest devils in Fort Worth and had written registered letters inviting them to be present to answer any charges he made and to defend themselves. They were all prominent men.

There was only one question in my mind. He wanted just exactly the thing I wanted to do. I had prayed for several years for some church that would give me enough financially to live on so I could demonstrate to my own satisfaction some important and vital things about the modern Sunday School. I knew very little about it and had had very little experience, and still I was lecturing all over the country on how to build and run the Sunday School. I wanted an opportunity to test some plans and methods I had in mind and prove their worth. The only question in my mind about coming to Fort Worth was the question of his character and integrity.

I never heard, in fact I never dreamed, of such a thing as the way he exposed that bunch of big, outstanding business men that night. It was the most terrific exposure of corruption and immorality conceivable. The biggest man among the bunch happened to be there when Dr. Norris got through and took the platform to defend himself. He did the unwise thing of asking Dr. Norris a question.

Dr. Norris answered it and then asked him a question that put him to shaking like an aspen leaf. He had to admit certain charges Norris had made against him and his paper that set the crowd in an uproar of applause. Many of them simply yelled, because for several years the charges he admitted were true had been vigorously denied.

### The Storm of Battle the First Sunday Night

He was in a terrific battle with the leading top men of the city, county and city officials, Chamber of Commerce and they were after him to run him out of the city. They had already dragged him through the courts, and, as I recall, there were a couple more indictments hanging over him. He fought back with everything at his command – he had no paper then, no radio, no influential members, and all this situation, conditions I found puzzled me, amazed me.

Here I was to cast my lot with a man who, humanly speaking, was at his row's end, who was not about to be put out of business but the majority of people I talked to said "He is already finished and out of business."

What I wanted to do was to build a great Sunday School and how could I do it under such adverse conditions?

## But That First Sunday Night

He had written ten of the supposedly top men of the city a registered letter telling each one that he was going to give publicly their records and connections.

The newspapers would not publish his announcements, not even paid advertisements, but he had a crowd that was faithful – they were Gideon's three hundred – and that's about all he did have.

He sowed the city down with circulars containing a copy of this letter together with the names of the ten top men.

I confess it made me tremble for I had never read nor heard of such daring.

Talk about a crowd – only a part of the vast multitude of thousands got on the block – the streets were filled all around.

The ten men had held a conference and agreed to ignore this meeting, and nine of them did; but one of them, the main one, came.

This man was sitting on the front porch of the Elk's Club across from the tabernacle, surrounded by a group of his friends, and, as we learned afterwards, they were imbibing rather freely.

Norris carried out his full announced plan on all ten of them, calling the roll and giving their records.

I confess it scared me for I wouldn't have been surprised at what might happen at any minute.

But Norris was perfectly calm and as the crowd would break out in applause he would quiet them. There was perfect order throughout until the final tragic climax.

This man, the top one of the ten, who had succeeded in getting all of the other nine not to come to this meeting – when Norris came to his name he proceeded to give his record.

I was sitting on the platform and trying to take in the whole situation, and suddenly I saw the group of men, about a dozen, come bolting in through the crowd and down the aisle, and there was commotion throughout the audience.

This man and his crowd came rushing up to the platform and Norris stood there very quietly while the crowd began to yell, "Put him out," "throw him out," et cetera.

Norris beckoned to the crowd and obtained order and said:

"I invited this man, (calling his name), to be here tonight. He is my guest and your guest and I want you to give him a respectful hearing." And then he walked over and touched this man on the shoulder and assured him, "You will be given a full, free hearing, and you can say anything you wish in reply to the charges I have made."

That amazed me still more and I wondered still more.

This man was very nervous and began to talk in a high, keen voice. Again the crowd interrupted and Norris stepped in front of him and made a passionate appeal to give this man a free and undisturbed hearing.

Then this man proceeded and when he had finished his harangue Norris stepped forward and quietly pointed his long finger in his face and said, "Now, you have had your say and I want to ask you some questions."

The man started to walk off the platform but Norris very gently but firmly took him by the arm and said, "Just a minute."

It is unnecessary to go into all the questions, but I remember one of them very distinctly. It pertained to the ownership of the morning paper. The issue was whether the breweries owned it in whole or in part, and Norris was fighting the liquor interest tooth and nail, and he wrung from this man a confession that the breweries owned no small part of the stock. When this man made that confession the crowd rose and roared and this man walked away, head down, and that ended the most dramatic hour I had ever witnessed in a public meeting.

Well, I wondered still more, but that meeting that night, the way he handled his chief antagonist and that multitude caused me to say to myself, "I am not afraid to tie my life to a man that has such courage, such convictions, and they have nothing against him and will never be able to defeat him."

That meeting settled the matter for me. I knew that a man who had a single skeleton in the closet would never do what J. Frank Norris did that night. And I was convinced, even as Dr. Gambrell said he was, that the whole conspiracy against Norris was a frame-up, and my appetite was really whetted to join in the battle with him. Therefore I accepted the work to begin the first of September.

I wanted to visit several Sunday reputation. I spent the first week

Schools of national in September going to New York and Chicago and several other places and arrived in Fort Worth September 9, 1913 to begin work as superintendent of the First Baptist Church Sunday School.

That was the beginning of 34 years' relations that have been strenuous, sometimes tragic, sometimes dark, not a star in our. Sky, sometimes on transfiguration heights, sometimes in the nadir of despair, sometimes, and often times, the most glorious soul winning campaigns I have ever witnessed, and going to this hour more glorious than ever.

I suppose Dr. Norris has been lied upon more about money matters and financial dealings than possibly any other one thing. I have been amazed at things that men have said about reports of his financial dealings.

As an intimate associate of 34 years I do not know of one single time where he hasn't measured up on the highest principles of honesty.

He has always, on every occasion and in every transaction, paid me more than he promised and I know of a large number of others who have worked with him whose testimony is the same. He gives with a generous hand.

I know personally of many sums of money he has loaned to befriend people which were never paid.

The first salary I ever drew for the first month's work I did with him in September, 1913 when the church was poverty stricken and he was worse than broke, that first salary was money he borrowed from a friend in Dallas personally to pay my salary.

Time and time again in those first four years of my association with him after all the wealthy people were gone I have known him to go and hold meetings and come back with offerings from $500 to $1,000 and $1,500 and $2,000 and put every penny of it in the hands of the church treasurer to pay bills.

If there ever was an honest soul in financial matters, I believe J. Frank Norris is one.

## The Choir of the First Baptist Church

It is larger than most congregations, and the happy thing is the huge platform which is 100 feet across from wall to wall is filled and often not room for those who wish to get in the choir.

Average Sunday congregation First Baptist Church, Fort Worth, Texas

The Choir, Temple Baptist Church, Detroit, Mich.

Morning congregation of Temple Baptist Church, Detroit, Mich.

Dr. Norris speaking to students at Paschal High School, Fort Worth. Invited by school authorities, all classes adjourned to hear him. Packed auditorium shows his popularity with the students.

# SECTION I

# CHAPTER I

THIRTEEN YEAR OLD BOY SHOT THREE TIMES BUT SAVED HIS FATHER'S LIFE

In the early days the State of Texas was infested with cattle and horse thieves. They were organized and went in gangs. The way they worked their stealing of horses and cattle, one or two men in the neighborhood who were well known and stood high, would do the immediate taking of the stock from the lot or pasture and drive them a short distance and would then turn them over to the gang and that was the last of them.

If anybody undertook to testify against the gang, his fate would be worse than what happened at the hands of Al Capone's gangsters. Norris' father was a witness against some thieves and two of the gangsters appeared at the Norris' front gate late one afternoon. The first the boy knew that they were there was when he heard the shooting. He was chopping cotton just across the fence and saw his father fall. He had his pocket knife and he jumped through the wire fence and against impossible odds fought for his father's life. One of the gangsters ran behind the boy and shot him three times. His father received only slight wounds and soon recovered, but the boy's life hung in the balance, gangrene set up; inflammatory rheumatism came as a result and for three years he couldn't walk a step and was rolled in an invalid chair. Two specialists went out from Hillsboro, Drs. Dudley and Roberts, and after diagnosing the case they went into an adjoining room, which had just a thin wall, and said to his parents: "He can't live and if he does he will be an invalid for life."

But his mother said, "No doctor, no doctor, he will get well."

The boy heard his mother say "No doctor, no doctor, he will get well."

During three years of the most excruciating pain there was born in his soul a determination and ambition, and whatever courage he may have exhibited in after years was born in those three years.

When he reached his majority he was very frail. He went through college and Seminary, and when he was called to Fort Worth to the First Baptist Church in 1908, there was little prospect of his ever becoming strong.

### Owes His Health to The Devil, The Machine and The Lord

J. Frank Norris often says he would be in his grave today if it had not been for three things.

First, the devil jumping on him and he summoned all the powers and principalities and wicked spirits that fill the air.

Second, because he would not bow the knee to Baal, the denominational machine conspired to destroy him, and

Third, but the Lord delivered him and he is a monument of grace both physically and spiritually. He has never been free from persecutions, slanders and attacks from the bottomless abyss.

With his most phenomenal success in winning souls and building churches, the Lord gave him the experience:

"And lest I should be exalted above measure through the abundance of the revelations, there was given to me a thorn in the flesh, the messenger of Satan to buffet me, lest I should be exalted above measure.

"For this thing I besought the Lord thrice, that it might depart from me.

"And he said unto me, My grace is sufficient for thee: for my strength is made perfect in weakness. Most gladly therefore will I rather glory in my infirmities, that the power of Christ may rest upon me.

"Therefore I take pleasure in infirmities, in reproaches, in necessities, in persecutions, in distresses for Christ's sake: for when I am weak, then am I strong." (II Cor. 12:7-10)

# HOW THE LORD OVER RULED THE DEMON OF DRINK TO MAKE A PREACHER

Unfortunately Dr. Norris' father was a drinking man most of his life and up to within a few years of his death.

One Christmas when the boy was 7 years old he emptied his father's jug of liquor and broke the bottle. When his father found the liquor was gone, the boy told him why he did it – "It's because I love you, and I love Mother."

The father was so enraged, as liquor will enrage a man, and he took a heavy blacksnake whip and nearly beat the 7 year old boy to death, and would have but for his mother's throwing herself between the boy and the enraged father.

His nose was broken, his head was lacerated, and his body was cut from head to foot. The doctor came and bandaged him up

And the next day was Christmas, and what a Christmas!

His father was a very tender hearted man, as most drinking men are, and when he came to himself and saw the lacerated body of his little boy he fell down on his knees by the bed, pulled back the bandages from his face and kissed him and said.

"Daddy didn't do it! Daddy didn't do it! Liquor did it!"

Then he prayed a prayer that has gone with the preacher all his life.

"O, God, liquor has ruined my life, and my home. Take this boy that I have been so cruel to and send him up and down the land to smite the awful curse that wrecked his father's life and broke his mother's heart."

When the boy was 14 years old at Hubbard, Texas – and many of the old timers will remember this – there were two wicked men that were running an open "blind tiger" and sold his father liquor. His mother wrote a note pleading with them not to sell her poor husband liquor and the boy carried the note to those wicked men and law breakers. When he went in and gave the note to them they grabbed him by his right arm, rushed him to the back door and kicked him out. He went home and told his mother, and here is where the boy gets his iron will.

The mother dressed and said,

"Drive me to town." It was four miles away.

It was on a Saturday afternoon, and the "blind tiger" was full of men. She told the boy to sit buggy and wait for her.

She took a heavy whip and went in and whipped both of those keepers of the "blind tiger" and broke up the place.

The keeper of this "blind tiger" was Newt Leftwich, and all the old timers knew what a dive it was.

## FROM VALEDICTORIAN OF GREATEST SEMINARY IN THE WORLD TO 13 MEMBERS AND A MULE BARN

J. Frank Norris' records were so high at Southern Baptist Theological Seminary, where he graduated in "all the schools," that he was valedictorian of the graduating class. He was called to two very prominent churches but declined both and went to Dallas and started a church located at McKinney and Routh. He had 13 members the first Sunday morning and in a little more than two years there were over 1,000 members and a $50,000 building. And that church has gone on gloriously through these more than 40 years.

## THE SECRET OF NORRIS' HEALTH AND GREAT ENDURANCE

When I first saw him I didn't think he could live six months, but today he is going stronger than ever. He could not speak but a few minutes without coughing and he was completely exhausted at the close of every message. But I have known him to speak as much as 14 hours in one day and he never knows what it is to be hoarse, even when speaking in the open air.

One of his favorite Scriptures is, "Who forgiveth all thine iniquities and healeth all thy diseases."

He can throw off worries quicker than any man I ever saw. He divides his troubles in two parts – first, those he can help, and, second, those he can't help. He leaves the second division alone.

I suppose that every mean thing that could be said about a man has been said, circulated, published and radioed concerning him, and I have never seen him one single time the least bit concerned or worried about all the calumnies and slanders hurled at him. I have seen him smile and sing when everybody around him was cursing him.

That's the secret of his good health.

Dr. Norris speaking to a huge overflow crowd in the streets in front of the building of the Temple Baptist Church, Detroit, Mich.

# CHAPTER II

## A HARD STUDENT AND READER

Dr. Norris has, perhaps, the most thoroughly equipped library of any preacher now living. He has a large room full of the choicest books, books that are out of print, in his office and at his home. He also fitted up a very fine library for his son George – he has bequeathed all of his rich libraries to George.

He secured the library from the home of that great layman and right-hand man of Spurgeon's, William Olney, and the very books that Spurgeon used. He is a connoisseur of the oldest and rarest books of theology, biographies and histories.

At the beginning of each Seminary year he gives a course of lectures on the history of the world from the beginning until now and gives it from memory and without any notes.

He has specialized on three lines:

1. The Bible.

2. The history of the world.

3. The present-day current affairs among all nations of the earth.

He has made four world trips and now plans to leave soon for another trip, preaching in several places in England, Scotland and Ireland and then, by special permission of the British Government, going to Palestine – this will make five trips to Palestine.

He absorbs information like a sponge absorbs water. He has been very fortunate in making contacts with the world's outstanding thinkers, heads of governments, Prime Ministers, three different popes, editors, industrialists, – he can walk into any circle anywhere and be at home.

How fortunate for the Bible Baptist Seminary to have such a man as president and lecturer!

He is going stronger today than I have ever seen him in the 34 years I have been associated with him.

New York City – Dr. J. Frank Norris leaving on Pan American Clipper for Lisbon, bound for London – 1941.

# CHAPTER III

### MRS. J. FRANK NORRIS

It would not be too extravagant for me to say that she is the greatest living woman I know anything about. I never saw her lose her poise or composure. Whether in the quiet home or in the midst of the greatest revivals or sitting by her husband's side in the court house or with the sick and dying in the hospital, she has always been the same. I could go to her for help, for teachers, for encouragement and she never failed me. What D. L. Moody's Emma was to him, what Suzanna Wesley was in her home, what Hannah was in her home, all these are Mrs. Lillian Gaddy Norris!

### Four Wonderful Children

All four of them have the same faith of their mother and believe the same gospel preached by their father.

The total family number 19 besides myself and I count myself one of this happy family circle.

Once a year all gather together at Christmas time and it is a riot of entertainment, of pleasure, of laughter and love.

Through the sacrifices of this great and good mother, all four of their children went through the highest educational institutions. The Christian characters of all four children, with their husbands and wives and children, have won high renown.

As with trees so with men, they are judged by the fruit they bear.

According to all rules, it would not have been a surprise if all four children had been wrecks mentally, spiritually and morally. What trials, when little, they faced! Such trials on small children would be calculated to wreck nerves; but all became strong, healthy and happy.

The oldest, a daughter, is the wife of one of the leading bank officials of Chicago. She and her entire family are all consecrated church members.

The oldest son is a successful lawyer and business man and was Commander in the U. S. Navy.

The second son also rose to the high position of Commender in the Navy, and is now one of the executive of the Ford Motor Company.

And the youngest is one of the truly great young preachers of my acquaintance.

## WHEN NORRIS PUT HIS OWN SON IN JAIL

A sensational and unfriendly press published big headlines "Son of J. Frank Norris Is In Jail," but they did not tell that his father had it done. This inside history spares nobody.

The lad was just in his early teen age and had been through many of the trials that his father had to face, and one day when he was only 13 years old, an old maid school teacher said, before the whole school, "You are a nice preacher's son." There was no justification for such a remark and the boy, with, perhaps, some of the spirit of his near ancestors, said, "You go to hell." She started after him and he went through the window, being on the first floor.

He did not want to go to school any more and would not and broke his father and mother's hearts.

Tarrant County had just built a fine new jail and Sterling Clark, the sheriff, was a personal friend of Dr. Norris', and he had Mr. Clark pick the boy up and give him free board for a couple of weeks.

It did the work for the lad went to the greatest military academy in America and went through three universities and received a law license from the Supreme Court and entered the Navy and came out a Commander.

He saved the First Church during the trying days of his father's absence while he was building the Temple Church in Detroit.

Incidentally, it was one of the ten thousand slanders that the denominational machine published all over the country about "Frank Norris' boy in jail."

But they would do anything to injure Norris. One of the first two denominational leaders of the state told me personally, "We are going to dehorn Norris; we have got to get rid of him." But they are all gone and he is still going on at last reports.

The Norris family Christmas day 1946

One of the meetings Dr. Norris holds for Railroad Shops. He goes to all shops, factories, packing houses, and all these shut down work in order to hear the Gospel by Dr. Norris.

# CHAPTER IV

## A TURNING POINT IN THE LIFE OF J. FRANK NORRIS – HIS WIFE'S PRAYERS

I quote from the close of one of his sermons:

I want to give you the greatest story of my life. I wanted my wife to come tonight – but she thought she ought to stay at home and help with the radio – and I wouldn't tell her what I wanted for if I had I knew she wouldn't come, but I want her to stand here on the platform some day and tell her side of this story. I want you to have it from a woman whose faith never fails.

In the darkest darkness of the tragic summer of 1912 – the reason why it was so dark – everything was gone, my health was gone – I looked like one of those scarecrows they put out to keep the crows out of a watermelon patch walking around – I looked like a poor old horse that was string-halted; with blind staggers, reeling around – I felt like that and I looked like it. I couldn't talk more than ten or fifteen minutes until I would begin to cough, and I would tremble like a twig in a March wind, and afterwards I would be so hoarse I couldn't speak above a whisper. Now I believe I could speak for twenty hours and never know what it is to be hoarse.

I want to say this to help somebody. Say, did you ever feel like your feet were going down and down and down? Well, beloved, I know how you felt.

Did you ever feel like everything on earth was gone and something had gone wrong upstairs? Well, I know how you felt.

Have you ever gone to bed and rolled from side to side, and the morning would come and you had not slept a wink? Well, I know what you are talking about.

Say, were you ever just worse than broke – I don't mean badly bent – my enemies said I was broke, they didn't know the half of it. I was – broke all flat. (Laughter.)

During that day when everything was gone, then something seemed to snap up here in my head and I felt like somebody had a sledge hammer hitting me on the back of the head. About that time a friend wired me to come help him in a meeting – I said I can't hold a meeting I haven't got the strength to hold a meeting, but I wired him I would come without thinking much about it. When I went down to catch the train, I missed it – I was glad of it, and went to send a telegram that I wasn't coming, and George Neace – if he were here tonight would perhaps remember this, said, "Brother Norris, there is another train going at 11 o'clock." It made me mad because he told me. I got on it and went down there and when I got there – a little town of about a thousand people – well it seemed like all the folks and all the dogs were standing there looking at me to see what kind of looking wild animal I was. Brother White came up and took my little old hand satchel – didn't have much in it – and he said, "You are going to be my guest" – well he was a nice looking, civilized man and I went along with him. When we got home he introduced me to his wife and took me to a room – a nice looking room, and said, "This is to be your room." We went out to the tabernacle that night and everybody was there for forty miles around, and when I stood up to speak I was so weak I couldn't stand without holding to the stand for support. I was absolutely exhausted. I read a few Scriptures and said, "Good night." I didn't make any appeal. I didn't have any appeal to make. When we got home that night, Sister White wanted to fix me something to eat – I didn't want anything to eat. I didn't have any appetite. I had a dark brown taste in my mouth. I went to bed. I tossed back and forth all night long – the next morning when I was shaving I noticed my hand trembling – my eyes were blood shot – I looked as if I had been on a month's drunk. We went down to the tabernacle that day, and talked a little while and quit. That night there was another big crowd – I preached the best I could and we went home – I had not been able to sleep and I was so tired – my breath was short, just cutting off right here – I woke up to the fact that unless that thing changed I would soon be in my grave or in the asylum. Later on that night – Oh, that night, it was the greatest night I ever experienced on earth, the darkest and the deepest and the saddest – the family went to bed – I tried to sleep but I couldn't. I needed sleep, I had lost several nights sleep I hadn't been able to eat and sleep all summer and I didn't weigh but 124 pounds, and I was as tall as I am now – that's a good deal less than what I weigh now – let me see, that's about sixty pounds less than I weigh now. After a while as the night rolled on and I tossed and tossed – my limbs from my knees down felt as I were standing in red hot fire, and my temples just felt as if somebody had my head in a vise bursting it wide open, and I felt as if somebody had tweezers pulling my nerves out one at a time. My body felt as if it had been flayed and cut to pieces – it was gone, wasted away. Finally I got up, put on my clothes, the window was open, I didn't want to disturb the family, and I took my shoes in my hand and slipped out, walked out. the back way out into the pasture, I walked along slowly until I got way out from the house and I sat down for awhile in the grass – and I sat there – thin, wasted away, broken, discouraged, overcome, overwhelmed – after a while I lay down on the grass like Jacob the first night he was away from home – I put my hands under my tired aching head and lay there looking up at the glowing stars on that hot July night, and I wondered why all these things had befallen me. What wrong had I done? I went to Fort Worth and made the best fight I could and I had lost – I didn't care for myself so much, but my wife and three babies, God pity them! My friends had turned away, everything was gone and I knew I was gone too – I am telling you I knew I would be in the asylum or in the grave in a short time. I felt myself slipping, and I was terribly alarmed about it. When I got up the cold sweat was on my brow. I started home and the gray streaks of morning were showing up in the eastern sky – I slipped back into bed, but I couldn't sleep. After a while that good old Methodist layman came and knocked gently on my door – I said, "Come in." He came in and said: "Did you have a good night!" "Yes, sir," I said. "Well," he said, "breakfast will soon be ready" – I didn't want anything to eat, but I went in and sat down at the table. I was so sad I couldn't think of a word on earth to say, and Sister White wanted to know if there was anything she could fix for me that I could eat. I felt like a man that was drowning and nothing to hold to – every friend I had on earth was gone. I said to myself, I am going home, get my family and I am going to Southern California where nobody knows me and I am going to get out there on a ranch, and I am through with the ministry – not that I had lost faith in God, but I had lost my fight, my courage was gone, health was gone, everything was gone.

When we started to church that night I told the family to go on that I would walk. After they had gone, I got my grip – I didn't have much in it, just a change of underwear and a necktie – and I said I am going home tonight and I am not going to tell a soul that I am going. I walked on to the tabernacle and went through a peach orchard and hid my grip in some weeds, and I went into the tabernacle. When the services were over I meant to slip out there, get my grip and catch the 11 o'clock train and come home.

When I got into the tabernacle and started to preach, the pastor leaned over and whispered to me, "Do you see that man sitting back yonder?" I had already seen him. He said, "That old fellow with the red bandana handkerchief around his neck – he is the meanest man in all this country, it is the first time I have ever known him to come to church – he has a half dozen notches on his gun. If you could reach that man you could reach this whole country." I can see him now as he sat rared back – he had on boots and spurs, and I learned afterwards bells on his spurs, and he looked at me and I looked at him, we were of mutual curiosity to each other. I stood up, tired and weak, and I looked at him and I thought – "You poor old sinner, it's the last time I ever expect to preach and I am going to give you the best I have."

So what happened? I looked at him and he looked at me – and I began, "A certain man had two sons: and the younger of them said to his father, Father, give me the portion of goods that falleth to me. And he divided unto them his living. And not many days after the younger son gathered all together, and took his journey into a far country, and there wasted his substance in riotous living. And when he had spent all, there arose a mighty famine in that land; and he began to be in want. And he went and joined himself to a citizen of that country: and he sent him into his fields to feed the swine.

And he would fain have filled his belly with the husks that the swine did eat: and no man gave unto him. And when he came to himself, he said, How many hired servants of my father's have bread enough and to spare, and I perish with hunger! I will arise and go to my father, and will say unto him, Father, I have sinned against heaven, and before thee, And am no more worthy to be called thy son: make me as one of thy hired servants. And he arose, and came to his father. But when he was yet a great way off, his father saw him, and had compassion, and ran, and fell on his neck, and kissed him. And the son said unto him, Father, I have sinned against heaven and in thy sight and am no more worthy to be called thy son. But the father said to his servants, Bring forth the best robe, and put it on him; and put a ring on his hand, and he made a great feast" – and about that time I saw that old red-faced sinner bury his face in his hands – it was a hot night and I didn't know what it meant, but in a minute he just reached up behind and tore that old red bandana loose and I saw him bury his face in it and his frame shook like a leaf in a storm – and folks, something happened in this tired weak frame of mine – and I stood up on my hind feet for the first time in a long time and felt strong – and I said if there is a man here who is a sinner, lost, and will come to the Father's house tonight, come on; come on! come on! and, my friends, I can see that old sinner now as he got up and started down the aisle – he had that old red bandana handkerchief in one hand and his cow-boy hat in the other, and you could hear his bells jingling as he came – listen folks, he didn't stop to shake hands with me, but he fell full length on his face – and when his little old Methodist wife sitting over there saw him, she let out a shout that you could have heard a quarter of a mile and came running and fell by his side (shoutings) and in five minutes there were more than fifty men and women in that altar seeking Jesus Christ, and salvation came down and that 11 o'clock train whistled and went on and they were still being saved, and twelve o'clock came and folks were still being saved, one o'clock came and they were still shouting, and two o'clock came and we were still there. When I got back home at 3 o'clock and walked in Brother White said, "Fort Worth is trying to get you" – well I knew who in Fort Worth wanted me. I went to the telephone and tried to talk – I have always been able to keep control of my emotions, but sometimes they get the best of me – this was one time they did – I got Fort Worth on the line and they told me Mrs. Norris was trying to get me, and I said, "Bless God, I want her too." When she came to the telephone and said, "Hello, is that you, Frank?" I just played the baby act, and I couldn't do anything but stand there and cry, and central kept saying, "Talk, talk, here they are." Well, I was doing my best to talk and I couldn't say a word. I turned to Sister White and I said "You tell her." She said, "All right, I will tell her," and she came and took that receiver out of my hand, and she drew back and slung it against the wall and shouted "Hallelujah! hallelujah! hallelujah!" and she just shouted all over the room. I said, "Brother White, you tell her" – he said, "All right," and he came to the telephone and he said, "Sister Norris," and that was as far as he got, he just bellowed as loud as he could – and their sixteen-year-old daughter came and she tried it and she just squalled and cried. And I said, "Give me that telephone receiver"—and all the time central was saying, "Talk, talk, talk!" Finally I got my feelings under control enough and I said, "Wife, wife, we have had the biggest meeting you ever saw, more than half a hundred sinners have been saved, and they are still shouting all over this country, and the best part of it is, wife, you have a new husband – he has been saved tonight, and he is coming home and we are going to start life over again and lick the tar out of that crowd and build the biggest church in the world." And she said, "I knew it was happening. I have been praying for three days and nights. I haven't slept a wink, and tonight I had the answer to my prayer, I have been praying that this thing might happen, and my joy is complete, my cup runneth over. " I said, "Wife, I will come home Sunday."

The next Sunday I preached at 7th and Lamar and the fire from heaven came down and we had sixty-two converts to walk down the aisle. Any of you remember that night? (Hands up.) Many of you.

To God be all the glory. I praise His name for good health and for the opportunity He has given me to testify for Him, and as long as there is breath in my body, as long as my tongue can proclaim, that long will I proclaim the unsearchable riches of Jesus Christ. My only hope of reward, my only ambition, my only joy, is to take some old boy like Shields and Jake Street out there and point them to the way of salvation that shall outlast the shining stars and a life shall be saved for ever and for ever! Who will come tonight! (People came from all the tabernacle.)

Dr. Norris preaching to the joint session of the State Legislatnre of Georgia

# CHAPTER V

NORRIS BELIEVES IN THE PERSONAL WITNESS OF THE HOLY SPIRIT IN THE LIFE OF THE BELIEVER

Because the burdens were so great, seven years ago Dr. Norris was compelled to resign the church in Detroit – he had been carrying the two great churches for six years.

He had been traveling night and day for the Mission work. He would leave Detroit Sunday midninght and travel and speak every day and night and return the next Sunday morning and then leave again that night for another portion of the country. He did this for five years, and all the travel and work he did for the Mission work he did at his own time and expense. The world-wide sweep of the Mission Fellowship stands today largely as a result of his tireless energies.

On the first day of the year, after a week of deepest Gethsemane, he asked his wife to drive with him out into the deep woods of Trinity Park. There had been no Christmas in their home – Dr. Norris had wired all the children not to come – but on that fateful first afternoon of the new year while sitting with his wife in the car watching a heavy rain fall in the clear waters of the Trinity, there flashed into his soul the words of the Lord to Paul at Corinth –

"Then spake the Lord to Paul in the night by a vision, Be not afraid, but speak, and hold not thy peace:

"For I am with thee, and no man shall set on thee to hurt thee..." (Acts 18 :9-10),

He was so everwhelmed he did not speak but drove back with his wife and wired the church at Detroit, "I am coming back."

When he stood before the great congregation and related that experience on the Sunday afternoon on the river bank, the great audience broke and wept as one man. It was the only message, it was the voice of God to the congregation! There was no sermon – no need for one. The deacons, teachers, officers, whole congregation fell on their faces and more than half a hundred souls were born into the kingdom of God!

Throughout his whole checkered, tragic and yet glorious ministry, I have known of many such transfiguration experiences in his life. He has said little about these experiences and I would not have known them except for my close relation and association with him.

Take another occasion. During the first months in Detroit we occupied the same room with twin beds. Many a night he would sit up through the wee small hours and I would wake up and find him still sitting up waiting for day. I have heard him cry, like a little child, "Who is sufficient for these things?"

Then, I have seen him when the storms were raging. He was not always the quiet and even-tempered soul. Talk about Martin Luther throwing ink bottles at the devil or John the Baptist calling the Sanhedrin at Jerusalem a generation of vipers – I saw it all in "the stormy petrel" many a midnight hour.

I have been with him through the Saturday nights when I would see the storms raging and I felt, "We will have no services tomorrow, no results, nobody saved." But I soon learned that these storms, these outbursts of his soul meant that We were going to have a greater day and larger results.

George White, one of the greatest laymen I ever knew, said to me one Saturday night, "What can you do to stir the preacher up, set him on fire, that we may have the greatest day in the history of the church tomorrow?"

Often in riding with him alone, I have heard him talk and cry aloud, pleading like a little child, for a merciful God to come to his help – and his prayers were answered!

# CHAPTER VI

## THE BIBLE BAPTIST SEMINARY

Started in 1939 with only 16 students, one instructor, the writer, and not one red cent of money.

Since that time it has enrolled nearly 2,000 resident students and 3,500 in Correspondence Courses, or a total of 5,500.

It now has over seventeen hundred thousand dollars worth of property that it has built, purchased or has a 199-year lease on, all located right in the heart of the business section of Fort Worth.

Its motto is: "ONLY SEMINARY IN THE WORLD TEACHING WHOLE ENGLISH BIBLE."

It gives the highest degrees that can be granted in the theological world and is so recognized by the Bureau of Education at Washington, which gives it the classification: "AN APPROVED THEOLOGICAL OR DIVINITY SCHOOL WITHIN THE PURVIEW OF THE FEDERAL LAW."

Dr. J. Frank Norris is president.

The Seminary specializes in evangelism. It is, indeed, the center and hotbed, like the church at Antioch, for missions and evangelism.

Large numbers of new churches have been built by graduates of the Seminary, and the students are in large demand everywhere, and even by Convention churches.

## "CONSISTENCY IS THE VIRTUE OF FOOLS" – BUT NOT ONE OF NORRIS' CHIEF CHARACTERISTICS

Deep down in his heart he is, I think, proud of his inconsistency. Many times he has had me going one way and the next morning I found he had reversed himself and was going in the opposite direction. But who can imagine Elijah or John the Baptist caring about "consistency"?

The most outstanding example of his inconsistency is the changing of the name of the Seminary from the "Fundamental Baptist Bible Institute" to the "Bible Baptist Seminary".

For many years he had made all manner of fun of seminaries and called them "Cemeteries", though he was a graduate with highest record from the outstanding Seminary on the American Continent, yet he never ceased to poke fun at the Seminaries.

And when he was made president of the Bible Baptist Seminary he confessed with no small humor saying,

"The last thing in the world I ever thought I would be guilty of was to be president of a Seminary."

But here is how it was brought about:

Having established the Fundamental Baptist Bible Institute with only sixteen students six years before the name was changed, I discovered that graduates of a Bible Institute had very little standing, could not go as chaplains from the armed forces, and that the draft law made no recognition of Bible Institutes, but only established and recognized seminaries.

One day in a restaurant I suggested, "Norris, there is something that I want to some time suggest to you. But I am not going to do it now because I am afraid you would pitch me out on my head."

Immediately he wanted to know and demanded what it was, and in his characteristic way gave me to understand there would be no peace in the family until I told him.

I saw I was already into it and I said:

"We should change the name of the Fundamental Baptist Bible Institute to the Bible Baptist Seminary.

Instantly he replied:

"It is changed."

He went over to the office and called up the directors by long distance telephone and submitted it to them and it was unanimously changed.

It was all done in a few minutes' time.

Take another case of his inconsistency. He has said many times, on many occasions, "I have no use for a census."

But he and I went to hold a meeting in a certain place. I went on ahead of time, and when he got there he said,

"Entz, have you taken a census?"

I replied, "Well, you said you didn't want any more census."

"Well," he replied instantly, "That was last year and that doesn't apply to this case."

So, therefore, I got out and took a census.

I do not want to leave the impression that he is not possessed of hard, stubborn judgment. But he is no slave to the grave clothes.

His motto is:

"Methods change every day and the message never changes."

The Office building of the Frist Baptist Church, two extra stories to be added which will be used for offices of the faculty and for Studios of the Bible Baptist Seminary. The building to the right, is John Birch Hall. To the left can be seen First Baptist Church Auditorium.

# CHAPTER VII

## WHY A LARGE NUMBER OF NORRIS' ENEMIES ARE BORN OF ENVY — "AND HE KNEW THAT FOR ENVY THEY DELIVERED HIM"

## "FOR JEALOUSY IS THE RAGE OF A MAN" Prov. 6:34

There are three ways to earn envy:
First, do more.
Second, know more, and
Third, have more.

Jealousy or envy reaches its highest and its worst form among preachers – even worse than among women.

Dr. Norris has helped many preachers out of trouble, got them on their feet, and (sad to say sometimes) then they would turn in a rage against him and say all manner of evil things about him.

For instance, in 1928 he helped a pastor in Dallas who was clear out, and one of the greatest meetings ever held in the history of Dallas was at a big tent meeting in Buckner Park, 636 people joined that church, and immediately the machine moved in and began to flatter this preacher who lacked backbone and he sold his birthright for a mess of pottage. He of course turned then and joined with Norris' enemies in order to justify his ill-fated course – and an ill-fated course it has been, for he is practically out of business.

Another case was over at Lexington, Kentucky, in 1925 when the pastor of the First Baptist Church of that city was a refugee beyond the Canadian border to escape the reach of the law. He was in other serious trouble, and he appealed to Norris for help, and Norris went and held a meeting that resulted in over 700 additions to the church. This pastor, right in the midst of the meeting, became so filled with the green-eyed monster – well, he has an empty house now. He too received the thirty pieces of silver.

So after surveying the whole record for more than thirty years I have found that his loudest critics have been those that turned and bit the hand that fed them.

But nothing new about that – "He that dippeth his hand with me in the dish, the same shall betray me." Norris is generous to a fault, and I have known him to take traitors back into his bosom, and he was always ready to forgive.

# CHAPTER VIII

## A GREAT SOUL WINNER

Why has Norris not only survived, but grown in stature through the years?

One of his favorite Scripture mottoes is I Peter 2:15, "For so is the well of God, that with well doing ye may put to silence the ignorance of foolish men."

He is a man of very strong convictions on all the fundamentals of the Christian Faith. He believes every one of them from Creation to the Second Coming of Christ. He believes that the soul that dies out of Christ is certain for hell. He preaches it. He lives it. He talks it.

When they had him in the court house for six weeks, as soon as court would adjourn in the afternoon he would bo making calls on the unsaved until midnight.

In the mornings before court convened he would call on people in their homes at breakfast.

And every Sunday during that six weeks court house conspiracy there would be forty, fifty, seventy-five to one hundred people saved and baptized.

He would go into the saloons and talk to the saloon keepers and drunkards.

He would go into the brothels and talk to the keepers.

He would go to the gambling dens and pool halls and talk to them and pray with them.

And I have seen this with my own eyes – when court adjourned he would turn the court into a prayer meeting and soul-winning service.

Temple Baptist Church, Corner 14th & Marquette Sts., Detroit

Baptizing in the Detroit River

Young People's Department No.1 Temple Baptist Church, Detroit, Mich. This Department covers the ages of 15, 16 and 17. They have an average attendance of 225.

# SECTION II

# CHAPTER I

A CALL TO THE FIRST BAPTIST CHURCH, FORT WORTH

Dr. Norris tells it better than I could so I'll give the story in his own words –

The preceding three years at Dallas as pastor of McKinney Avenue Baptist Church and editor of the Baptist Standard furnished the background to the call to Fort Worth.

Not sparing myself, I am giving this testimony, with the hope and prayer that it may help some young preachers to avoid my mistakes.

I graduated from Southern Baptist Theological Seminary, Louisville, Ky., in May, 1906, having finished all the courses required for the Master's Degree in Theology. I finished the three-year course in two years' time. I had a wife and one-year-old baby. And that was the cause of the shortening of the course from three to two years.

When I finished at Baylor, I had a call to the First Baptist Church at Rockdale, and the Pulpit Committee of the First Baptist Church, Corsicana, also wanted me.

My wife's father, Jim Gaddy, and Dr. B. H. Carroll, wanted me to take one of these important pulpits, and I wished afterwards I had. But it would have been a mistake.

It is a doubtful question as to whether a man should marry before he finishes his education. I wondered about it before I married, and my wife wondered after we married.

Because of my record at the Seminary, I was appointed by the faculty to deliver one of the graduating addresses. And no question about my address; it was a "hum dinger." I had a great subject – "International Justification of Japan in Its War With Russia."

The Louisville Courier-Journal thought this address was statesmanlike and had international merit, for they published it in full.

I was broke but I bought an armful of this great paper and sent a marked copy to all my kinfolks and acquaintances.

It was a gala occasion the night of the graduation and, of course, the most important event of that occasion was not the address by Dr. Mullins or the giving of the diplomas, but my address in defense of Japan. Ever since I was a boy on the farm I was a close student of international affairs, in fact I became an "expert" before I left the farm – I mean on international affairs.

When I graduated the McKinney Avenue Church at Dallas called me; they called me sight unseen before I graduated – and I accepted sight unseen. Talk about marrying by correspondence, that is nothing. They thought I was some pumpkin, and I thought they were some pumpkins, because they were in Dallas. No young Roman Catholic priest ever looked with stronger devotion towards St. Peter's at Rome than I looked on the denominational headquarters at Dallas. What disillusionment was awaiting me!

I landed in Dallas the first Sunday in June, 1906. And the thermometer was – well, I think it set the record for all that summer. I went to the St. George Hotel, sent my double breasted, long tail Prince Albert coat and striped trousers down to the pressing shop – I delivered the address on Japan in this same outfit.

The coat was a heavy winter coat, and came down almost like the skirts of the robe of Aaron, had satin lapels, and the pants – the trousers, breeches – whichever called – had stripes as big as a lead pencil. I had a white vest also. And with it a heavy black silk tie. But the most important part about the regalia was the stove pipe collar. I was long and slender, wore a 13 collar – now $16\frac{1}{2}$ I was as tall as I am now – think I was taller – and weighed about 130 pounds – some 50 or 60 pounds lighter than at present. And that coat was made to fit me tight.

All the distinguished city pastors wore long tailed coats – they carried their theology in their coat tails. That is where I carried mine.

Dr. Norris on Graduation Day

Incidentally, I wore this same suit when I preached the annual sermon at the Baptist General Convention of Texas the next year.

I had some "standing" in those days. I remember after preaching the sermon, Dr. George W. Truett came up to me and put his arm around me and said, "My lad, the world will hear from you." (Of course, he has forgotten the prophecy, but I haven't.) That may be the reason why I have done some things that I perhaps ought not to have done. Great preachers should be very careful how they put their hands on young ministeral sprouts.

I went to the church at McKinney and Routh. It was a flat topped tabernacle – looked like a hay barn. And I could stand on the platform and touch the ceiling with my hands. There were thirteen present – the thirteen original colonies.

I had a prepared sermon for that occasion, all written out. For had not I just finished a course in Homiletics? And I was an expert Homiletician, too. Dr. E. C. Dargan, the professor, said so. He called me in one day and said, "My young brother, the world will hear from you"

Dr. E. Y. Mullins called me in his office one day, showed me my grades in theology – I had perfect grades in all my subjects. He also made a very extravagant prophecy.

I believed all these great preachers said. And still have some of it left.

But I didn't preach that prepared sermon that day I don't know whether it was the heat – for my stove pipe collar melted down as soon as I got in – or whether it was the vacant wood yard, or whether it was the deacon that leaned up against one of the posts and went sound asleep, I didn't mind his going to sleep, but he snored. The rest of the crowd were used to it and didn't pay any attention to it, but it got on my nerves.

There I was, a highly distinguished preacher, valedictorian of my class, having delivered a great "statesmanlike" address on Japan. And Theodore Roosevelt who settled the war between Russia and Japan – why his coat wouldn't have made me a neck tie.

I had that manuscript, the prepared sermon in the inside of that long tailed coat. And it stayed there, too.

I shall never forget my first message. It was impromptu. It was spoken out of a heart of distress. And I meant every word of it. It was from the text, Mark 11:22, "Have faith in God."

There wasn't anything else around there to have faith in then. I was on four flats – worse than that, I was wilted.

The first month I got $12.50. The next month I got $22.50, and I owed over $800 and had my wife and baby girl on my hands.

I couldn't get away to hold meetings to supplement with, because if I had gone, there wouldn't have been anything there when I got back, so I had to stay.

But we got along fine. Somehow they gave me enough to live on, and no finer, nobler set of people ever drew the breath of life. They built a magnificent building at McKinney Avenue. And the church grew to a thousand membership. And they are a great church today. I love them very tenderly.

Right in the midst of the rapid growth of this church Judge T. B. Butler, former business manager of the Baptist Seminary and a director at the time of the Standard, called me before a group of men to take over the management of the Baptist Standard.

I was not thirty years old. I had never written an article in my life for a paper. Didn't know what a printing press looked like. I didn't know what a Mergenthaler linotype machine was. But it wasn't long until I knew – bills, bills! And I was fool enough to take it, or rather let it take me. Talk about a fellow getting a bear by the tail!

But the brethren wanted me to take it. Dr. J. B. Cranfill and Dr. S. A. Hayden were still on the scene. Dr. Hayden published the "Texas Baptist Herald," and Dr. J. B. Cranfill was coming rapidly back in power with his paper, "The Advance."

And right here I want to say that the greatest injustice ever done any man was the way the Texas Baptist machine treated Dr. J. B. Cranfill. It was his pen that fought their battles. And he is the greatest religious editor of this age.

I bought the whole outfit of the "Texas Baptist Heraid" for $30,000, including its machinery. And that was $29,999.90 more than it was worth – I am just telling of my fool mistakes.

I bought out Dr. Cranfill's, "The Advance," and the condition of sale was he signed a contract he would not go back into the Baptist paper business for ten years – and that was another mistake I made.

But I bought out both Drs. Hayden and Cranfill because the brethren wanted me to do it. That is what they got me for.

I did only one smart thing in the whole business, and I don't know why I did that. I got the stockholders to transfer to me in fee simple 54 per cent of the active voting stock. There was $7,000 "preferred stock" which Mr. George W. Carroll, a noble man, who had given large sums to the denomination, in his financial embarrassment had put up for collateral. And I didn't know anything about this $7,000. But I heard about it later to my great sorrow. No man was ever talked about or misrepresented so much as I was on the whole transaction.

I had a perfectly corking good time while running the Standard. And I ran it, too!

I decided the thing needed some new life in it, something to stir up its dead bones. So I put a lot of news in there, and the circulation increased from 16,000 to 38,000.

I made one advertising contract with Jacobs and Company for $40,000.00.

So I was flying high.

I believed all the prophecies that had been made concerning me. If I had consulted the Sybillian Books of ancient Rome I am sure I would have found something in there concerning my destiny.

## My First Big Fight

One day I got a letter from a country mother, twelve pages, from a little town in Southeast Texas, telling of the suicide of her only son. He was cashier in the bank, and he played the races and lost. He embezzled the funds of the bank. He wrote his mother and said, "I am sorry, but this is the only way out. I would rather be dead than in the penitentiary."

I laid the letter aside after writing her a word of sympathy. What could I do? But the thing got on my mind and I took Deacon H. Z. Duke, as fine a man as ever lived, and went out to the Dallas Pair with him. And we counted forty-eight book-making stands, and saw five thousand men and women in a drunken gambling debauch, women's hair disheveled, hanging over their shoulders – it was in the days before bobbed hair.

I found the city of Dallas got $125,000 annually out of this gambling. I went and had the whole thing photographed, and wrote it up in the Baptist Standard, front page, this title. "Racing at the Dallas Fair Gambling Hell."

Hon. T. M. Campbell was governor at that time. A Baptist deacon by the name of Greer from East Texas was in the Senate, and Judge Robinson, a Methodist, in the House of Representatives. They introduced the bill to stop race track gambling. The first thing I knew I was called before the Judiciary Committee. The greatest and most famous criminal lawyer, Hon William Crawford, was there to defend the gambling. All the members of the legislature read my exposure and it stirred things up.

Colonel Crawford, through long experience at criminal law, made an attack on me, evading the issue of gambling. That was the first public cussing I ever received. I wasn't used to it then.

He denied all that I had published, and the committee asked me for the proof. I went back to Dallas and brought it down. Dr. W. D. Bradfield, (now deceased) of Southern Methodist University, joined with me, and things were stirred up. They were red hot.

We spent seven weeks in Austin. And the brethren everywhere would write us wonderful letters, but didn't enclose any checks. They always said, "God bless you." I learned then for the first time the meaning of the song, "Jesus Paid It All." My friends, don't think that I am irreverent. I am simply telling some of my fool mistakes.

The General Ministerial Association of Dallas was called in special session. All the big preachers were there. Dr. J. Frank Smith of Central Presbyterian Church, Dr. Thornton Whaling, Dr. George W. Truett, Dr. J. W. Hill of the First Methodist. There were about a hundred in all. I was there.

I remember Dr. Jeff D. Ray was a visitor, and he had some things to say.

A committee of seven was appointed – I thought to help me in the gambling fight, but I found out differently afterwards.

The first thing I knew there was a called meeting in the Dallas News editorial office. I was not invited to this meeting.

Present at that meeting was the editorial staff of the Dallas News, Messrs. Tooney, Clark and Lombardy, and President of the National Exchange Bank, President of Chamber of Commerce, and several other representative business men. Among the distinguished divines, Drs. Thornton Whaling, J. Frank Smith, George W. Truett, G. C. Rankin, and J. B. Gambrell. The meeting was called to put a "kibosh" on me, and when Dr. Gambrell found it out he would not go any further until they phoned me to come.

I went.

I arrived, not knowing that my execution had been arranged, like the two noted former associates of Stalin who were shot this week.

Dr. Gambrell got up and said, "Gentlemen, this institution is on one corner of hell. The gambling at the Fair is a disgrace and ought to be stopped. That is all I have to say."

He reached down and picked up his hat and walked out. I followed him. And the meeting adjourned sine die. Dr. Truett condemned gambling in principle and also condemned my "methods."

One night in the Driscoll Hotel at Austin adjoining my room I heard my name used. I never heard so much cussing in my life, before or since. They didn't know I was in the adjoining room. It scared me. They told what they were going to do to me. For the first time since I was grown I felt a challenge to become religious. I saw I was into it. What could I do with all that crowd? Two whole train loads came down from Dallas to defend the gamblers. And they were all present at a joint session of the Legislature, House and Senate, Supreme Court and the Governor were present.

And I shall never forget what a knock-down, drag out fight we had. I closed the argument about two o'clock in the morning.

The bill was passed and race track gambling stopped in Texas for twenty-five years.

Governor Campbell called me into the governor's office and presented me with the pen he used to sign the Law.

I was not strong physically, and when the fight was over I was over. My health was gone. I had a good friend, Dr. J. H. Wayland, who wanted me to come out there and take charge of Plainview College, and that would have been a sure enough mistake. But I went and wife and I stayed with him awhile. He had a fine herd of thoroughbred cows grazing on the rich alfalfa and I got myself together.

During this time things went awry with the printing business.

But we got out the paper.

Concerning the fight against race track gambling in Texas the Literary Digest published, "Two ministers, Drs. J. Frank Norris and W. D. Bradfield, fought the combined forces of book makers, and what former governor, Charles E. Hughes, did for New York in 1905 these two Texas ministers did for the Lone Star State four years later."

There are some who see no humor in anything. They never laugh – neither do the people in the lower world – and some married people. But everybody is in a good humor in heaven. Even the Lord Himself laughs – "He that sitteth in the heavens shall laugh."

Therefore it is a free country and every man can take his choice. In hades they remind one of candidates for the divorce bill – chewing on each other and gnashing with their teeth. But in heaven they rejoice always. And if you expect to enjoy heaven, or even go there, better get in a good humor here.

I read a very able discussion by one of the world's outstanding psychologists, a very wonderful book, recently, on the effect of good humor and bad humor on the physical condition, and how the humor of the soul affects a man's features. A lot of women throw away their money going to beauty parlors, when if they would get in love with their husbands and enjoy life – in other words if they work at it from within – a woman who is ugly as home made sin could be as beautiful as Raphael's Madonna.

In giving the background to the call to Fort Worth, I left out an important chapter, and I give it because of its effect on my inner life.

As I said, I didn't want the Baptist Standard, but was persuaded to take it, and knew nothing in the world about the publishing business. I was thrown in the midst of the Atlantic Ocean without any life preservers and with a hundred pounds of lead on both feet and a ton around my neck.

Dr. Truett informed me that he would not write any more for the Standard.

And I told him that I needed the space anyhow. And I told him two things:

First, if it were an honor to be in the Standard each week, it should be passed around, and

Second, if it were a burden, it was a shame to overwork him.

But the Standard grew.

It wasn't long until Dr. Truett wrote a wonderful letter to the membership of the First Baptist Church, urging them to take the Baptist Standard. And I was paying for a shorthand reporter to take down his sermons. And everywhere he went, he would always send me the daily papers giving wonderful accounts of his great crowds and meetings, and I published them. I thought that was what he sent them to me for. I knew he never sent me these clippings before I was editor, and he hasn't sent them to me since. And I remember his meetings at Atlanta and Brooklyn, and other places, greater or lesser.

There would be no comment, just a large envelope of clippings from the daily papers. And the boys in the forks of the creek wondered how I got hold of these papers. Of course, Dr. Truett "detested the publicity."

Another thing I found out while editor of the Standard, namely, that all denominational bishops were just humans – they had feet of clay and lips of clay, just old East Texas red clay. That was a great shock to my young faith, for no young Israelite ever looked upon Aaron on the day of atonement with priestly garments down to his feet, going into the Holy of Holies, with greater reverence than I, as I stood at a safe distance, and eyed the denominational leaders. It took me several years before I felt comfortable in their presence – I was such a sinner. They filled me with awe.

I had heard somewhere George Elliott's expression, that there were three orders of creation – men, women, and preachers. But here was a fourth order, a sort of annex to the heavenly world, let down by a sheet, like the animals to Peter on the house top in Joppa.

Take this instance:

One time, before the Convention, the leaders called the brethren – the rank and file – to a special prayer meeting. There was a great crisis on. Deep anxiety prevailed. And the main High Priest got up before the prayer meeting and said:

"My dearly beloved brethren, we must keep step; we must have one mind; we must have heavenly guidance. The issue that is before the Convention presents the greatest crises – it is indeed an epochal hour. We are at the cross roads of Texas Baptist history." The Holy Father had spoken.

And I believed every word of it.

Why shouldn't I?

The brethren prayed, and then prayed some more, and prayed until everybody had his handkerchief out – I had mine out too – and we pulled our noses until they were as red as a turkey gobler's snout on the day before Thanksgiving.

Now the thing that they were praying for was already set up in type in the Baptist Standard office!

The prayer meeting adjourned about midnight. I went to my room, but I couldn't sleep. I was still in my twenties, and I wondered what it was all about. My disillusionment was on, and I felt something going on inside of me that I wasn't expecting.

Praying for what!

I soon found out that the leaders were not praying for objective results, but for subjective effects; that is, getting the brethren in notion to follow the leadership, not from above, but at the headquarters.

I tried my best to adjust myself, but it was like fitting a square stick in a round hole. I was as unreconstructible – this is a new word – as my granddaddy was at the close of the Civil War when he refused to be reconstructed to the Union. Both of us were wrong, my granddad and I. I know it – and I knew it then.

Praying for a matter that was already fixed!

But I am glad I found this out, because it has helped me a great deal to understand a lot of things since.

Incidentally that is one reason why I have never been afraid of the Sanhedrin. I soon found out that the little tin gods were like Dagon when the priests went in and found him on his face one morning, and took the old man and set him back on his pedestal. The next morning they came in and found him not only down on the floor, but his legs, arms, and head were off, and nothing but his trunk was left, and the Scripture says. "And they left and haven't been back until this day."

They didn't have much suspicion as to his impotency the first time they found Dagon on his face, but when they went back and saw his whole anatomy dismembered, their suspicions were aroused, and hopelessly so.

In all seriousness it was a terrible shock to me. There was a San Francisco earthquake inside. And it nearly destroyed my faith – I didn't have much to destroy.

# How I Helped to Establish the Southwestern Baptist Theological Seminary

This is one thing that I have never been accused of. But in order that the record might be complete I want to make another confession. I should not say confession, because that is a great institution. And in this day of world wide sweep of atheism and communism, even though we may not agree with all of its teachings, yet on the whole, we rejoice that the Gospel of salvation goes out from this great institution, the Southwestern Seminary.

While I was editor of the Standard, Dr. B. H. Carroll came to Dallas and called me to room 303, Oriental Hotel – the site is now occupied by the Baker Hotel. I went to his room and was happy to do so. What a giant figure he was, standing way above six feet and with long venerable white beard – and I thought I was standing in the presence of Samuel. And he was, indeed, a prophet for his day and generation.

He ordered refreshments – two bottles of Apollinaris water, one for each of us. It was the first time I had ever tasted any. I liked it, and it is good for what ails you. It will blow the top of your head off.

He said, "Frank, how much of the stock of the Baptist Standard do you own? And what is your legal relation to it?"

I said, "Dr. Carroll, I own the majority of the stock, and can control its policies."

"What do you think of the establishment of a seminary here in the Southwest? You were my student for four years, and you took my English Bible course. There is a great crisis coming, and it may not come in my day, but it will in your day. I see a dark cloud on the horizon, it is German Rationalism. It has already struck our Northern schools and seminaries, and it will soon come South, and the only way to meet it is to establish a Gibraltar of Orthodoxy in the Southwest."

I was for it and told him so.

Then he told me that the other denominational leaders were opposed to it, and he named Drs. A. J. Barton, S. P. Brooks, and George W. Truett.

But this family row among the denominational leaders didn't concern me any more than an ancient Athenian was concerned about the war among the gods of Olympus.

I was for him, and told him so.

He said, "All I want is plenty of space in the Standard – not much to begin with, but more later on. And if you will stand by me I will go afield and raise $55,000.00 to endow the chair of the English Bible.

"What I want you to do at present is to print the telegrams that I will send each week, giving full report of my work and of money raised."

I told him he could have the space, and soon the telegrams signed, "B. H. Carroll," appeared on the front page of the Standard.

Immediately the other denominational leaders got their heads together and called me into a conference and told me what would happen to me if I didn't stop it.

It was all funny to me.

But the telegrams kept coming from Dr. Carroll.

Then Dr. Carroll would get various brethren to write articles advocating establishment of the seminary. And the first argument that was published was from the able pen of W. K. Penrod, the pastor of the First Baptist Church of Cleburne, Texas. He is now in glory with Dr. Carroll.

The opposition to the establishment of the seminary began to pour in arguments, and I poured everyone of them into the waste basket.

They said I was partisan, that I was running the Standard with an iron hand, and I was accused even of being a dictator. That was a long time before Mussolini and Hitler got on the scene.

It didn't make any difference with me. I told Dr. Carroll what was going on, and he told me just to stand pat and publish what he sent in and what he got his supporters to send in, and to continue to throw the opposition in the waste basket. However, he said once, "Frank, perhaps you had better let some of the articles opposing the seminary be published, but send them to me before you publish them, and I will write a reply, and you can run it as an 'editorial'."

I picked out a typical article of the opposition and forwarded it to Dr. Carroll, and he annihilated it.

I ran it as an "editorial," and my, how many comments I got! There were quite a number who wrote and one brother said,

"You are the most brilliant editor in the religious world!"

And I believed it – this was another one of my fool mistakes, to believe it.

I did feel a little mean about it, but it is now over forty years ago, and I am glad the Lord says, "I will remember your sins against you no more forever."

But I did a good deed. And so I have some part in the Southwestern Baptist Theological seminary, even though some of the members of the faculty may not appreciate it.

They have had a little hard time getting their salary and per diem and I wish I could get Henry Ford or somebody to send them a million dollars. And If he knows what is good for him he will do it, because if you destroy these seminaries and churches, the Reds will hang Henry Ford and Sloan higher than Haman.

Incidentally I had some "standing" among my denominational leaders in my youth.

Oh, I forgot to say, Dr. Carroll had me as his assistant before I became editor of the Standard while I was in the seminary at Louisville. He also, like the other leaders, made most flattering prophecies concerning my future. He said one day, "Frank, you have in you the making of a great preacher."

I believed it then. And this was another mistake of foolish youth.

Of course, the other denominational leaders never did forgive me for siding with Dr. Carroll. But some of them are dead, and all the rest of us will go to our reward. And in the ages upon ages we will rejoice together.

## Call to Fort Worth – 1909

When Mr. G. H. Connell called me to come to Fort Worth to supply, I accepted and they gave me $25.00 for that Sunday.

Evidently they liked the sample and asked me to come back the next Sunday.

But I had made all arrangements to leave Dallas and go to the far West to regain my health. But the pulpit committee asked me to supply again, which I did. And there was some time required to wind up my affairs with the Standard, and they asked me if I would supply during this time.

There was a pulpit committee of thirty, and the committee had voted unaminously to call Dr. Samuel J. Porter, than whom there was never a nobler, finer man, preacher, scholar, and he was a great orator. He had been pastor of the First Baptist Church. San Antonio, then he went to the Roger Williams church. Washington, from which place he went on to glory.

One morning the chairman of the pulpit committee got up before the church and said,

"The pulpit committee is ready to report on the call of pastor next Wednesday night, and everybody should be present." I thought, of course that Dr. Porter would be called. And I know we preachers do like the old maid when proposed to – "This is so sudden and unexpected, and I am surprised." But certainly this was true when near midnight Judge R. H. Buck called me in Dallas and said,

"As chairman of the notification committee I am happy to tell you that you have been called to the pastorate of the First Baptist Church, Fort Worth."

Judge Buck was a great lawyer, occupying the high position of Judge of the Forty-eighth District Court, and then went to the Court of Civil Appeals, from which honored place he went to his reward.

The committee went before the church and said, "We have no recommendation to make concerning any man, and recommend that the church proceed by ballot."

There were 334 votes cast by ballot.

There was opposition to the call, and only one whole family, and that was J. T. Pemberton and his family.

Mr. Pemberton said, "I am not opposed to J. Frank Norris; I am for him, but this church is not in condition for his type of ministry. If he comes there will be the all firedest explosion ever witnessed in any church. We are at peace with the world, the flesh, and the devil, and with one another. And this fellow carries a broad axe and not a pearl handle pen knife. I just want to warn you. But now since you have called him, I am going to stay by him."

And he stayed by me. He is the best friend I ever had. At a later time I will give his whole connection and loyalty.

Not sparing myself, I had very little faith. My experiences above related with the denominational leaders shattered my soul to its deepest depths. I wanted to quit the ministry. My dad always told me that I would make a great lawyer, and so did everybody else. That was my boyhood ambition. And now what was I going to do?

I was utterly disgusted with churches, the ministry, and the whole machinery.

But I went back the next Sunday, and to the great surprise of the First Church I didn't accept it. I only referred to the call and said, "I thank you." And they were amazed that I didn't jump in head over heels. It was the richest church in the city, or the state, or the South. Millionaires hung in bunches. It was the church known as "The Home of the Cattle Kings."

I shall never forget my first text: – Job 19:25 – 26, "For I know that my redeemer liveth, and that he shall stand at the latter day upon the earth: And though after my skin worms destroy this body, yet in my flesh shall I see God."

Job was in the deepest, darkest depths of despair when he uttered these words, which I consider the highest height of Old Testament revelation. The only difference between me and Job was he came up from the bottom to the highest heights, but I stayed down there. Every time I would start to climb up I was like the proverbial frog which crawled up out of the well two feet every day and fell back three feet every night. How long did it take the frog to get out?

I was pale, wan, worn, and weary. I had a terrible cough. And because of my condition I was greatly surprised at the call.

A large group of men, among them three bank presidents, quite a number of capitalists and cattle kings met with me for a conference. They told me what a wonderful church they had – and it was all true. They did the talking. They had no idea what was going on in my soul. My faith – what little I had left – was fast ebbing away; my unbelief changed into contempt. The darkness of Gethsemane was fast settling over my soul.

When they finished the long conference of eulogizing the great church, its wealth, its prestige, its standing, et cetera, ad infinitum, ad nauseam, I rose and said just one sentence:

"Gentlemen, if I come to you I don't know what will happen. All I know is we won't look like we do now when we get through with each other."

I had forgotten the expression, but many years afterwards Mr. J. W. Spencer who went out with the exodus and later became my good friend before his death, and we often laughed about it afterwards – he reminded me of what I said.

It was a typical church with the B. Y. P. U's, Ladies Aid, W. M. U's, Boards, Gee-whiz "high-falutin" choir, pipe organ, ushers, and twenty some odd committees.

I had a literal contempt for the whole machinery.

But I went on with it, and for two years did my best to fit into the program. They were exceedingly lovely to me and my family. They showered their gifts, they gave the largest salary of any church in the state or South. And if they heard of anybody giving one larger they would raise mine – and I never objected – they furnished me a home, paid all the bills, I never bought a suit of clothes, overcoat, hat, necktie, or even a pair of socks. They remembered my family on Thanksgiving Day, Christmas, birthdays, and between times. The chairman of the board of trustees drove up one day with a handful of twenty dollar gold pieces and gave everybody one, including the cook and the yard man. My rich officials had one of the finest cars ever made driven up to my door, and the fellow told me to get in – and I did. And that was the first time I had ever sat in an automobile. He drove me around, and asked me "How do you like it?"

Well, I told him what Mark Twain said concerning Niagara Falls – "It's a success."

He said, "It is yours." And then he explained to me how it came, and then the best part, explained to me how he was to keep it up.

It was customary for the pastor to take a whole summer vacation, not one month, but the entire summer. At the time for the first vacation the chairman of the finance committee gave me a morocco bound book of travelers checks, $20.00 each. I had never seen one of them before, never even heard of them while I was down there in the black lands of West Texas pulling the bell cord over the gray backs of Beck and Jude from the break of day until dark.

When I got home I counted these twenty dollar travelers checks, and it was just even $1000. I took a trip, but I couldn't spend the amount, and they would have been insulted if I had given any check back. And I never liked to insult people deliberately.

The next summer my wife and children and myself all went up into Colorado and they paid all expenses.

No danger of anything happening to the church while I was gone – no more than there would be a corpse.

I was a typical city pastor. I was the chief after dinner speaker. I had tuxedoes, swallow tail coats, a selection of "biled" shirts, several of them, and I would give $10.00 for the latest joke. I was, as I said, the main attraction at all the gatherings of the Rotarians, Lions, Kiwanis, Eagles. I was Will Rogers and Mark Twain both combined; they thought so, so did I.

It made little difference to me what the church did. Thus I spent my first two years.

I went home one Sunday night and told my wife, "I am going to quit the ministry."

She said, "When did you ever begin?"

Such unkindness!

I agreed with her and said, "I am going to quit before I begin. I didn't want to come here, I have had no faith. I don't even know whether I am a Christian. I thought I was once – fact is don't know whether there is a God. I am going to leave it all."

My good friend Charlie Carroll, son of Dr. B. H. Carroll, was then pastor in Owensboro, Kentucky, and wanted me to come for a meeting, and I wired him I would come. I didn't go for the meeting, just went to get away from things, and meet myself coming, or find out which way I was going.

I was in the same fix I was up here not long ago in Detroit when I made the wrong turn, didn't know the traffic rules. I saw the policeman and thought I would beat him to it, and called out to him, "Mr. Officer, do you know where I am going?"

He said, "Yes, you are going with me down to the City Hall."

I pulled out a letter from Colonel Heinrich Pickert, the Police Commissioner in which he told me he would do everything he could to help me. The officer relented and stood on the running board to the next corner.

I thanked him.

Incidentally, I used that letter several times afterwards until Entzminger borrowed it, and then he lost it.

Before I went to the Owensboro engagement I was in a very bad state of mind. I didn't care what happened – mark you there was perfect peace in the church – just as there is in a grave yard. The only difference between that church and the grave yard was the people iii the grave yard were buried and everybody knew it, but in the church they were dead and unburied and didn't know it.

The Ladies Aid – and don't anybody get the idea that I have it in for the Ladies Aid – I just haven't anything for them – they were very nice to cover the platform and pulpit with a lot of pot plants – ferns – geraniums – gladioli – palms – chrysanthemums – it was decorated the same way for weddings, funerals, and preaching. And there I stood straight up, all embalmed, and all that was needed was that peculiar scent of the mixture of roses and carbolic acid. I had on my long tail coat and striped breeches – I had several suits by that time.

I did a very mean thing, but I think the Lord forgave me, even before I did it. I went down in the poor section near the Trinity River and got a whole crowd of poor people with their children, and got them all up in the church one night and gave them free entertainment – ice cream was served, as well as some other things, and they got it all over that fine heavy carpet.

The next day when the diamond bedecked sisters of the Ladies Aid came and saw how their rich, highly colored carpet was ruined – "It is terrible – It is terrible – It is terrible" – "He is going to ruin our church, going to make a regular Salvation Army out of it."

When I came back from Owensboro, after a month's meditation on the banks of the Ohio, I decided I would enter the ministry.

I began to preach the gospel after the fashion of John the Baptist in the wilderness of Judea. I didn't use a pearl handle pen knife; I did what J. T. Pemberton said, I had a broad axe and laid it at the tap root of the trees of dancing, gambling, saloons, houses of ill fame, ungodly conduct, high and low, far and near. And you talk about a bonfire – the whole woods was set on fire and it looked like the forest fire I saw in Northern Michigan once when it appeared that the infernal regions below had burst through the crust of the earth and painted the lurid flames of the inferno itself on the clouds above.

With all the intensity of my soul I waded into the thing, right and left, fore and aft, inside and outside. I asked no questions for conscience's sake or stomach's sake. I got me a Scotch tweed, salt and pepper suit of clothes and went in arm and hammer brand style.

The crowds came, large numbers were saved.

First thing I knew I got a call from the chairman of the board of trustees. He was in the wholesale grocery business, a very domineering type of man, and he had been one of my closest friends. He was the one who gave the twenty-dollar gold pieces on Thanksgiving. He called me up as if I had been a negro janitor and talked to me with less respect than I would speak to the janitor. He said in a few curt words: – "I want you to come down here right away. I want to see you."

I started to tell him to go where the fires don't go out, but fortunately I decided otherwise, and I went.

I knew then I had put my foot on the edge of a bottomless abyss covered with flowers.

I knew then I had entered the ministry.

I knew then that I was in the supreme fight of my life.

Before I got there he had told all his office force, and everybody on the outside heard him say it, "We are going to fire that blankety blank preacher, and I am going to tell him what I think of him."

I went into that office as a lamb led to the slaughter. Only afterwards did I find out what he said. When I went in he never even asked me to sit down, had his feet propped up on his desk, and he just rared back and they heard him all over the place as he began to tell me what a fool I was, and what a mistake they had made, and closed by saying, "Norris, when we called you we thought you had some sense, but you are a D—— fool! And this is to notify you that you are fired!"

I walked up close to him, and if the Lord ever helped a poor preacher He helped me that noon. I was made over. There was something beyond human power and wisdom that shot through my soul. I looked him squarely in the eye, and I wasn't afraid of him. I had already come to the point where it mattered little what happened to me. All sense of fear was gone.

I said, "Mr. W——, No. You have not made a mistake. I thought you made a mistake in the call, but you are the one that is fired!"

He had objected to the crowd of poor people I was bringing to the church, and even went on to say, "I noticed the other night where you baptized a notorious street walker in the very same baptistry where I was baptized."

I said, "You are mistaken. There was not one; there were two. And I don't know how you know who they are, but last Sunday night they came to the church and it was crowded and they couldn't get in, but stood on the outside and heard the message. And the next day they came to my house, and one of them had a little girl five years of age. And they both in the presence of my wife and me related the story of their sin and sorrow and wanted to be saved and start life over again. We prayed, and they were both saved. And I want to say to you, Sir, that I would rather have my church filled with publicans and sinners that come to hear the gospel, than to have it run by a worldly, ungodly crowd of officials that have their automobiles full of liquor and women and go out and spend all night on the lake and then come around the next Sunday and pass around the bread and wine at the Lord's table. You are fired! And next Sunday I am going to tell the whole world your threats!"

And I did, and the fight was on, and it has been on ever since.

Dr. E.Y. Mullins, President of Southern Baptist Theological Seminary, Dr. J.B. Gambell, President Southern Baptist Convention, and Dr. J. Frank Norris, pastor of First Baptist Church. This picture was in London in 1920 when Dr. Norris arranged an appointment for them with David Lloyd George.

The picture was taken in London in 1920. Dr. E. Y. Mullins was president of the Southern Baptist Theological Seminary, Dr. J. B. Gambrell, President Southern Baptist Convention, and Dr. J. Frank Norris, Pastor of the First Baptist Church.

Drs. Mullins and Gambrell were touring Europe in behalf of the Baptists, and the day before the three met. Through the courtesy of Sir Arthur I. Durrant, Commissioner of His Majesty Works, I was carried to 10 Downing Street and introduced to David Lloyd George, the Prime Minister. He gave me an autographed photograph which I still have.

Drs. Gambrell and Mullins had been waiting in London for three days seeking an interview with David Lloyd George, and they could hardly believe it when they were informed of my interview the day before.

I immediately called up Sir Arthur I. Durrant and he arranged for their meeting with Lloyd George the next morning. I was on my first visit to London on my way to Palestine. Through the courtesy of Mr. John Coutts I was brought in contact with Sir Arthur I. Durrant who in turn secured a special permit through the War Department which at that time was closed and no passports were issued in Palestine.

The three of us had many happy experiences in London. The following letter from Dr. Mullins has always been prized very highly:

"Louisville, Kentucky
May 9, 1912.

"My dear Dr. Norris:

"I have followed the newspaper accounts of your trial with keenest interest and will say that I am delighted at the outcome expresses it mildly.

"I have read Dr. Gambrell's review in the Standard and I quite concur in his judgment that it was a 'Colossal frameup.'

"May this sorrow turn to the deepening of your Spiritual life and thereby enlarge your ministry.

"Yours very cordially,
"E. Y. MULLINS."

When the fire destroyed the magnificent auditorium of the First Baptist Church in January 1929. When the pastor returned next day the Dallas news said, "Dr. Norris stood on the corner across the street from the ruins of the magnificent auditorium where he had preached to multiplied thousands, and tears cursed down his cheeks as he stood in silence for several minutes". It was late Saturday afternoon and no place to worship the next day but he called his workers around him and in a few minutes more than 100 men were working to enclose a big tabernacle at Lipscomb&Morphy. They worked all night while the pastor superintended the job and by 10 o'clock next morning a place was prepared, ready and heated for the 5,000 people, and the pastor preached on the text: "And he thanked God and took courage". More than 60 people were saved and came onto the church a great revival followed.

Former building with radio towers destroyed by fire.

# CHAPTER II

### DEMAND NORRIS LEAVE CITY IN THIRTY DAYS OR ELSE

One of the most trying experiences in all my life was when there was a red hot local option election on in Fort Worth and Tarrant County. The financial and liquor interests united, and most preachers were in complete silence. But not Norris.

He spoke in every school house and community throughout the county.

In the midst of this red hot campaign a hundred and sixty-five men met in the dining room of the Metropolitan Hotel where the Chamber of Commerce now holds its office.

They appointed a committee to wait on Norris and they came to his office, three of them, and delivered an ultimatum and said, "We Will give you thirty days, time to wind up your affairs and leave town or else take the consequences"'

Norris thanked them for giving him thirty days and said,

"I will give you twenty-nine of them back."

Excitement was running high. You could see knots of people standing on the sidewalk and there was but one theme.

Norris had no radio, had no paper, and the daily papers refused to take his advertisement for pay. He struck off circulars by the tens of thousands and published and printed the demand that he leave town and gave the names of the men who were back of the demand at 15th and Main Streets that night.

Talk about crowds! It seemed as if everybody in town was there, and a lot more.

Norris arranged for a truck to be at this corner before sun down.

Talk about seared! I didn't want to be in it. I knew there would be wholesale killing. But on the other hand I was not coward enough to forsake my partner. I went.

From what I heard and understood, I think everybody was carrying his gun that night. But Norris didn't have any.

The police tried to clear the streets, but in vain

The fire company tried it, but in vain.

For blocks and blocks they were stacked.

Norris wore white trousers, white shirt, white tie and was in shirt sleeves. Didn't even have a pen knife.

He tried to force his way through that mass of packed humanity, and one man who owned the saloon across the street – Norris pushed up against him and he turned and ripped out an oath and said, "What do you want?"

Norris said, "I want to get to that corner down there where I can speak."

He looked at him and said, "Who are you?"

"I am Frank Norris."

This big strong 225 pounder whirled around with a forty-five in his hand and said – and everybody heard him – "I came out here to get the first shot." And he turned to Norris and said, "follow me! The first man that lays a hand on this preacher I will shoot a hole through him you can drive that truck through."

He went through that crowd with the gun held before him, Norris hanging on to his coat tail.

This big fellow walked up, climbed up on the truck and sat down with that gun across his lap and said, "Frank, give 'em hell."

He stood there on that seat and said,

"I have nothing against you, and I call on the God of Elijah, the God of my mother to lay bare His mighty arm in judgment in this city."

And then he led the huge crowd in singing, "There's a Land that is Fairer Than Day." And when he had finished he said, "Good night." Everybody quietly stole away and nobody was hurt.

The next morning this big saloon keeper came to the church office and walked in, and I was scared again when he pulled out that long gun and he laid it on Norris' desk and said,

"I am through. I want you to pray for me, and I want to give you this gun as a memento." And he knelt and was gloriously saved and Norris baptized him.

Of course he went out of the saloon business.

## WHEN NORRIS MADE A JUDGE CANCEL AN INJUNCTION

Just an example of the many difficulties the First Baptist Church had to overcome in the years of struggle. The First Church bought 100 feet square on Fourth and Taylor, where the present entrance to the main auditorium is. A woman ran a two-story "rooming house" and the church needed possession to build. They offered to pay her a handsome bonus to give possession but instead the opposition on the outside, led by three deacons on the inside, backed by the denominational machine, persuaded the district judge to issue an injunction against moving this house off the property of the First Baptist Church. That meant a long delay.

Norris had the record of this judge where he owned a certain resort out on the lake where he frequently was found, and not in condition to teach a Sunday School class.

Norris went to see this judge in his private office and told him, "I will give you twenty-four hours to dismiss that injunction." That was on Saturday morning, and the judge didn't wait twenty-four hours, he dismissed it in twenty-four minutes.

Again, Norris was criticized for talking to the court in such a fashion, but he was fighting a hard fight against overwhelming odds.

Incidentally, that judge died a sudden death three weeks afterwards.

Temple Baptist Sunday School Building – Detroit

# CHAPTER III

## WHEN THE PASTOR WAS FIRED IN THE SALOON AT $808\frac{1}{2}$ HOUSTON

It was known as the "University Club." It had a retail liquor license on the door.

One of the deacons of the First Baptist Church at that time was president of the club, and two other deacons were directors.

Twenty-six men, deacons and prominent members of the First Baptist Church, had a specially called meeting at this place, $808\frac{1}{2}$ Houston Street, upstairs. The same number $808\frac{1}{2}$ can be seen to this day!

They called the young preacher in and bluntly, coldly said, "You are fired." Only one man stood by him – "Only Luke is with me" – and that man was J. T. Pemberton.

The young pastor said, "Gentlemen, I will answer you next Sunday night."

They flew into a rage. The young pastor wrote each of them a letter and gave their connections – it is best to pull down the curtain.

Three of these men called on the pastor and told him,

"If you call our names and tell what you said in that letter there will be a funeral in town the next day."

The young pastor quietly asked, "What text do you want me to use at your funeral?"

He carried out his purpose and called the names and gave the records. Of course things broke loose on every hand.

He was severely criticized. I suppose if I had been present I would have joined in the criticisms. All the denominational leaders joined in against him. Remember, these men were rich men and there is not an exception when a pastor has trouble that the denominational leaders will always line up with the wealth that is against the pastor.

Ahe leading stores closed their doors and called all their employees together to hear the Gospel by Dr. Norris. The above picture os of the Monning Dry Goods Company, several hundred employees listening to Dr. Norris.

# CHAPTER IV

## WHEN THE CHOIR WAS FIRED – THE BEER-GUZZLING DUTCHMAN LEADING

After two years just marking time – a typical city pastor – the young pastor put on the new program, preaching the full gospel, multitudes came and the church was too small.

There was a beer-guzzling Dutchman with a bunch of frizzled hair as long as Samson's hair – he led the choir on Sunday and played for dances and beer gardens during the week.

The first night of the new full gospel program the church was packed and the aisles were packed early.

The choir director with some dozen were in the alley on the outside behind the church and sent in a "Please open the way so the choir can get in."

The pastor wrote on the bottom of the note, "Wait till I send for you."

If he had waited till the pastor sent for him he would be standing there yet, and, like Lot's wife, turned to a pillar of salt.

The next morning this frizzled-haired Dutchman came dashing into the pastor's office – he was knock-kneed and couldn't get his heels within a foot of each other. In his rage he said, "Vot does dis mean? You ruined my choir program last night."

The pastor said, "Professor, it means that you have resigned."

"Vot? Me resign? I have been here twelve years!"

The pastor: "That is long enough. I am going to be here the next twelve years."

The frizzled-haired choir director shouted, "I vill take it up with the deacons!"

The pastor said, "Take it up with the deacons. " And he did.

Late in the afternoon Dr. Norris met J. T. Pemberton who said to him,

"Well, I will see you at the deacons meeting tonight."

That was the first the pastor knew of a specially called meeting of the deacons. And that was just about as much as the pastor had to say on how things were run around the First Baptist Church. He had about as much to say about it as a weaned calf tied to a post outside the cow lot, looking through the cracks of the gate where his mammy was and he wanted to be and could not even stick his nose through the crack.

The pastor waited until the proceedings were in full headway and then walked in unannounced. Talk about a hot time!

The pastor rose and said, "I told the Professor this morning that he had resigned."

Immediately three of the rich deacons leaped to their feet and took the side of the choir director. The young pastor said,

"Gentlemen, you have also resigned."

And they did resign and stayed resigned. And there was a house cleaning in the choir.

## A Typical City Church Program

They are all alike – all in the same rut – and a rut is a grave with both ends knocked out.

And the program – all sessions, was as follows:

1. Organ Prelude.
2. Doxology.
3. Invocation.
4. Hymn.
5. Anthem.
6. Offertory – organ music in B flat – all soon flat.
7. Solo – starting in G and ending in G-whizz.
8. Prayer (make it very short)
9. Duet.
10. Sermonette.

11. Benediction.
12. Postlude.
13. Get-away-in-a-hurry, go home, come back next Sunday and do the same thing over again.

And when the young pastor put the kibosh on whole cut-and-dried program – cut in two in the middle and dried at both ends – he called down on his head maledictions of all compartments, and "compoodlements."

# CHAPTER V

## WHEN THE W. M. U. LADIES AID "RESIGNED"

They were typical. "Women's organizations," and I have never known a single one to be a soul winning organization. As I often heard Dr. Norris say, "They will meet and gossip about everybody on earth and under the earth."

He called all the ten groups of organizations together at one time, and they thought he was going to make one of his typical "lady finger'" addresses that the average pastor is supposed to do.

He left his car running, held his hat in his hand and said,

"Ladies, I have no address to make, only an announcement. You have resigned sine die."

Talk about trouble breaking loose and brick-bats flying in the air! It was worse than when Jezebel got after Elijah, and no flaming chariot to take the pastor home to his heavenly address! He never stopped until he eliminated all "organizations" and put everything in Sunday School classes and Sunday School departments. He took the Great Commission literally when it said,

First, Make Disciples.
Second, Baptize them, and
Third, Teach them.

This platform explains the two greatest Sunday Schools in the world – and they have been the two greatest now for many years.

During his 38 years in Fort Worth Dr. Norris conducted 120 tent or open air meetings. The above picture was taken of his meeting on East Weatherford Street, Fort Worth, 1934.

# CHAPTER VI

## HOW GEORGE WHITE SAVED J. FRANK NORRIS FROM ASSASSIN'S BULLET

George E. White was one of the greatest laymen of my acquaintance. He was one of the leading business men of Fort Worth. He lived at 917 West Second Street where recently a new dormitory was finished for the Seminary.

Late one night George White and J. Frank Norris were walking from Fifth Street through the back way to White's home where Norris and his family were living after their home had been destroyed by fire.

Suddenly the would-be assassin sprang upon Norris from the rear and George White knocked the gun up and grappled with the assassin who tore loose and lacerated Mr. White's hand.

Mr. White was, indeed, a father to the pastor and but for his intervention that would have been the last night of the pastor on earth.

## PANTS AND SLEEVES TOO SHORT – SUIT BORROWED FROM A. F. PLUNKETT

Why would there be a story in pants too short and sleeves too short? Isaiah speaks of a bed too short and cover too narrow, but here a preacher wore a suit of clothes that was three or four numbers too small or too short.

Twenty different suits and overcoats, that had been given him by his rich members, had all been burned and the young preacher borrowed a suit from his closest friend, Andrew Plunkett. The pants hardly reached his shoe tops and the sleeves were three inches too short, but the preacher brought a message to the overflowing Byers Opera House – now the Palace Theater – on I Cor. 15:19 – "If in this life only we have hope in Christ, we are of all men most miserable." More than ten thousand people packed the streets and the preacher appeared on the outside and preached to the overflow a few minutes, and large numbers were saved.

People soon forgot to laugh at the pants and sleeves that were too short but they thought only of God and how to meet Him. More than 100 souls were saved.

# CHAPTER VII

## THE MAYOR WHO CUT THE TENT DOWN, AND AFTERWARDS WAS LED TO CHRIST BY DR. NORRIS

In 1911 there was a state-wide fight to rid Texas of the curse of liquor. W. D. Davis was mayor of Fort Worth, a very strong, dynamic and colorful personality. He built many public works for the City, among them he constructed the huge dam at Lake Worth. He was a liberal of the liberals, and believed in a wide open town.

Norris secured a permit to put up a big tent at Tenth and Houston, the whole block was vacant at that time, where now is located the Telephone Building. Sarah Bernhardt toured America to break the theatre trust and had a huge circus tent and Fort Worth was the last place she gave her concert, and she stored the big tent here, and years afterward Norris bought it for storage.

A great revival broke out and there can be no revival without naming and fighting every manner of evil, and this Norris did.

One day Mayor Davis called him up and said,

"You have got to take that tent down, it's causing too much trouble."

Norris went down to the Mayor's office and there was a red-hot argument, and the Mayor sent the Fire Department and cut the tent all to pieces.

Norris stood under the clear sky and preached that night, and talk about excitement!

Norris went after the Mayor and his crowd.

The Mayor retaliated and went after Norris.

W. P. Lane, State Comptroller, reported to Norris how the City was $400,000 short in its public funds.

Norris demanded that the Mayor give an account of it.

The Mayor called his crowd of 3,000 together and said,

"No boys under 21, no women allowed."

And of all the vile, bitter denunciations that were ever heaped on a man Bill Davis did on the head of the pastor of the First Baptist Church. And he closed by saying,

"If there are fifty red-blooded men in this town a preacher will be hanging from a limb before daylight!"

Someone who was present, heard the Mayor's in flamatory speech, and called Norris and told him to leave home. He did leave home and came up to the crowd where the Mayor was holding forth, only a few blocks from his house, and when he walked up the group quickly dispelled and he returned home. The next night the First Baptist Church was burned, and then excitement, recriminations, mass meetings, counter mass meetings, and the Mayor's crowd raised $20,000 and brought the head man of Burns Detective Agency to Fort Worth to frame Norris.

Dr. J. B. Gambrell published all that Court House conspiracy. He was the greatest Christian statesman of that time or of all time.

Time marches on!

Afterwards the Mayor was suddenly stricken with appendicitis. He waited too late, peritonitis had set in. The surgeon told him,

"Mr. Mayor, if you have anything to attend to you better do it at once."

The Mayor said (he was not Mayor then), "Call Frank Norris"

It was one A. M. Dr. Norris lived a short distance from the Harris Hospital on Fifth Avenue. When he went into the room Davis was having hiccups and a cold sweat of death was on his brow and he said,

"I want you to get those good women in your church to pray for me, and pull old Bill through for I'm not ready to go. They prayed and pulled you through when I was after you."

Dr. Norris called his wife and she called up several of the most faithful women and men, and they not only prayed, but gathered at the church, between two and three o 'clock m the morning.

Dr. Norris started to leave, and the Mayor said,

"Don't go, stay with me."

When it was morning the surgeon came into his room and said,

"Mr. Mayor, you're a whole lot better, the crisis is past!"

He said, "Yes, Frank has had a large group of his men and women praying for me and their prayers have pulled me through. God has given me another chance."

Dr. Norris led his bitter enemy to Christ and he became his warmest friend, and he stood before the First Baptist Church he tried to destroy and told the simple story, how God snatched him from the jaws of death and gave him another chance, and now he was happy in the faith of the Lord Jesus Christ.

"That a notable miracle had been wrought, none could deny."

Intermediate Department Sunday School crowd in temporary tabernacle after the first fire 1913

# CHAPTER VIII

"NO DOUBT THIS MAH IS A MURDERER" – Acts 28:4 – THE CHIPPS CASE

Many good men have been accused of murder – some innocent, some guilty.

Moses was accused of murder, and was guilty.

Paul was a murderer and confessed his guilt – "And I persecuted this way unto the death, binding and delivering into prisons both men and women."

There are murderers who never kill any man – I John 3:15,

"Whosoever hateth his brother is a murderer: and ye know that no murderer hath eternal life abiding in him" – a hint in this scripture for certain denominational leaders.

Not every man who kills another is a murderer. It is true soldiers kill other men, but it is without malice and in defense of their native land.

A man may kill another in an accident, but he is no murderer. The great and beloved George W. Truett killed the Chief of Police of the city of Dallas while out hunting. But he was no murderer.

At 10 A. M. Friday morning July 16, 1926 two city officers, Harry Conner and Fred Holland, warned Dr. Norris that D. E. Chipps had made repeated threats, and before many others, in the Texas Hotel the night before, he said, "I am going to kill J. Frank Norris."

Norris had never heard of Chipps, knew nothing about him, and therefore could have no malice or hate towards him.

On the fateful Saturday afternoon Chipps walked up Main Street to the Westbrook Hotel where he was staying and told many people, "Sunday morning the Star-Telegram will have front page headline,

**"D. E. Chipps Kills J. Frank Norris."**

Those were the exact words in the Star-Telegram and his prophecy came true except their names were reversed.

At 3:30 P. M. he asked the PBX operator at the Westbrook Hotel, "Get J. Frank Norris on the telephone." He was impatient and cursed her because she did not get Norris quickly enough. The name of this operator was Mrs. J. H. Greer and she still lives. She testified,

"Because of Chipp's anger and abuse I listened to the conversation. Everybody in the hotel was afraid of him. I heard him call Dr. Norris many vile names, and he was very profane. I heard him repeat several times, "You blankety, blankety, blank, I am coming over there and kill you."

L. H. Nutt, a deacon in the First Baptist Church was in the office of the pastor at that time. He was teller in the Farmer's and Mechanics Bank, a very honorable man. After those violent threats from Chipps over the phone, Norris turned to Nutt and asked,

"Who is this man, D. E. Chipps?"

Nutt told him the reputation of Chipps, that he was a troublemaker and had had many escapades with the police.

Before Norris knew it Chipps kicked the door open – it was only a block away from the Westbrook Hotel – and announced so all could hear, "This is D. E. Chipps, you blankety, blankety blank – I am going to kill you."

The night watchman of the church always left his gun in a drawer in the pastor's office for safe keeping. It has always been a joke how it has been published "Two gun Norris," "Pistol Packin' Pastor," et cetera. He never carried a gun.

Norris sought to quiet Chipps and succeeded for a moment. Then he saw that Chipps' anger and abuse increased – and Nutt testified that Chipps kept his hand on his right side, with his coat pulled back, and kept moving it – finally Norris said,

"There is the door and I don't want any trouble with you."

Norris was standing with his back against his desk and had his hand on the gun and did everything he could to avoid trouble.

Chipps went out into the hallway and the mayor of the city and some others who had sent Chipps to Norris' office were waiting in the car across the street in of the First Baptist Church office building where Norris' office was.

No doubt Chipps' mock pride got the best of him and he whirled around and started back into Norris' office and said, so the testimony shows, "I will kill you, you blankety, blankety blank!"

And quick as a flash it was over.

Immediately the mayor, the city manager and other henchmen were up the stairway. Norris had gone into the larger office to phone his wife.

The testimony showed there were two guns found on the floor in the room and they were never presented in the trial. And why?

The testimony showed that at the morgue, the Mayor, H. G. Meacham, said,

"Poor Chipps, I sent him to his death."

Of course Norris was quickly vindicated, and notwithstanding all the dregs of bitterness and passion of years that entered into it.

Norris went before the congregation the next Sunday morning and said, "It is a great sorrow, but I have no apology for what I have done. I could not have done otherwise. I was forced to defend myself, my wife and children," and he offered his resignation.

The church leaped to its feet and refused to accept his resignation. Those present will never forget the first Sunday morning afterwards.

Of course the secular press sent out many distorted and untrue stories. Some of them continue to do so. Last year a fine daily paper at Abilene published an untrue statement concerning the Chipps tragedy, but afterwards made the following apology:

> **THE ABILENE REPORTER-NEWS**
> Sunday Morning, March 24, 1946
>
> # Dr. J. Frank Norris Not A Gun Totin' Parson
>
> In our issue of December 2, 1945, we published an article entitled "NORRIS TO SPEAK AT BAPTIST MEET."
>
> This article, on the whole, was laudatory of Dr. Norris, and we deeply regret that the statement occurs as follows: "known as the gun totin' parson." This is not true, and there is no record in any court of law where such was ever charged, much less proven.
>
> Dr. Norris is pastor of the two great churches, First Baptist Church of Fort Worth, where he has been for thirty-seven years, and pastor of Temple Baptist Church, Detroit, where he has been for twelve years, alternating between these two great churches.
>
> He has the distinction of being pastor of the largest combined membership in the world under one minister, and has the two largest Sunday Schools in America.
>
> The following is a report of the twelve years' joint pastorate: Twenty Thousand Five Hundred additions to both churches; $2,300,000 raised for all purposes; two and a half million, six hundred forty-four thousand copies of Fundamentalist, weekly paper, has carried the gospel to the uttermost parts of the earth; during the time (thirty-seven years in Fort Worth, twelve years in Detroit) the pastor has traveled 864,000 miles.
>
> Both Sunday Schools use the Bible only as a textbook in all classes, instead of hop-skip International lesson series. Both churches support New Testament Fundamental Baptist Missionary Fellowship, and have no part or lot in any ecclesiastical machine.
>
> The year just closed, the two churches had the remarkable record of over 2,300 additions, and over $400,000 raised. Dr. Norris is also President of the Bible Baptist Seminary and Editor of the Fundamentalist.

The Chipps affair was a great sorrow to Norris and his family and will be.

# CHAPTER IX

## AND JUDGMENT CAME – BRAINS SCATTERED FOR 100 FEET ON TRACK

The man who presided at the meeting when a hundred and sixty-five banded themselves together to run Norris out of town – this man was a powerful and influential man. He was chairman of the Democratic party of Texas. He lifted his glass of liquor and said to the crowd,

"Let's stand and drink to the death of our enemy."

Six days after that night – he lived out on the Interurban then – he and his negro chaffeur were driving to town and crossed the Interurban – the two-story brick house still stands – there was not a curve in the then double track of the Interurban between Dallas and Fort Worth. The motorman on the front end said,

"I saw the car moving slowly and thought surely it would stop, but it came onto the track." And that Interurban coming sixty miles an hour hit that car amidship and smashed it to smithereens and the two Interurbans plunged from the track and there were more than sixty people in both cars. Not one person on the Interurban had a broken bone. The negro chauffeur was unscathed. But the insides and brains of this man who had drunk the toast to the death of Norris six days before – his brains were scattered for a distance of a hundred feet on the track.

He lay in state in the auditorium of the Chamber of Commerce – "And great fear came upon every soul."

And the revival increased.

One of the main men in the conspiracy to run Norris out of town came to his house at two o'clock the next morning. Norris lived at 1201 Sixth Avenue. I have been there many times. When he rang the bell Mrs. Norris said, "I'd better go."

But Norris said, "No, I'll go." And there stood one of his bitterest enemies. And he said, "Let me come in."

And there that man knelt in Norris' front room with him and God and was gloriously saved and became one of his strongest friends and supporters.

## BROKEN QUART BOTTLE OP LIQUOR WITH BRAINS OF DISTRICT ATTORNEY

It would be now in order to tell the fate of the conspirators.

Take the District Attorney who was a tool of the liquor interests. After the conspiracy trial had come to nought – and only a short time afterwards – this prosecuting attorney loaded his fine new Cadillac car with liquor, two women and another man. They were going across the North Main Viaduct at a terrific speed and ran head-on into an on-coming street car. This District Attorney and the other three in the car were killed instantly, and nobody was hurt on the street car, only shaken up.

There was a half quart bottle of liquor broken and it was sitting straight up on the pavement, and it had a lobe of brains in it.

This bottle of liquor and brains was carried to Dr. Norris and he took it to the pulpit and preached a sermon on it the next Sunday night on the text, "The Wages of Sin is Death."

Of course it created a great sensation. Norris was severely criticized. Some women fainted in the audience. And some men did too. You talk about "Great Fear coming upon every soul!" It scared me almost to death.

He fought on. He preached on.

# CHAPTER X

## "RAZOR BLADES THOUSAND FEET HIGH" – ANOTHER CHAPTER OF "INSIDE THE CUP"

To use a well known expression of my lifelong friend, I. E. Gates, "Razor blades were flying a thousand feet high."

The year 1911 arrived, and that was the reddest hot prohibition fight in the history of Texas, and I was pulled into the fight, and here is how it happened.

There was a statewide gathering of the saloon crowd held in the Coliseum in Fort Worth, and the papers reported over 10,000 in attendance. All the red-nosed saloon keepers, white-apron bartenders, and all their henchmen – they were all on hand.

On Sunday morning I picked up the Fort Worth Record, which has since gone out of business for reasons that will hereinafter be stated, and saw where there was a big "Committee of prominent citizens," for the arrangement, entertainment, and handling of this liquor convention.

And the first three names of the committee were three deacons in the First Baptist Church! I will not call their names for they have passed to their reward, and notwithstanding a very bitter fight that became intensely personal, I am happy to state that all three died my good friends.

I won't carry anger long. I don't want to carry it. I believe the Scripture that says, "Be ye angry, and sin not: Let not the sun go down upon thy wrath." It has not always been easy for me to carry out this Scripture. I am just as human as the humanest. There are some "pious," superlatively pious, preachers who go around and yam about it, but I am not going to commit two sins, have anger and wrath, then lie about it. One sin is enough.

I believe the Lord is gracious enough to forgive, yet I don't want to overdraw my bank account.

When I read that account where my three deacons headed this committee entertaining the liquor crowd, I went down the list showing several other members of the First Baptist Church. The chief spokesman, the editor of the Fort Worth Record, who at that time was a member of the First Baptist Church – he was publisher as well as editor, a very brilliant man, and a remarkably gifted man.

What surgings of soul! What conflicts I had. One voice said, "Now you are the pastor of a great city church, and don't stir up a row over this liquor question. These men are men of wealth and prestige, bankers and capitalists and you will make a fool of yourself to say anything about it – besides you can't do anything about it."

But another voice said, "You, the pastor of a great church – will you permit officials and deacons to remain on your official board who are personally responsible before the world for this liquor convention? Have you forgotten the rivers of tears that liquor caused your own sainted mother? Have you forgotten how it wrapped its slimy coil around one of the best, and one of the most brilliant men who ever drew the breath of life and wrecked him? Have you forgotten that liquor knows no race, no color, no wealth, no poverty?"

I was brought up when a small boy on the editorial writings of Henry W. Grady, and I recall how he said:

"My friends, don't trust it. It is powerful, aggressive and universal in its attacks. Tonight it enters an humble home to strike the roses from a woman's cheeks, and tomorrow it challenges this republic in the halls of Congress.

"Today it strikes the crust from the lips of a starving child, and tomorrow levies the tribute from the government itself. There is no cottage humble enough to escape it – no palace strong enough to shut it out...

"It is the mortal enemy of peace and order. The despoiler of men, the terror of women, the cloud that shadows the face of children, the demon that has dug more graves and sent more souls unshriven to judgment than all the pestilences that have wasted life since God sent the plagues to Egypt, and all the wars since Joshua stood before Jericho...

"It can profit no man by its return. It can uplift no industry, revive no interests, remedy no wrong... It comes to destroy, and it shall profit mainly by the ruin of your sons and mine. It comes to mislead human souls and crush human hearts under its rumbling wheels.

"It comes to bring gray-haired mothers down in sorrow to their graves. It comes to turn the wife's love into despair, and her pride into shame. It comes to still the laughter on the lips of little children, and to stifle all the music of the home and fill it with silence and desolation. It comes to ruin your body and mind, to wreck your home."

My decision was made; I acted promptly. I called a meeting of the deacons in the old church – just had one small office in the corner – and that meeting was held just before the morning service. I held that paper in my hand, with their names on the Liquor Committee, and I never shall forget my experience, my feelings. I had come to the do-and-dare decision. It was life and death. God was good to a young preacher that morning.

I knew then for the first time a little something of what Daniel must have felt when he stood before Belshazzar and read the handwriting on the wall. I knew then something of what Peter must have felt when he stood before the Sanhedrin at Jerusalem, and said, "We ought to obey God rather than men." I knew something of what the Apostle Paul must have felt as he stood before the Roman Courts, and even Caesar himself.

I was entering into a new world, but I didn't know one tenthousandth part of the things that awaited me. How wonderful that a gracious God keeps the future from us! I am so glad I didn't know what was ahead.

I threw the issue right square on the table, before these men. Of course, they could not defend the liquor business.

But as usual on such occasions there was the counsel for "caution and conservatism."

I gave them the ultimatum of choosing between the church and the liquor crowd, and right now, and not tomorrow. I made a most dangerous decision as it proved afterwards.

I am happy to say they resigned from the Board of Deacons.

But you talk about that warm country, spelled with four letters that sometimes breaks loose over in Georgia – the whole region broke loose in the First Baptist Church.

They dared not say what the real issue was.

They attacked my "methods." They objected to my sermons. They accused me of being "sensational." They said I was a "disturber of peace," a "divider of the brethren," an "agitator," and even went so far as to say I was a "public nuisance."

And I didn't deny anything, and I am not denying now, all they said, for I recall how they said the same things about the men of the Old Testament and the New Testament.

That's why they called Elijah – "A troubler in Israel."

And Paul – they called him a "pestilent fellow."

If any body has any idea that I wanted to fight, they are just ten thousand times mistaken. I never had wanted to fight; never did start one, but I have been there when several have been finished.

Talk about the "timid soul" – I had a copyright on it.

But something happened in the church besides the row. The Lord came around and paid us a visit.

And the folks came.

And salvation came.

And hundreds were saved.

Yes, I preached on sensational subjects – Hell and Heaven.

I saw the ball parks, the barber shops, the theatres and every other place full, and I was preaching to an empty wood-yard on Sunday nights.

I wouldn't preach now on some of the subjects I did then, and I wouldn't advise any other young preacher to do it. I am just telling about some of my mistakes, hoping they may help some other young preacher.

The fact that I got by with it – well, I might not get by with it now; no, I should say I didn't get by with it, the Lord just pulled me through it. It was the same God who pulled Jacob out of his trouble, and who delivered Simon Peter out of the hands of Herod and the Jews. On more than one occasion He has pulled me through. I confess it and deny not; yes, more, I am happy to state that He did it. I know He did, and I expect Him to do it again.

I don't know what close places I will be in during the rest of my earthly journey, but I am dead certain to be in several. And I still believe that "He is a very present help ill time of trouble."

That's why I have a through ticket from the beginning of my earthly journey clear through to the end of eternity. And I am very glad that ticket is all paid for; even meals provided for; even lodging, clothes, armor – everything from helmet to shoes on my feet. Even the wells of water of salvation are overflowing, and an abundance of honey is found in the dry carcasses of lions on the roadside.

Yes, I preached on sensational subjects. But always on salvation.

Oh, the "high-falutin" lorgnetet-sisters were terribly shocked. They threw up their hands in holy terror. The General Pastors Association had many things to say about it, just like the Detroit Council of Churches put in much of their time discussing my ministry in Detroit. Newspaper editorials were very caustic in their criticism. I intended that it should be discussed, and my intentions were more than abundantly realized.

Everybody was talking about the First Baptist Church.

When I first came here I went down Main Street, and asked five business concerns – one a popcorn stand, another a news stand – where the First Baptist Church was, and there wasn't a one of the five could tell me. I made up my mind if I stayed in Fort Worth it wouldn't be long until they would all soon find out. And they did!

The same thing has already happened with the Temple Baptist Church in Detroit. But like the fellow who had delirium teremens, who said to the globe trotter when he returned, "You ain't seen nothing yet."

My message was on the prodigal's return. That was the answer to critics of the new plan. My text was, "I will arise and go to my father."

Walking up Main Street, two blocks from the church, was a Lieutenant and recruiting officer of the Marine Service. He saw the crowd standing on the outside, couldn't get in, and he said afterward, he wondered whether it was a fire or fight, so he came over. It happened to be both a fire and a fight. He was a great big, strong, strapping fellow, 34 years of age, a native of Connecticut. I never shall forget the name, Charles G. Fain. He had on the full uniform, brass buttons, braid, and everything else that goes with it. He elbowed his way into the vestibule of the Sunday School annex, and stood there towering over everybody. When I gave the appeal for the prodigal to come to God for mercy and salvation, this strong, athletic, military figure, pushed his way through the crowd, down the aisle. Of course he attracted everybody's attention. Standing before the crowd, erect, as fine a specimen of physical manhood as I ever laid my eyes on – I said to him, "Do you come accepting my proposition, taking Christ as your Saviour!"

He said in a clear voice, "I do."

I took him by the hand and said, "Get up here on the platform, and tell this crowd why you have come."

I didn't know what he was going to say. I remember, as if it were yesterday – he stood there and began to weep, and said:

"My friends, I was walking up Main Street, saw the crowd, wondered what was happening, whether it was a fight or a fire. I came over. I haven't been to church in many years. I left my home in Connecticut when eighteen years of age. The last night I was home, my mother, who is now in heaven, came into my room, and knelt by my bed. As she tucked the cover in and kissed me, she said, 'My boy, you are leaving home tomorrow, and I want you to know wherever you sail the wide seas your mother's prayers will always follow you.' She put a little Bible in my trunk on top of my clothes. I went into the service. Time rolled on, one day while in the harbor of Osaka, Japan, on one of Uncle Sam's battleships, I received this cablegram, 'Your mother passed away.' I went into my room, fell on my knees, lifted my heart to God, but I was surrounded by evil associations. Time rolled on – I have been a prodigal. I have lived the life of a sinner, but tonight as I stood yonder in the corner it seemed just as real, as I am looking in your face, my mother stood by me saying, 'Remember, wherever you go Mother's prayers will follow you.' I am happy to tell you I am now ready to meet my mother in the home beyond the skies."

Of course, the effect was electric. You could have heard a pin fall – sinners were coming from the right and from the left – "Wisdom is justified of her ways."

Results? Oh, the results when souls are saved, all hell cannot gainsay. That should have been enough to convince the most ungodly gainsayer.

But it added to their hatred. Their opposition grew, and I knew for the first time, the spirit of hell that took Stephen outside the gate of Jerusalem and gnashed on him with their teeth and stoned him to death.

(Reprinted from the Evening News, London, England)

# WHO IS THIS AMERICAN?

"Who is this American, this country Baptist preacher? Why has he taken top headlines of the British press throughout the whole realm? What has he, in the most terrible war in the history of the Empire, that challenges our attention? He comes not as a special ambassador or official representative, not as an ecclesiastical dignitary.

"But he says things, and he hits straight from the shoulder. His language is unique, it is of the ranch, the farm, yet he has world events, of history and international events at his finger tips. He has made us laugh in these drab days. He captured the British press association, called in special meeting by the Ministry of Information to hear him.

## Preaches Hell Fire and Brimstone

"He is a Fundamentalist of the John Wesley order, and preaches hell fire and brimstone. One may not agree with his theology, but none can escape the contagious passion of his own conscious certainty of convictions on what he believes. Perhaps, we need again to hear the voice of no uncertain authority in matters religious.

"Sent and credentialed by the highest officials of his government, and immediately is the guest of the Prime Minister, the Right Honorable Winston Churchill. He is sponsored throughout Britain by the Ministry of Information, Honorable Brendan Bracken; and the guest of Honorable Alexander, the First Lord of the Admiralty, and other Cabinet Ministers. He is received, entertained, and dined by the Lord Mayor of London in the Mansion House, and other Lord Mayors and by Lord Provosts of Glasgow and Edinburgh.

## Pastor of Two Churches

"He preaches to overflowing crowds in the famous Spurgeon Church (Metropolitan Tabernacle) and to other large congregations. He was the guest of the Dean of St. Paul's Cathedral for a day, and spoke to the large ball room of the Savoy Hotel, filled with clergymen of all faiths. What has he, this man, this plain everyday Texan, the pastor of the two largest congregations on the American Continent?"

# CHAPTER XI

## THE FATE OF THE CONSPIRATORS

"So, they hanged Haman on the gallows that he had prepared for Mordecai."

It is with no small hesitation that reference is made to the unfortunate fate of the men who conspired to destroy the pastor of the First Baptist Church. It is no small ground for gratitude that many of them have not only ceased to be his enemies, but are very warm personal friends.

A large number have been saved and been baptized and are now the most active members of the First Baptist Church, and it is a regular occurrence to hear the testimony in both churches of hardened sinners saved, and who declare to the whole world, "I once hated Dr. Norris, but through his preaching I have been saved."

As an example of how things have changed in Fort Worth, during the dark days of 1912 and 1913 the pastor of the First Baptist Church went into one of the leading clothing, stores, of, Fort Worth and not one clerk would even approach him to wait on him. He stood there and waited and then walked out while the clerks cast suspicious glances at him. But today when he goes into that same store, the same proprietor and same employees, it is like holding a family reunion, proprietor, clerks and the pastor all join in happy, cordial good humor.

During those Same dark days, there was not a business house in Fort Worth that would give credit to the pastor of the First Baptist Church and, today he does not need their credit and his name is riot on the books of any business concern for credit, "Behold what God hath wrought?"

It is true that he had no credit and, worse than that, he was broke, and still worse he was an absolute bankrupt and owed $12,500.00, and had a wife and three little children. This was in the dark days of 1913, but every cent was paid and today in both Detroit and Fort Worth he can borrow on his own note $10,000.00 and has borrowed as much as $25,000.00 to go into the building program of the two churches.

Reference is made to the Detroit Bank which declined to loan Temple Baptist Church any money on the grounds that the churches of Detroit were in default over $7,000,000.00 to the banks, but the bank did loan $25,000.00 upon the name of the pastor. To God be all the glory! (For full information, ask the bank or the finance committee.)

"Vengeance is mine; I will repay, saith the Lord." What has been the fate of the conspirators? No names will be called, but old timers will readily recognize the characters.

The District Attorney, who was the tool of the liquor interests, and who framed and forged the indictment in 1912, met with a horrible death, driving in an eight cylinder Cadillac over North Main Street Viaduct, with his lady companion, and his automobile full of liquor, a head-on crash with a street car and both were hurled into eternity and their blood, brains, and the broken bottles covered the pavement.

One of Fort Worth's richest citizens was the "expert witness" on hand writing in the framed testimony and later, he walked out on the railroad track, near his house, and laid down, and a long line of freight cars cut his body half in two.

The president of a bank swore he would spend every dollar he had or "send Frank Norris to the penitentiary." He proclaimed these words to every customer and to all his acquaintances. This bank went broke and when he died, his relatives had to buy his shroud and casket.

Another capitalist, who was deep in the conspiracy and made large contributions, his bank went broke and, at that time he lived in the costliest home in Fort Worth. One morning before breakfast, he blew his brains out in his garage with a 38 Smith & Wesson.

The president of another bank where the brewery and liquor interests deposited their money and where the funds were raised to "prosecute" the pastor of the First Baptist Church, this bank also went broke and one afternoon when the president and his wife started for a drive, he went back into the house and she heard the crack of a shotgun and found him with the top of his head blown off by his own hand.

Another prominent citizen, who helped to raise the funds by personal solicitation to "prosecute" the pastor of the First Baptist Church, went broke and he has joined the others, waiting the hour when the leaves of the Judgment Book unfold.

The mayor of the city, at that time, called his crowd, some 3,000 or more, together and delivered such a bitter vindictive address on the pastor of the first Baptist Church, and closed with these words, "If there are enough red-blooded men left in Fort Worth, a preacher will be hanging to a telephone post before daylight." (The church was burned the next night.) That mayor was relegated to private life but died a warm friend of the pastor.

Another man, a wholesaler, who had spent large sums of money in the "prosecution" of the pastor – he died suddenly under circumstances that charity would forbid to be published.

Another lawyer who was in the Grand Jury, a member of the District Attorney's office force, that framed the indictment – he has long since become a pitiful spectacle, all that is left of a drunkard's life. The Deputy Sheriff who came to the pastor's home to serve the indictment and who brought along a crowd of hoodlums to stand outside and look on, and who invited the newspapers that they could take flashlights of the scene, six days afterwards was driving across the railroad on South Hemphill and ran head-on into a fast north bound train and never knew what hit him.

The chairman of the board of deacons, a good man, but was influenced and became very bitter, as is the case of good men when they go wrong, and who did the pastor much injury because of his high standing, it took him a year of long lingering suffering to leave this world, and before he passed away he called for the man he had persecuted and wept and said "The saddest tragedy that ever happened was when I and others who ought to have stood by you forsook you."

A number of pastors, especially Baptist pastors, were used by the ex-members of the First Baptist Church, who had money, to do harm to the pastor of the First Baptist Church. They passed many resolutions and gave these resolutions to enemy papers and Associated Press, but they have all gone.

For example, the leader, the man who was brought to Fort Worth with the avowed purpose of fighting Norris, he was fired out of his pulpit and was given a denominational pallet.

During the meeting conducted by Mordecai F. Ham in 1916 the police commissioner joined with the underworld, of which he was the representative, and undertook to harass the meeting by having a large number of automobiles to circle the tabernacle with horns wide open. In vain we begged for police protection but this police commissioner met with a horrible fate too gruesome to describe.

The most powerful firm of criminal lawyers in the state who received big money to act as the hired prosecution – that firm of lawyers is no more and the remnants are scattered.

The famous brewery investigation by the Attorney General of Texas, the correspondence was unearthed showing where the Anheuser Busch Brewing Company, through its president, August Busch, wrote letters to the Texas Brewing Company in Fort Worth, giving instructions on how to stop Norris, and also the letter said, "spare no expense." The interesting thing about the Texas Brewing Company, the president of this brewing company was one of the main directors of the bank where several deacons of the First Baptist Church were also officials and directors, and which caused the pastor so much trouble.

But August Busch, the big St. Louis brewer, blew his own brains out with his own gun.

A young preacher who lived in Norris' home and was sent to school by him, was promised promotion if he would turn against Norris and he accepted the 30 pieces of silver. The ecclesiastical power in alliance with the powers of darkness promoted him to a prominent pastorate, but soon thereafter he became involved, his wife divorced him and he was driven from the ministry and in later years walked into the offices of the pastor of the First Baptist Church and begged forgiveness, which was readily granted.

A capitalist with a string of banks, he and three of the other above referred to bankers were members of the First Baptist Church. His entire fortune was swept away, he moved West, and died under circumstances that are well known to the old timers.

156 men, including the Chief of Police, Sheriff, Constabulary, City and County Officials, met in the Metropolitan dining room and voted a demand that the pastor of the First Baptist Church leave Fort Worth in 30 days and so notified him. The man that presided over that meeting – in six days, a fast interurban limited struck his car and not a bone was broken of one of the more than 40 odd people on the two cars, the negro chauffeur was unscathed, the motorman was unhurt, but the brains and blood of this man who presided over this meeting was scattered for more than 30 feet on the tracks.

Immediately after the fire of the First Baptist Church in 1912, there was a hurried meeting called in the Chamber of Commerce and $22,000.00 was raised for the "prosecution" and the man who presided over that meeting lived only a short time and died a horrible death.

The foreman of the Grand Jury that returned the indictment in 1912 was the editor of Fort Worth's leading paper and was one of the most popular political figures and the most influential editor of the State. He was also a member of the First Baptist Church. His paper went broke, and he was driven from public life, and while he still lives, he is long since forgotten.

One of the richest property owners in Fort Worth went to one of the closest friends of the pastor and threatened the shotgun route, he has long since gone – peace to his ashes.

Another editor of a daily paper in Fort Worth wrote very bitter editorials and his paper misrepresented day after day, issuing as many as ten extras on the pastor of the First Baptist Church and sent out, also, many false representations and reports to the various news agencies – he went to his long home after more than a year of lingering illness.

Another very influential man, attorney, newspaper proprietor, came to the First Baptist Church one night with his crowd to reply to the pastor and caused no small disturbance and commotion. It was the beginning of his end and after a long, lingering illness, mind gone, he passed to the long eternity.

Another capitalist, also member of the First Baptist Church, played double. He, too, went broke and after a long seige, he went over the river.

Another capitalist, who was chairman of the Board of Deacons of the church when the first row broke between the pastor and the ungodly element – this deacon owned buildings rented to the wholesale liquor houses – he, too, waits the hour of judgment.

The Fort Worth Record issued extra after extra on the pastor and would send them by the bundle all over the country for free distribution – that paper went broke three times and even the name is no longer seen, except when referred to as past history.

Fort Worth Baptist Pastors' Association, controlled by the rich, ungodly element of their churches, in the absence of the pastor of the First Baptist Church, excluded him from the Pastors' Conference and not a single one of those dear brethren reside in Fort Worth and haven't for some time. The minister who led the conspiracy left his church financially bankrupt and as a reward for his hatred and attack on the pastor of the First Baptist Church, he was put on a pension by the denominational machine. And long since the machine said to him "See thou to that."

Another mayor, who was known for his hatred of preachers and churches, took his special spite out on the First Baptist Church and pastor and sent a would-be assassin to the study of the pastor of the First Baptist Church – this mayor was driven from office, lost his fortune, and the once magnificent store that ran from street to street and blocks of valuable property are all gone.

**Why the First Baptist Church Turned Out of Convention**

The First Baptist Church was turned out of the *Association* and Convention and among the nearly sever pages of printed "charges" the two principal "charges" were that the pastor of the First Baptist Church,

First, "opposed the 75 Million Campaign." And on this charge, the minutes of the Convention show the following on page 22 of the Galveston Convention: "Second, concerning the charge of opposition to the 75 Million Campaign, your committee believes that the charge is true, and that the challenge should, therefore, be sustained, and it submits the following proof: 1. That the pastor and church did not co-operate in putting over the 75 Million Campaign. 2. The pastor has misrepresented the campaign by declaring it to be an ecclesiastical machine which made assessments on the churches. Proof: In the Searchlight of September 29, 1922, page 2, we quote, 'They sent me an assessment of $100,000, and I said, Thank you, then they said, 'Do it this way, or you are not co-operating.' The tragedy of the hour is that preacher after preacher has been crushed by this ecclesiastical machine... This ecclesiastical machine wants money, money, money'."

The 75 Million Campaign was the most disastrous campaign that ever happened to Southern Baptists, and the whole denominational machinery has completely collapsed and wrecked itself and the First Baptist Church, which refused to bow to the ecclesiastical machine, is today as glorious as the sun, as fair as the moon, and as terrible as an army with banners.

Another "charge" was that the First Baptist Church refused further to use the denominational literature and took the Bible as its only textbook. This is found also on page 22 of the same minutes of the same convention.

Eighteen of the signers of the "charges" against the First Baptist Church, including laymen and ministers, have either gone into bankruptcy or been driven from the ministry, or passed to their rewards.

It is interesting that only a short time ago the pastor who was the chairman of the committee that brought in the false charges against the First Baptist Church to the Convention – he was forced to resign from his church in Houston under circumstances about which the least said is best.

THE SECRETARY OF STATE
WASHINGTON

*Personal*

August 28, 1941

My dear Mr. Churchill:

The bearer of this letter, Dr. J. Frank Norris, is one of the great pulpit speakers of this country. He is doing marvelous work to arouse the American people from their complacency and to develop a thorough understanding of the world war situation and of America's intimate relation to what Hitler and Hitlerism means for civilized countries.

I am glad thus to speak of Dr. Norris and to express my thanks in advance for such courtesy and cooperation as you may find it consistent to extend to him in connection with the great work he is carrying on.

Sincerely yours,

Cordell Hull

The Right Honorable
  Winston Churchill,
    Prime Minister,
      London.

# CHAPTER XII

THE FATE OF THE CHAIRMAN OF THE COMMITTEE WHICH TURNED NORRIS OUT OF THE CONVENTION

There were seven on the Committee, the Chairman was H. W. Virgin, who held a very high place in the pulpits of the denomination.

He was pastor once of the First Baptist Church of Amarillo, and for several years afterwards he was pastor of the North Shore Baptist Church, Chicago (we are not certain about the name but it was the largest Baptist Church in Chicago.)

We do not take any satisfaction over the downfall of any man but since it became a matter of record, his wife, the wife of his youth and the mother of his children, had to divorce him and he married his stenographer, and his church fired him.

Another member of the Committee of seven which anathematized and turned the First Baptist Church out of the Convention on trumped up charges. He was pastor of the South Main Street Baptist Church at Houston at that time and one of the largest churches in the state. His name was M. M. Wolfe and he "resigned" under well-known conditions that charity forbids publicity.

The list of casualties is multiplying very rapidly in Detroit and Isaiah 54:17 is true in the twentieth century and in the north as well as the south, east as well as west.

"No weapon that is formed against thee shall prosper; and every tongue that shall rise against three in judgment thou shalt condemn. This is the heritage of the servants of the Lord, and their righteousness is of me, saith the Lord."

The chairman of the board of trustees for Temple Baptist Church for many years, a man with a small clique ran the church. He led a very vicious fight against Norris and it has now been brought out that he sold $20,000.00 of very valuable property belonging to the church and for which the church only received $4,000.00 but judgment has come to him.

Another former and prominent official of the Temple Baptist Church, the head of the Detroit Baptist machine, the minutes of the church show that in 1922 as chairman of the committee he spent "$31,005.00 on improvements" made on the church but now a check by competent and reputable architects show that $7,000.00 is a maximum price for the "improvements." He was excluded from the Temple Baptist Church after the present pastorate began.

The Executive Secretary of the Detroit Baptist Union was very active in opposing the call to Temple Church of Dr. Norris and constantly hindered the work of the church even during the great revival on Oakman Boulevard, but he ceased his interference and opposition to the church after he made a signed, sweeping and public retraction and apology of the things he said against Dr. Norris and made this retraction and apology on February 13, 1936.

Why add to the list? It is with great hesitation that these matters are referred to. This is "Inside the Cup." The outside world has not known these things. But what has been the effect on the growth of the church?

"And great fear came upon all the church, and upon as many as heard these things." – Acts 5:11.

# CHAPTER XIII

HEAD OF RETAIL LIQUOR DEALERS' ASSOCIATION SAVED AND BAPTIZED

(I am still quoting from book "Inside The Cup.")

But there is another and glorious side. Multitudes of the bitterest enemies have been converted and baptized by the very man they fought. For example, the founder and head of the Retail Liquor Dealers' Association of Texas, a saloon keeper for 40 years, was gloriously saved and baptized in the First Baptist Church and seat on the front seat at every service until the day he went home to God.

His name is William Blevins. A stenographic report of his testimony is as follows:

"I was in the liquor business for 40 years. I organized the Malt and Retail Liquor Dealers' Association of Texas and was its only head until it went out of business. When J. Frank Norris came to Fort. Worth it wasn't long until I recognized that he was going to put us out of business unless we put him out of business. I called our gang together and we got in touch with the leading business men and they in turn called the representative churchmen together of the various denominations, and it wasn't long until we had all the preachers silenced except this young fellow Norris. I went out to hear him and I was convinced that we had a dangerous foe. He would never let up. We thought we had him down and out when we got him indicted and tried, but he was vindicated so overwhelmingly and then his church grew as never before and we were in worse fix than ever. Then he did begin his war on us in dead earnest.

"He went and brought that fellow Mordecai Ham here and he was as bad or worse than Norris. So something had to be done. We thought we had Ham put out of business when a fellow jumped on him and knocked him in the head one night and we were soon through with Ham and Ramsey, but Norris was still fighting away and we called a representative group of 150 or more of the leading business men of the city together at the Metropolitan Hotel dining room and Paul Waples presided. We lifted our glasses at the close of the fireworks when we decided to finish Norris', and gave a toast to his exit or finish.

"A few nights afterwards we called a huge mass meeting in the auditorium of tie Chamber of Commerce, one block from the First Baptist Church, and Mr. George Armstrong presided and called for fifteen men to go and take Norris out. I was heartily in favor of taking him out and so was everybody else, but we could not get the 15 men.

"And ladies and gentlmen, I believe the hand of God interfered that night and I am so glad that we didn't deprive his wife and children of their husband and father, and this church of its pastor, and I could not put him out of business, I decided to join him. I came to the church, walked down to the front and got down on my knees and he got down with me on his knees and put his arms around my shoulders while I prayed, and I prayed the prayer 'God be merciful to me, a sinner,' and He heard me and this man that I so hated and tried with others at every foot of ground at my command to put out of business, baptized me and I am now past my 80th milestone and in the course of nature will precede him to the other shore, and when I get there I am going to hunt up the Superintendent of that fair land and make two requests of Him.

"First I want Him to let me know the day that Frank comes, and second, I want Him to let me off that day that I may be standing down at the beautiful gate and be the first to put my arms around him as the man who led me to Christ, by whose grace I am saved."

William (Bill) Blevins, who organized the Retail Liquor Dealers Association of Texas, and one of the crowd that called a mass meeting to get rid of Dr. Norris, but who later was saved and baptized on the first Baptist Church.

## DR. T. T. SHIELDS OF TORONTO, ONTARIO, CANADA WRITES AS FOLLOWS ON THE FIRST BAPTIST CHURCH, FORT WORTH

It Is always a tonic for jaded spirits to come into the presence of Dr. Norris. He is always bubbling over like a mountain torrent, and radiates energy like the summer sun. We do not know much about the constitution of radium, but when it was discovered years ago by the Curies it was hailed as a new element. We understand, however, that one of the characteristics of radium is that it never diminishes, it never burns itself out. We have seen many human dynamos, many men of abounding energy, but almost invariably after a while their energy diminished, their pace slackened, they reached he crest of the hill and descended; and by and by they passed from public memory.

Dr. Norris is, of course, still a young man. It would therefore scarcely be appropriate to quote what is said of Moses in relation to him, that "his natural force was not abated." We have a suspicion that, were it possible chemically to analyze Dr. Norris' constitution it would be found to contain a large proportion of radium. At all events, we found it most refreshing to meet him again. It was like getting into a new atmosphere, electrically charged.

We were last in Fort Worth in 1926, when the old auditorium of the First Baptist Church was still standing. Dr. Norris and his people have seen strenuous times since then. Their building was destroyed by fire, and through failure of the insurance companies they received little insurance. For more than a year now they have been in their new auditorium. It has an enormous area. We shall not say what it will seat, although we know within fifty. The average estimate of a building's seating capacity is so far from being accurate that to give exact numbers would have the effect of misrepresenting things as they are to the popular mind. It is enough to say that from our count the First Baptist Church auditorium seats approximately the same as the Metropolitan Tabernacle, London. There is, however, this difference, Spurgeon's Tabernacle has two galleries, the Fort Worth auditorium has none; the people are seated on one ascending floor.

We have heard Dr. Norris many times, and in many places, under varying circumstances, but we were never more thrilled by his messages than we were when we heard him from his own platform in Fort Worth. Evidently he is a larger figure in Fort Worth than ever before. He enjoys a larger measure of public esteem, and is, therefore, more popular than ever before. In this, we greatly rejoice. There never was but one Dr. J. Frank Norris, and the passage of time serves only to endear him to the multitude and more firmly to establish him In public confidence. May his bow long abide in strength.

# CHAPTER XIV

## CHIEF DETECTIVE FROM NEW YORK A. J. RITCHIE BROUGHT TO FORT WORTH TO FRAME NORRIS

His enemies raised $22,000 one Sunday morning in the building of the old Board of Trade to prosecute Norris with. The Burns Detective Agency of New York sent their top man to Fort Worth and he was given $10,000 to make the case against Norris.

Norris was quickly vindicated and this chief of the Burns Detective Agency was converted under Norris' ministry.

### Sample of Testimony of The Conspirators

The First Baptist Church, the old church, was located at Third and Taylor – the church that was burned.

Across the street was what is known as the Alta Vista Creamery. The drivers would leave the creamery from midnight to four o'clock delivering their milk in various sections of the city.

The star witness of the hired prosecution was driving one of the wagons, and he swore,

"That he saw Norris at the First Baptist Church a few minutes before it burst into flames around 2 A. M,"

And when he was asked how he knew it was Dr. Norris over two hundred feet away, he swore,

"I saw him standing under the electric light at the entrance of the church."

An immediate check was made and the record of the light company showed the lights had been turned off at 8 P. M., six hours before.

And when the hired prosecution found out that their witness had perjured himself, they put him back on the witness stand and then he swore that the electric lights were not on, but that the moon was shining.

The weather bureau testified that the moon was not shining.

Dr. Norris' attorney asked this perjurer one question, "Who told you to change your testimony?"

He pointed to the hired prosecution and called his name.

Judge James Edward Swain was presiding at this trial and the jury brought in the verdict of "Not guilty" and the trial was quickly over.

"THE WHOLE BUSINESS A COLOSSAL FRAME-UP OF WICKEDNESS IN WHICH THE MACHINERY OF THE LAW HAS BEEN SEIZED AND USED TO RUIN AN INNOCENT MAN IN ORDER TO SCREEN GUILTY MEN"

May 2, 1912, Dr. J. B. Gambrell, then editor of the Baptist Standard, on this whole conspiracy published the following editorial in the Baptist Standard:

"The remarkable trial in Fort Worth, which has held the attention of the State and country for weeks, came to an end in a most triumphant way for Pastor J. F. Norris of the First Baptist Church, Fort Worth. The indictment was for perjury, but the trial was for perjury and arson. The verdict was 'Not guilty.' The whole country had rendered the verdict on the in advance of the jury.

"Not in the history America perhaps, was there ever an indictment brought in by a grand jury on as flimsy and shadowy pretense of evidence. Nor was ever an indictment framed under more questionable circumstances. But that a grand jury would bring in an indictment against one occupying a place so exalted as that of pastor of a great church, and following a series of such crimes as had been committed in Fort Worth gave the country pause. The trial revealed a condition in and around that grand jury reprehensible and regrettable to the last degree.

"Not doubting for a moment that the underworld was beneath the prosecution of the pastor, making the atmosphere for it and filling Fort Worth with its spirit; and not doubting that Pastor Norris was innocent of the charge laid against him, I nevertheless felt that prudence, a decent regard for even the forms of law, as well as the ends of justice, dictated an attitude of waiting. This was the attitude of the country at large and of ministers in particular. The comparative silence of the Standard was in deference to civic decorum. But, now in words as plain as can be written, I give my conviction that

"That indictment was an outrage.

"The situation in Fort Worth was unfriendly to a fair trial. Passion was deeply stirred. Prejudice was rife. The forces of evil in Fort Worth are very strong, with ramifications widespread, personal matters, no way related to the case, unhappily became involved. The long and persistent war of Brother Norris on the allied and shameful vices of the city lay in the background. Putting everything together the situation did not promise well for the defendant. That a verdict of 'not guilty' could be had under the conditions obtaining is highly gratifying and honoring to the spirit of justice which rose superior to partisan prejudice, and pronounced a righteous judgments. Great credit is due the twelve men who measured up to a high trust and vindicated the right.

"The First Church, as a body, stood by the pastor, and were present in large numbers when the verdict was brought in. The Dallas News correspondents thus describe the scene that followed the announcement 'not guilty':

"Following the" tending of this verdict there was a remarkable demonstration. Dr. Norris Was not in the court room at the time, having gone to the home of a friend to rest; but scores: of women and other friends crowded about Mrs. Norris, sobs shaking their voices as they extended congratulations. Others were more demonstrative and gave a shrill cheer. In a moment this had swelled to what might have been called a storm of rejoicing. Almost hysterical laughter, cheers, handclapping, the stamping of feet, all contributed to the noise.

### "Demonstration Renewed

"Finally order was restored sufficiently to permit of the formal discharge of the jury, with the thanks of the court. This done, the demonstration was renewed. Some one began to sing 'Old-Time Religion' and scores joined in until the swelling chorus reminded one of the singing at a revival meeting. That hymn was succeeded by 'We Shall Meet on the Beautiful Shore'; 'Nearer My God to Thee'; 'There Is a Great Day Coming,' and 'Are You Ready?'

### "Dr. Norris Arrives

"It was at this juncture that Dr. Norris arrived at the court room. He had been notified by telephone of the result and had responded in great haste. As he came in the door he was greeted with the Chautauqua salute and cheered. After greeting Mrs. Norris very affectionately, he personally thanked the jury, while the crowd sang 'We Praise Thee, O Lord,' 'Revive Us Again' and 'How Firm a Foundation.' This last hymn was started by Hon. O. S. Lattimore. Mr. Norris was called upon to speak, and at last, replying to some utterance by Mr. Lattimore, said:

### "Confident of Acquittal

" 'Yes, I will say something, and it will be the first time I have had anything to say publicly in this matter. I have been confident of the result all alone, and this ending today simply confirms that confidence. I am only going to say a few words, but I will have something to say next Sunday night. I will have a few plain words to say, then, just a few.

### "Victim of Prejudice

" 'My friends, when fifteen years ago I went down into the water as a symbol of Christianity, I never even imagined that I could ever by any possibility stand before any of my fellow citizens as one accused of crime. And now, the victim of passion and prejudice as I have been, I want publicly to express my appreciation of the friends who have stood by me. But, first of all, I want to lay the crown of laurels on the head of my wife, whose sustaining cheer, comfort and strengthening can simply never be told.

### "Thanks His Friends

" 'To my friends who have gone down in this valley of trial with me I also give thanks. I can not undertake to name them. There are too many. But to one and all of them go my heartfelt thanks.

" 'To my counsel – the fifteen lawyers who struggled for the right – there was much comment on the number, fifteen, but it could just as well have been five hundred as fifteen if I had taken them all – also go my thanks.

" 'To the jurors who have so nobly done their duty to themselves, to justice, and to their State, a jury of the fair, honest, impartial citizenship of Tarrant County, who have given their aid in the vindication of my good name, that of my wife, that of my children, that of the pastor of the First Baptist Church and the membership of that church – to them are special thanks due.

" 'As to the enemies – '

### "Forgiveness for Enemies

"Here Mr. Lattimore and Mr. Doyle, of Mr. Norris' counsel, made some suggestions that could not be heard. Mr. Norris made a low-voiced reply to them and then said aloud: 'I know just what I am going to say, and I am not going to say too much. As to the enemies, I have none but the kindest feelings and not a harsh or unkind word to say. Some have been swept from their feet in this matter, influenced maybe by loud and continued talk, misrepresentations in newspapers or by other influences. Whatever the cause, I repeat I have only the kindest, charitably feelings.'

### "Dr. Gambrell Pays Tribute to J. M. Gaddy

"Such a scene is not often witnessed in this world, and no heart can resist its pathos. I can but enter into this joyous scene to the full. The woman most conspicious in it is the daughter of J. M. Gaddy, than whom Texas never had a more valiant soldier for the right. He was brother to my soul. I joined this woman in holy wedlock to the man by whose side she walked these days in the fiery furnace of trial and all the time in the dauntless spirit of her noble sire.

"The verdict might have been properly instructed by the Judge, for the prosecution stood at the end with not the decent shadow of a case. The defense not only destroyed the case of the prosecution, but on the arson part of the case, made out an affirmative case as impregnable as Gibraltar.

"This is an hour for forgiveness and forgetting. In the stress of the battle natural friends may have wounded each other. Vision was blurred. Mischief makers have been in their heydey. Pastor Norris's words of forgiveness suit a great hour. They were well and nobly spoken. Let all hearts respond and all live up to a high duty and privilege. There is no time for personal wars. The great church must go on with its work. The preacher must proclaim the divine message of peace, and good will, living it as well as preaching it. The work of Controlling evil is ever with us and must be pushed. Fort Worth has a duty to perform to herself. She ought to inaugurate a campaign for civic righteousness to redeem herself from her bad conditions.

## "A Colossal Frame-Up of Wickedness

"It has beep given out that the arson indictment against Pastor Norris is to be prosecuted harder than the perjury indictment was. The country has come with great unanimity to the belief that the whole business is a colossal frame-up of wickedness in which the machinery of the law has been seized and used to ruin an innocent man in, order to screen guilty men. The complete playout of the perjury case, the utter inefficiency of the evidence, even total lack of evidence in the case, has settled public opinion as to the grand jury, the legal adviser of the jury and the whole business. Hon. O. S. Lattimore did not put it too strong when he said it was a disgrace to the State."

## "Nothing Against Norris, But Indict Him and It Will Ruin Him and We Will Be Through With Him" "

We have no evidence, but if we indict him it would ruin him and we will get rid of him." This is what the foreman of the framed and packed grand jury was forced to admit on the witness stand.

It took only nine men out of twelve to frame an indictment, and one of the three that voted against the indictment was a great citizen, Joe East of Everman.

During the long session of the Grand Jury of the framed and perjured testimony, of the secret session of the grand jury, the foreman of the grand jury said,

"I know we have nothing against Norris, but we have got to get rid of him, and if we indict him that would ruin him. No man, much less a minister, can survive the stigma of an indictment." Joe East swore this on the witness stand before the grand jury and confessed it.

Is it any wonder that the First Baptist Church grew so mightily during those days?

It is just like it was in the Acts of the Apostles. The Apostles would spend half the time in jail and the other half preaching the gospel of Christ and the resurrection, on the streets of Jerusalem and the porch of Solomon's Temple – "So mightily grew the Word of God."

A part of the crowd assembled in the 17th District Court, Tarrant County to hear Dr. Norris bring a gospel message. All courts assembled for this special message. It was in this same court room that the conspiracy against Dr. Norris was tried 36 years ago.

# CHAPTER XV

## WHEN DR. NORRIS REFUSED $1,000 FOR CONDUCTING THE FUNERAL OF A WICKED MAN

He owned what was known in Fort Worth as the bucket of blood – the red light district.

He was Vice-President of one of the big banks of the city.

He lived in a mansion on Pennsylvania Avenue now used as an undertaking establishment.

He was killed at a crossing of the Katy Railroad near Mt. Olivet Cemetery.

The lawyer representing the estate of the deceased came to Norris and said,

"He left $1,000 to the man who preaches his funeral and here is an eulogy that we want read at his funeral.

The eulogy put him with the white winged crowd.

Norris declined both the thousand dollars and the eulogy.

Several of his deacons were officers in the bank with this notorious character and they got mad and took Norris to task.

The funeral was had and high banks of floral wreaths, among them was a large horseshoe wreath ten feet high and had in the center of it "Gates Ajar."

Here's one of the things for which Norris was criticized severely. Next Sunday night he preached on "Gates Ajar" and he said that it should be very clearly understood what gates they were talking about. He spoke of the "gates of hell," the "gates of Paradise" – his real sermons was Luke 16:23:

"And in hell he lift up his eyes, being in torment..."

A section of the large crowd that Heard dr. Norris in Berlin in 1937

# CHAPTER XVI

## THE BIG BANKER WHO BOUGHT A DOZEN PAIR OF HIGH PRICED HOSE FOR ANOTHER MAN'S WIFE

As I said before, Norris did many things that I did not approve or understand, perhaps I had better say.

The picked and stacked grand jury indicted him without any evidence but indicted him for the purpose of ruining him, as the foreman confessed on the witness stand. Norris did not take it on the chin – he fought back.

He got the record of all these perjurers and all these stacked grand jurors and threw everything at his command at them. He had them jumping sideways, turning somersaults and there were none too high, too wealthy, too influential, provided they had tried to destroy him.

He did exactly what Mordecai did to Haman.

He did just exactly what Moses did to Pharaoh at the Red Sea.

He did just exactly what Samuel did to Agag.

Just exactly what David did to Goliath.

Just exactly what John the Baptist did when he pointed his unerring finger of judgment in the guilty face of Herod Antipas.

There wasn't any cheap sentiment in it, none of this lovey-dovey, milk and cider business with him.

His enemies were like David's enemies, the enemies of the Lord.

I have heard him quote scores of times the 27th Psalm.

"The Lord is my light and my salvation; whom shall I fear? the Lord is the strength of my life; of whom shall I be afraid?

"When the wicked, even mine enemies and my foes, came upon me to eat up my flesh, they stumbled and fell.

"Though an host should encamp against me, my heart shall not fear; though war should rise against me, in this will I be confident."

And perhaps his favorite scripture is Romans 8:31-33;

"What shall we then say to these things! If God be for us, who can be against us?

"He that spared not his own Son, but delivered him up for us all, how shall he not with him also freely give us all things?

"Who shall lay anything to the charge of God's elect? It is God that justifieth."

It mattered not what happened to him, what slanders, what indictments, what conspiracies, what lies, he could preach with added boldness on Philippians 1:12:

"But I would ye should understand, brethren, that the things which happened unto me have fallen out rather unto the furtherance of the gospel."

His crowds increased and conviction deepened, multitudes were saved at every service. His ministry was a perennial fulfillment of the words of Jesus when He said:

"Go your way, and tell John what things ye have seen and heard; how that the blind see, the lame walk, the lepers are cleansed, the deaf hear, the dead are raised, to the poor the gospel is preached." – Luke 7:22.

And his people were poor!

They were laughed at, ridiculed, criticized, his enemies said,

"What do these feeble Jews? will they fortify themselves? will they sacrifice? Will they revive the stones out of the heaps of the rubbish which are burned?"

He boldly answered I Cor. 1:26-29:

"For ye see your calling, brethren, how that not many wise men after the flesh, not many mighty, not many noble, are called:

"But God hath chosen the foolish things of the world to confound the wise; and God hath chosen the weak things of the world to confound the things which are mighty;

"And the base things of the world, and things which are despised, hath God chosen, yea, and things which are not, to bring to nought things that are:

"That no flesh should glory in his presence."

## But To The Banker, And The Silk Hose For Another Man's Wife

Mrs. J. D. Garrett, one of the greatest women of my acquaintance, a great Bible student, built a large Sunday School Class and won many souls, she came to Dr. Norris one day – she worked in the leading department store of the city W. T. Burton & Co. – and said:

"Do you want something on (naming this prominent banker) who was on the Grand Jury that framed the indictment against you?"

Dr. Norris welcomed the information.

Then she said, "This banker bought a dozen pair of high priced hose, drop-stitch silk hose for another man's wife."

"How do I know? Because the next day after he bought them a woman brought them back and said, " 'I want to exchange these hose I bought from you yesterday for another size.' "

I told her that "while you didn't buy them I will be glad to exchange them."

Dr. Norris said, "Mrs. Garrett, would you be willing to, stand before the congregation and testify to that?"

Mrs. Garrett said, "Yes, if it costs me my job."

And her courage was characteristic of his whole crowd.

Dr. Norris had a big black board out in front of the church and had printed in large box car letters that could be read across the street these words,

"Next Sunday night – Should a prominent Fort Worth Banker buy high priced silk hose for another man's wife?"

Crowds gathered across the street from the church all during the week. People would drive slowly by and read that sign.

Sunday night not half the people could get in.

But something happened before the next Sunday night.

Another banker, not the one in question, went to J. T. Pemberton, president of the Farmers & Mechanics National Bank, Dr. Norris' friend, and said,

"Jess, I am into it, Norris is going to expose me next Sunday night, my wife will quit me and there'll be a run on my bank. I made a mistake when I gave that woman the silk hose."

Then a third banker came, who was not the one in question or under suspicion, and came to J. T. Pemberton and pled for him to plead for him.

But what is still more surprising, the man in question came to see J. T. Pemberton and said,

"Jess, I'm ruined, it will break my bank – (he was president) and I don't care for myself but for the sake of my family..."

Pemberton said to him, "I'd go straight to Norris' office and tell him the whole story. You'll find him to be very generous as well as courageous, and confess it all."

He said, "I don't care for myself but I have got one precious daughter and it will be a blot on her forever."

Contrary to what Dr. Morris' enemies say, he is a very generous man, I have known him to forgive many bitter enemies, many who sought his life, and baptize them.

Sunday night came, the crowds were there, and quietly Dr. Norris asked, "Will Mrs. J. D. Garrett come to the platform?"

She told the story of how the silk hose were bought as above described but he asked her to withhold the name of the banker for the present.

After she finished Dr. Norris quietly said,

"Ladies and gentlemen, instead of one banker guilty of buying silk hose for another man's wife three have made confession, and the guilty banker in question has thrown himself on my hands and asked the God of the Universe to forgive him, and he has asked for the sake of his family that I withhold his name.

"I cannot and I will not lift my hand against a man that I believe is sincerely penitent and the matter is a closed incident."

But that bank did go broke. Of course, everybody found out who it was.

That man died, one of the best, warmest friends that Dr. Norris ever had.

Dr. Norris went on and preached that night on "Whatsoever a man soweth, that shall he also reap."

A prominent businessman from Minneapolis, Minn, was in the city and saw the announcement and came to the First Baptist Church as a matter of curiosity. Of course, a subject like that hits everybody more or less.

Dr. Norris, in his characteristic manner, as he only can do, took the great audience to the flaming bar of God Almighty's judgment, sinners trembling, came running to the front, asking for salvation. This man from Minneapolis, a stranger to Fort Worth, was among those saved, and he went back to Minneapolis and Dr. W. B. Riley baptized him into the First Baptist Church, and he wrote his full testimony.

Thus one of the so-called "sensational" subjects or exposures of sin resulted in large numbers being saved.

But I would not advise any other preacher in the world to follow Norris' methods. Some few fools have tried, yes, just tried it.

**THE SECRETARY OF THE NAVY**
WASHINGTON

August 29, 1941

My dear Mr. Alexander:

This letter will serve to introduce to you Dr. J. Frank Norris, a prominent clergyman who is the head of a very large congregation here in the United States.

Dr. Norris expects to spend about a month in England where an extensive speaking tour has already been arranged for him. Dr. Norris is a powerful orator and throughout the years has developed a very large radio audience. Upon his return to the United States, he expects to make a speaking tour of the entire country and will do much toward promoting the right kind of sentiment over here.

Anything you can do to promote the purpose of Dr. Norris' visit to England will be deeply appreciated.

Yours sincerely,

Frank Knox

The Right Honorable A. V. Alexander
First Lord of the Admiralty
London, England

# SECTION III

# CHAPTER I

THE BAPTIST STANDARD PUBLISHED THE FOLLOWING:

"DR. J. FRANK NORRIS LEADS FIRST BAPTIST CHURCH OF SAN ANTONIO IN THE GREATEST REVIVAL MEETING EVER HELD IN TEXAS, AND, AS FAR AS I KNOW, IN THE SOUTH.

## By I. E. Gates

"I have been pastor of the First Baptist Church of San Antonio for nearly six years, and, only attempted one revival meeting in all that time. However, we have had great ingatherings all through the months and years, from the regular services. But I felt, and my church felt that the time had come to have the greatest meeting in the history of this city. We have tried evangelist after evangelist, but we always failed to do what we had hoped to do. In making preparation for this meeting, my heart turned to my old boyhood friend, Dr. J. Frank Norris, as the only man who could lead us in this great revival, and do for us what we wanted done. I have known Dr. Norris for twenty-seven years. I knew he had built a great church in Fort Worth – the greatest in America. But I did not understand fully how he could hold, for fifteen years, such multitudes every Sunday.

"I found out the past six weeks more than I ever knew about him.

"The First Baptist Church made the greatest preparation for this revival that any single church in America has ever undertaken to do. We erected a tabernacle, costing $5,000.00, with a seating capacity of around 5,000. We conducted pre-revival services for weeks ahead, making the best preparation possible for this great meeting.

"After we had engaged Dr. Norris to hold the meeting in the Spring, he felt that he ought to go to other engagements and postpone our meeting until fall. I was determined that this should not be done, for so much depended upon a great revival just now. My church building program was hanging in the balance, and so many other things were depending upon this meeting that I got on the train and went to Fort Worth and spent some time with him. I told him we could have five hundred additions, and stir all Texas. And when I laid out my plans before him, thoroughly, he agreed to come.

"I never saw a campaign in my life, and never hope to see one that has produced so many results. We had more than six hundred additions to the First Baptist Church alone, most of whom came by baptism, while hundreds of others joined other churches – Methodist, Baptist, Presbyterian, Campbellite, etc. We did not count the 'reclamations,' 'reconsecrations' and 'conversions' as is commonly reported by the thousands in many of the modern evangelistic campaigns. We could have made a greater show, but the church, myself and Dr. Norris were unanimously against it.

"I was not prepared to appreciate what was coming, for I never heard such gospel preaching in my day. Dr. Norris is the greatest Bible preacher that I ever heard. He is familiar with every book of the Bible, and can quote more Scripture in every sermon than any man I ever heard. He made all of his evangelistic appeals on the Word of God. He preached one whole week on 'Hell,' until I could hear the wails of the damned, and smell the smoke of their torment. And upon his first invitation, on Sunday night, one hundred and seven people joined the church. I never heard such sermons on 'Hell.'

"I am convinced that we are preaching too little on the doctrine of 'Hell.'

"He gave one whole week on 'The Work of The Holy Spirit,' and I never heard a man magnify the Holy Spirit as he did in Creation, in Regeneration, and in the Resurrection.

"He preached on every doctrine held by Baptists, including three sermons on 'Baptism'; two on 'The Lord's Supper' and one on 'The Final Preservation of the Saints'; several on 'The Church' and a dozen or more on 'The Second Coming.' He named and denounced every modern sin in no uncertain terms. I never saw people cringe and tremble under the power of the Gospel like they did under this modern John the Baptist preacher. I saw men rush up to the mourners' bench and cry out, 'Men and brethren, what must I do to be saved?' I saw men and women who couldn't speak the English language, come to the front under the power of one of his sermons, and ask 'What must I do to be saved?'

"He spared nobody. He denounced sin in high society, in low society and in no society; in deacons, preachers and elect sisters, until all of us came to the mourners' bench and got fight with God.

"He preached a whole week on 'Roman Catholicism.' I never heard such an exposition as he poured out his soul. He preached on:

"'The Romanists versus the Bible on the Lord's Supper.'

" 'The Romanists versus the Bible on Papal Infallibility.'

" 'The Romanists versus the Bible on the Confessional of the Priesthood.'

" 'The Romanists versus the Bible on Saint Worship.'

" 'The Romanists versus the Bible on The Purple, Scarlet-Robed Woman of Prophecy and History.'

"I never dreamed that any man had the courage to stand up before thousands of people in San Antonio, dominated by Romanism, and speak out as clearly as he did for one whole week.

"His sermon on 'The Infallibility of the Pope' was a masterpiece. I have heard B. H. Carroll in his palmiest days, but I never heard a sermon with more fire and logic than when he exalted Christ and proved that the Papacy is unscriptural. I did not know what might happen, but I sat behind him and gripped my chair with my hands and prayed God to give him the message, and he put it across and settled for all, times the Fundamentals of Protestantism in San Antonio, till Christ comes. Large numbers of Roman Catholics have joined our church and. I have baptized them. This series of sermons was the talk of the town. In fact, the whole meeting was the talk of the town. Never did a man dominate a city like Frank Norris dominated San Antonio. Of course, the devil got busy, as he always does, when God's people move.

"His first great fight was a newspaper fight, and what he did to the Express Publishing Company cannot be written down. The night he took them to a skinning, it seemed to me he had five acres of people present, besides those who were on the roof, trying to look over the banisters to see what was going on. Razor blades were in the air, one hundred feet high, as this John the Baptist with his broad axe, stood up there before ten thousand people and denounced the Express Publishing Company for boycotting the meeting.

" 'About a week later, we had another great fight, brought on by a combination of a Jewish Rabbi and the Knights of Columbus, and when he got through with them, the dust was settled in San Antonio for the rest of the meeting. He gave them 24 hours to apologize, and the last paragraph in their apology is as follows:

" 'For all of this, as well as any and all words of criticism direct or implied, I have ever expressed concerning you, I again sincerely and unqualifiedly apologize, and I fully retract any and all derogatory statements made by me concerning you as unfounded and unjustified.

" 'Again expressing my deep regret and apologies for this entire unfortunate affair, for which and its consequences, I accept full personal responsibility I am,

" 'Very sincerely yours,

\* '(Signed)_____'

"I never saw a man who could keep his head and speak with such deliberation and calmness and courage as Frank Norris can, in a great battle. I think he is the most courageous Baptist preacher living on the face of the earth. He looks like a timid, modest man until he becomes aroused, and then his eyes flash fire and his words bite and sting those who are guilty of sin.

"Sometimes I felt like pulling his coat tail and asking him, 'Is there no mercy?'

"No other man living could have done for San Antonio what ought to have been done right now, but Frank Norris. We have been dominated in this city so long by Romanism, that large numbers of our people felt that there was no use to protest. But this great meeting has put new courage and fighting spirit in every Protestant and Baptist within one hundred miles or more of this place.

"I will never be the same man any more. I have always been a peaceable man, and tried to get along with people, but my firm conviction is that Gospel preaching ought never to be defensive, but offensive, and aggressive, with the fighting spirit of a Savonarola, Martin Luther and John the Baptist. This is Frank Norris' style and manner of preaching. He never pussy-foots. He never compromises, he never palliates the Gospel, he never spares anyone's feelings, because he knows he is right, be knows his Bible, and he knows the Lord, and loves His Church.

"He preached three times a day while he was here and gave conference lectures on the side, to our Sunday School teachers, officers and deacons. He taught us more how to organize and make effective the working forces of a great church, than any man who ever came to see us. His plans are the most simplified I ever heard expounded, and when you have heard him, you know it is the only way to make it go. He never theorizes, he never tells you what tie book says – he talks from experience, but he knows what he is talking about, and he makes you feel it. I never heard a man, in my twenty-five years of ministerial life, who knew as much about church life and organization, as Frank Norris I do not wonder now why he holds the multitudes in Fort Worth, and has the greatest church in America.

"Of course, nobody can do exactly as Dr. Norris does. He would be a fool to try it. But a man can be himself and take his methods and double any church in the world. I have found out several things from him that are the secret of any pastor's success.

"There must be a Spiritual leader somewhere, and the pastor is that man. Several of my deacons learned that while be was here. Some of the elect sisters and the choir director, and the pastor.

"He is the most loyal man to a pastor in a meeting, that I ever had to help me. He allows nobody to talk about anybody else in his presence, nor to criticize and find fault and grouch around.

"He is the most untiring worker that I ever knew, and he has no patience whatever with men and women who will not work, but who seek to give advice. He just cuts them off at the knees and lets them alone.

"When I asked him to came and hold this meeting, I made up my mind fully to let him be the boss and give his directions, and there I showed sense. I never crossed him in any suggestions; I tried to do what he wanted done, for I knew that he knew what ought to be done.

I backed him up to the limit, in all of his fights, and urged him on – and our people did likewise. I found no white-livered cowards among our crowd when he got in a scrap with the devil, or the. forces of evil.

"Of course, there was some prejudice on the part of some people in San Antonio, to Dr. Norris' coming here. But when they heard him, they became, his most enthusiastic admirers, and so far as I know, everybody here is for him now – Baptists, Protestants, and the man of no church. I never saw such a campaign, going six weeks, with such sustained interest. The fact is, the last week was the greatest of all, and he did his best preaching that week.

## "Some of the Results

"I repeat, over six hundred people joined our church, most of them by baptism. I am not counting 'reclamations' and 'conversions.' If we had counted these the results would number into the thousands. Our church was completely reorganized, with doubled efficiency. The great doctrines of the Baptist Church were emphasized as I never heard before, in a revival. The cause of Christ was put forward in this wicked city, as no man had ever done or could do. Our new church enterprise was brought to completion, with the breaking of dirt, and the raising of the money to build the first unit of a million dollar enterprise.

"After we heard Dr. Norris for six weeks, we were ashamed that we had done so little, and we have undertaken a ten year program, with a million dollar objective, and with ten thousand membership in the First Baptist Church.

"All these things were made possible by this great revival. There will not be bad after-effects, for his sermons were not sensational, yarn-telling and clown performing; nor were they a bundle of graveyard stories.

"He built his sermons on the Word of God, and our people will never be the same any more, and will never put up with sop and cider preaching.

"One of his greatest sermons was one on 'The Bible Versus Evolution.' That sermon attracted as much attention as any sermon ever preached here, and it was unanswerable. I know the fight, I know the big fight we are in now is between Fundamentalism and Modernism, and I am lining up, and my church, with the Fundamentalists.

"The revival will continue, for we are going to move our platform and seats out into an open lot near the church and continue this meeting until Christmas, and the First Baptist Church expects to have 1,200 additions, or more, this year. We have had over 800 up to now, with half the year to go. We are going to set the world's record for 1924, in church additions.

"When the new church is done, I have invited Dr. Norris back to hold another meeting, and he has agreed to come, and I look for the next meeting to go beyond the present one. I want everybody to know that San Antonio appreciated Dr. Norris beyond words to express.

"He not only captured the Baptists, bag and baggage, but all other denominations, and thousands of Catholics as well."

**"Signed I. E. Gates."**

*Dr. Norris appointed ambassador of good will by Chamber of Commerce, Fort Worth*

February 19, 1938

Dr. J. Frank Norris
Pastor First Baptist Church
Fort Worth, Texas

Dear Dr. Norris:

As president of the Chamber of Commerce of this city, representing all the various business enterprises, factories, banks, and trades, I am appointing you and Mrs. Norris as ambassadors of good will of our city in your contemplated tour around the world.

While you are pastor of the great First Baptist Church, and have been for twenty-nine years yet you belong to the whole city, and we regard you as one of us. The whole citizenship rejoices in the opportunity that comes to us in that you will put the name of Fort Worth happily before all nations, citizens, peoples and rulers.

Yours very sincerely,

FORT WORTH CHAMBER OF COMMERCE

PRESIDENT

Gaylord J. Stone/d

# CHAPTER II

THE FOLLOWING WAS PUBLISHED IN THE BAPTIST STANDARD

"THE HOUSTON, TEXAS, REVIVAL

### By J. B. Leavell

In the midst of the red hot controversy, my two good friends, who are both now in glory, Rev. I. E. Gates of First Baptist Church, San Antonio, and Dr. J. B. Leavell, First Baptist Church, Houston, asked me to hold meetings for them, which I did.

Then the Sanhedrins did gnash their teeth – "When they heard these things, they were cut to the heart, and they gnashed on him with their teeth."

Dr. E. C. Routh was Editor of the Baptist Standard and got fired because he published the following account of those two great revivals, which are as follows:

(It is no secret that one man in Dallas did the firing. Ask Dr. E. C. Routh of Oklahoma City, and ask Dr. F. S. Groner of Marshall, Texas, who also was fired by the same man.) "

"Houston has just seen pass into history what is probably the greatest evangelistic meeting in the history of Southern Baptists. The meeting was under the auspices of the First Baptist Church of Houston. Dr. J. Frank Norris was the preacher.

"Mr. J. Dalbert Coutts led the choir, furnished wonderful music at the piano, and throughout the campaign directed the orchestra and large choir of two hundred or more voices. Other members of the working force from Fort Worth assisted in the campaign. All the forces from the First Church, Houston, stayed faithfully in the campaign from start to finish. The meeting was planned for six weeks, but was continued through its seventh week. Dr. Norris preached twice each week day and three times each Sunday for the eight Sundays.

"1010 Added to the Churches.

"I wonder if any meeting ever saw as large and definite results. 720 people united with the First Baptist Church alone. Most of these came by baptism. This brings the total membership of this church to nearly 5000. 1010 chine to all the churches in the city. All the Baptist churches in the city received additions, and probably every Protestant church. Pedo-baptists were borrowing baptismal pools to take care of those who came to them and would not be satisfied with anything but immersion for baptism. The work was definite and thorough with all who came forward. The pastor had a conference with each one individually at the front seat before they were received into the church. People joined from every faith and sect. Every Pedo-baptist denomination made its contribution, and many Roman Catholics. Christian Scientists, Russellites, Spiritualists, etc., made profession and received baptism.

"The Tabernacle was the largest ever built in Texas; seating capacity estimated at from six to eight thousand. It overflowed several times, was always taxed to its capacity on Sundays, the crowds were vastly increasing on week days during the entire period. The Tabernacle was situated at Main and McKinney – in the very heart of the business section. A building had just been torn down for larger construction, and we fortunately used this strategic point during this interval.

"The meeting presented many unique features. Notable among these are the following:

"That a campaign of such proportions should be launched and carried by one church. The magnitude of it will compare favorably with any big campaign in which all denominations and churches participate.

"The expenses of the meeting ran to over $12,000. This was cared for by plate collections.

"Again it is noteworthy that the evangelist received not one cent personally for his services. It was Dr. Norris' proposal that the meeting only take care of such expenses as were incurred in his own church because of his absence, stating that he felt the prolonged absence had encumbered upon him to supply the program at his own church. Every personal contribution went in this ion, the checks were made payable to the First Baptist Church of Fort Worth amounting to approximately $2,000.

"Another notable feature was that Dr. Norris felt that his greatest compensation was in the fact that his labours went to the establishment of the life of a downtown church. He shares the conviction, with many, that the down-town church is the greatest factor in modern church life. Never did a man find a more critical need in a great church, and never was a church more firmly established by an evangelistic effort. During the meeting it was announced that the pastor had fully refinanced the entire project and included in the deal was sufficient funds to guarantee the completion of the large auditorium. This auditorium will seat 3,400 people. This unit of construction will complete the actual needs of the First Baptist Church, at least, for the present. It leaves also a valuable lot on Main Street, which carries a potential value of nearly a fourth of a million dollars.

"Probably the most prominent and glorious feature of the meeting was the exaltation of the Word of God. Few, if any, living preachers have so mastered the Book. Surely no living preacher is so zealous in its defense. The preacher not only unfolded the Word in a most masterful fashion in every service, but flayed error and the enemies of the truth in the most fierce and fearless fashion, that the mind could imagine. Even the old soldiers of the cross would cringe in the midst of these attacks.

"Again, there was a total absence of emotionalism. The appeal was rather made to the intellect; often more than half of the time used by the speaker would be in reading the Word of God.

"During the campaign the people were led through the Books of Genesis, Revelation, Daniel, Malachi, Acts, and in almost every sermon there was reference made to every portion of the Book from beginning to end. The issue was clearly drawn in the Word of God, and the fruitage from such sowing will be flowing in for years and years to come.

"Dr. J. Frank Norris is a unique man. He is a far broader and deeper man and more resourceful than anyone could ever imagine except through a period of association, fellowship and service. It seems to me that any unbiased student of his life testimony and tactics would be forced to the conclusion that he is actuated by the holiest and purest passion for the Cross, the triumph of the Word and the hastening of the return of the coming King. Amen."

# CHAPTER III

## SEVENTEEN BAPTIST PREACHERS WENT IN FOR "THE KILL" – THE RADIO HATE FEST

For seven long years there was the bitterest denominational controversy, which culminated in the bitterest radio debate. One hour for the denominational leaders, followed by one hour by Norris.

Dr. W. B. Riley, now 86 years old, pastor of the great First Baptist Church, Minneapolis for forty years, well known and well beloved, published the following in his magazine, The Pilot;

### "The Texas Baptist Controversy"

"The air in Texas has been blue during the month. Six or eight outstanding Baptist men connected directly with the Texas Baptist machine, undertook to give Norris a black eye over the radio. It would seem that they went in for a straight killing. Norris, in order to put past dispute what they said, arranged for a wax cylinder reception, and he gives the following as samples of speech employed: 'Malicious,' 'diabolical,' falsifier,' 'perjurer,' 'liar,' 'thief,' 'scoundrel,' 'reprobate,' 'despicable,' 'damnable,' 'devilish,' 'infamous,' 'murderer,' 'criminal,' 'dastardly,' 'heinous,' 'infamous liar,' 'malicious falsifier,' 'wicked,' 'corrupt,' 'hellish,' malicious liar.' At the close of these addresses delivered by Drs. Brooks, Scarborough and others, Frank was immediately upon the air for an answer. We heard him but once, but were told by those who listened in nightly that this time was a sample of his regular procedure. He begged the air audience not to think hardly of his opponents, to remember that they were excited and heated up, and that their strong language did not represent their better spirit. He ignored very largely their hard names and malicious charges, and moved straight to the preaching of a first class evangelistic sermon, concluding with a soul-winning appeal.

"We say without hesitation, that, while we have heard of men building platforms, adjusting nooses about their own necks, tying the upper end of the rope over a limb, and then kicking the platform from beneath themselves to dangle till death, we have seldom seen so many high class and apparently sensible men commit the same folly at one time as occurred in this procedure. Since it began, I have been in Kansas, Oklahoma, Arkansas and Tennessee, and everywhere there was one judgment of 'a foolish procedure injurious to those who inaugurated it,' and advantageous to their enemy.

"The procedure can be explained, however, on the same ground that is going to render desperate leaders in the Northern Baptist Convention in the near future. The whole Southern machine is badly crippled; and when men's vested interests are touched, they lose equanimity and often behave foolishly. We predict that the comparative good nature of the Northern modernists among Baptists will not last much longer."

## THE RADIO HATE FEST

By Beauchamp Vick

**"I Expect to Look Over the Parapets of Heaven and See Frank Norris Frying in the Bottomless Pits of Hell"**

I heard the entire radio debase, and here is a sample from the records as taken down:

That is a quotation from the address of President J. L. Ward of Decatur College in the ill-fated radio hate fest where the denominational leaders went on the radio for eight nights to damn dr. J. Frank Norris. Their addresses were all taken down on max cylinders and the air was blistering with the bitterest epithets ever heard or spoken.

There is no hate or malice equal to religious persecution. Seventy millions of human lives have gone down to death on the field of battle because of religious wars. There is no hate equal to the hatred of a church row.

Dr. Norris fooled his traducers and did not answer them in kind. They rented the time from the KTAT Broadcasting Company. They contracted for it, but never did pay for it, and after they had made the announcement they were going to expose Dr. J. Frank Norris, he secured the hours immediately following and as they signed off he signed on. He advertised their time for several weeks before over the radio, in the Fundamentalist, and even took paid advertisements in the daily papers. That a great crowd heard goes without saying – both friend and foe.

As soon as the first speaker, Dr. L. R. Scarborough, was through, telling the world all the mean things he ever heard, thought or felt about Dr. Norris, and that everybody else ever felt, thought, published, circulated, whispered publicly or privately, and there was no prayer, no Scripture, no song.

Immediately when the distinguished President of the Seminary signed off, four young ladies stepped to the microphone in Dr. Norris' study, without any announcement and sang in perfect harmony:

"For you I am praying, For you I am praying,

For you I am praying, I'm praying for you."

Without a word of announcement there stepped to the microphone a number of sinners who had been redeemed under Dr. Norris' ministry – men who had been saved from drunkards' graves, saloon-keepers, gamblers, and they all with one accord told the listening audience in a score of statements:

"Go home to thy friends, and tell them how great things the Lord hath done for thee, and hath had compassion on thee."

Then Dr. Norris went on and said: "These men are good men but are mad. I feel sorry for them and I want you to forgive them. I have been mad myself and I know how bad it makes one feel.

"You are not interested in what they think of me, or what I think of them, but I want to take this occasion to call this great listening audience to repentance, and after the world is on fire and the heavens have passed away with a great noise, out in the eternity of eternities, you will have no concern about a denominational row between one insignificant preacher and a group of denominational leaders. Therefore, I want to talk to you on:

### "The Great White Throne of Judgment"

"I quote to you these solemn words from Revelation 21:11-15,

" 'And I saw a great white throne, and him that sat on it, from whose face the earth and the heaven fled away; and there was found no place for them. And I saw the dead, small and great stand before God; and the books were opened: and another book was opened, which is the book of life: and the dead were judged out of those things which were written in the books, according to their works. And the sea gave up the dead which were in it; and death and hell delivered up the dead which were in them: and they were judged every man according to their works. And death and hell were cast into the lake of fire. This is the second death. And whosoever was not found written in the book of life was cast into the lake of fire.'

'This is the final verdict and doom of the universe. Time is no more. And I pray tonight for some prodigal boy that is away from home, some gray haired father who has gone down in sin, some unfortunate girl without hope, and the moral man without Christ, I pray you and all to listen to these solemn words, when every one of us, these preachers who are saying all these mean things about me, and I with them, together we will stand before the flaming bar of God's eternal judgment.

> "ETERNTIY! stupendous theme!
> Compar'd here with our life's a dream:
> Eternity! O awful sound:
> A deep where all our thoughts are drown'd!

### Facing the Mob At Decatur

(Still quoting from "Inside the Cup")

Dr. J. L. Ward, president of Decatur Baptist College called a mob together to "hang Norris" on the court house square in the city of Decatur. He sent wide announcements, circulars, newspaper notices and told in blunt speech that the purpose of the gathering was to "hang Norris."

Hearing about it I drove to Decatur, 40 miles from Fort Worth and pushed my way through the mob and stood in front within ten feet of Dr. Ward while he was making his inflamatory speech.

They refused to give me the chance to reply, but I had already arranged for a truck to be parked on the other side of the square and after three hour of denunciation, I walked out and went around and got up on the truck and the crowd broke from Ward like a stampede of cattle and I had a lot of good humor and told many amusing stories and after a time of laughter and genuine Texas good humor I preached a sermon on 'The Prodigal Son," and there were many saved.

### Another Mob At Waco

"Whom the gods would destroy they first make mad." This was the slogan, though unannounced, of the Texas Baptist leaders. In the midst of the red hot evolution fight which ran for a period of seven years, during which time the Baptist convention did two things every year, "Hang Norris," and whitewash evolution. However, the convention would pass strong resolutions denouncing evolution, while saving the evolutionists. Debts piled up by the millions, confidence was broken down, but the First Baptist Church grew by leaps and bounds and great crowds turned out to hear me where ever I went.

### "Take the War Into Africa"

I called up the auditorium in the city of Waco and rented and paid for it at a cost of seventy-five dollars and announced that I was going to "hang the, apes and monkeys on the faculty of, Baylor University." The President of Baylor called a mass meeting at the Chapel, and not only did all the students attend, but they came from down in the various sections of the city, Jews, Gentiles, Protestants, and Catholics, and the chapel was packed while they "hung Norris in effigy."

When I arrived in Waco the sherriff and chief of police came to the hotel and said, "You had better not stay here five minutes, Norris, we cannot guarantee you protection and you must not dare to speak tonight." These two officers, sheriff and chief of police, were quietly informed that this was still a free country and that there was a contract with the auditorium and the address would be delivered.

I arrived at the auditorium an hour ahead of time and every available space was taken and it was impossible to get in through the main door and I had to go into a side entrance and never was there such cat calls, hooting, booing and yelling. They were plainly, sympathetically, and bluntly told: "You are running true to form and are giving the finest evidence that your ancestors were braying asses, screeching monkeys and yelling hyenas."

Soon howling mob spent its force and the address was delivered calling the names and giving the records of the evolutionists and at the close of two hours and ten minutes address the audience was in profound silence and their hearts were moved and when the question was put to them whether they believed the Bible versus evolution the entire audience leaped to its feet as one man.

This two hours and ten minutes address was published and it was the end of evolution in Baylor University.

At the next session of the convention Dr. J. B. Tidwell read the clearest address that perhaps was ever delivered against evolution and that address is the official statement of the Baptist Convention of Texas and Baylor University; and the evolution discussion swept through the entire Southern Baptist Convention and at the Houston session I had a huge tent and the leaders were seized with panic and stayed up all night long and the late George W. McDaniel, president of the convention told the leaders the convention would stampede to the tent unless they passed a resolution against evolution. Dr. McDaniel himself opened the convention by offering the following resolution:

"This convention accepts Genesis as teaching that man was the special creation of God, and rejects every theory, evolution or other, which teaches that man originated in, or came by way of, a lower animal ancestry."

# CHAPTER IV

## HOW FORT WORTH PASTORS KEPT NORRIS OUT OF THE LINCOLN McCONNELL MEETING

It was in 1914, and Norris wired Lincoln McConnell, one of the outstanding evangelists of this generation, to come to Fort Worth and hold a meeting. McConnell accepted. It was announced.

There were forty-nine pastors of all denominations who met and voted they would go into the meeting provided Norris would stay out, and they sent the Y.M.C.A. Secretary, Sam Bryant, a very high class Christian gentleman to see Norris. And he readily agreed that, to quote his exact words, "If the preachers of Fort Worth would get rid of Norris and the devil they ought to have a good meeting."

They built a huge tabernacle on the block now covered by Cox's Dry Goods, the Fort Worth Club, and the Worth Hotel.

There were some forty odd committees – Committee on Advertisings Committee on Signs – Committee on Ushers – Committee on Music – Committee on Personal Work – Committee on Entertainment, et cetera, et cetera.

The names of the forty-nine cooperating churches and pastors were printed on the Seventh Street side and the Throckmorton side of the, big tabernacle. Of course the First Church and pastor's name was not in the list. And people wondered. And even the First Church members wondered. I myself wondered. But Norris said nothing.

He had a very peculiar way it seems, after the fashion of Nehemiah he keeps his counsel to himself till the time to act. He often says that he has a meeting of his "Board" at 2 A. M. every morning and it is unanimous.

The meeting came and started with a bang. Large crowds, big advertisement, and there were forty some odd banners throughout the big tabernacle where each church was assigned to its place to do personal work.

There were forty-nine pastors on the platform behind the pulpit with their name and number. Of course there was no place for Norris.

On Sunday before the meeting was to start he called the whole church together and told them the whole inside story and then said, "I want you to meet with me and Entzminger for five nights and learn how to do personal work." And also he said, "Follow me."

Not being on any committee we were free to work and to do as we pleased, and Norris said to me, "Entz, this meeting is ours. This bunch of back slidden preachers are so filled with hate and envy against me that they cannot win souls, and we will go in to win souls as the Lord will give us power."

He and I were at that tabernacle the first half of the afternoon, and then he had a group of workers nearby and he would meet everybody as they came in, and when it was found to be a good prospect he turned it over to me or one of our workers.

That meeting came and went, and it wasn't long after the first week that that bunch of back slidden preachers slid out from the meeting and Norris and his workers literally took charge.

They had – that entire bunch of forty-nine preachers, a grand total of forty-seven members, and the First Baptist Church received six hundred thirty-six!

That bunch of preachers – those that are still living – and all of them are gone from Fort Worth – were perfectly furious, and said, "Norris tricked us."

Many of the outstanding people of the city were saved, notable sinners.

Norris baptized over five hundred.

The above picture is Leonard Brothers employees listening to Dr. Norris preach. He has standing invitations from all places of business in Fort Worth.

Dr. Norris and Dr. Graham Scroggie, Pastor Spurgeon's Church, London, England.

# CHAPTER V

"We Question Whether Any Book Outside the Bible Was Ever Published So Full of Inspiration and Suggestion and Explicit Direction to Sunday School Workers as This Latest Book by Dr. Norris." – The Gospel Witness.

The Editor of the Gospel Witness, Dr. T. T. Shields, Is Known for His Conservatism. All the More Valuable,

Therefore, Is His Testimony

January 13, 1938　　　**THE GOSPEL WITNESS**　　　343 7.

### "INSIDE HISTORY OF THE FIRST BAPTIST CHURCH, FORT WORTH, AND TEMPLE BAPTIST CHURCH, DETROIT—LIFE STORY OF DR. J. FRANK NORRIS

This is the title of a new book of three hundred and thirty pages, by Dr. Norris, generously illustrated with cuts of his great, buildings in Fort Worth and Detroit.

Its' value as an epitomized biography of a great preacher, and the condensed record of the unprecedented achievement of the same great preacher in the leadership of two great churches fifteen hundred miles apart, cannot possibly be estimated. We remember to have read a statement by Dr. A. T. Pearson, about Spurgeon, to the effect, that after the Lord had made C. H. Spurgeon, He broke the mold. There is only one J. Frank Norris. So far as we have been able to observe, in many respects he is unlike any other man we have ever known.

Some years ago a southern friend remarked to us that when the Lord made Norris, He found that He had run out of the element of fear, so He made him without fear. It reminded us of a certain man who used to attend Jarvis St. prayer meetings, a very precise man, who was biblically well-informed. For a good while he attended the meetings, and delivered himself of fifteen or twenty minute prayers, until we could endure it no longer. But his prayers were very thoroughly prepared in advance, and were extraordinary essays, evidently prepared to exhibit the prayer-essayist's ability. He was very fond of recounting the wonders of nature, and we recall a sentence from one of his prayers to this effect: "We thank Thee, O Lord, for the percolating power of a sunbeam." On another occasion he had evidently been delving into Job and his prayer was largely a dissertation on leviathan; and we recall that he reminded the Lord that leviathan was "the only creature whom Thou hast made without fear." It may have been quite fortunate for us that that particular gentleman was unacquainted with Dr. J. Frank Norris, for he would have had to make an exception in his case, and include him with leviathan – and then the usual twenty-minute prayer must have been extended for an hour or so.

Dr. Norris is a fearless man in more ways than one. We have known men who seemed to have any amount of moral courage, who were physical cowards; and we have known men abundantly endowed with physical courage, who were moral cowards. But Dr. Norris is afraid of nothing, either in the physical or moral realms. Who but Dr. Norris would have dared even to attempt what, by the blessing of God, he has achieved in Detroit? Even the most daring of other men would have been afraid to try.

It was this Editor's privilege and honour years ago to enjoy the warm personal friendship of the late Russel H. Conwell, in many respects, in his day, the world's greatest lecturer. We never heard Dr. Conwell lecture without feeling at the end that nothing was impossible. We have the same feeling when we read this record of the achievements of Dr. Norris. It gives us a feeling that there is no enemy physical or moral that may not be defeated and utterly routed; nor any task in our Lord's service which may not be accomplished.

Dr. Norris has been subject to trials that were no easier to endure than those of Job, but he has triumphed over them all. In Fort Worth, twice his great church was reduced to ashes – each time to rise from the ashes greater than ever. Some people in this northern part of the Continent would be inclined to say, "Yes, of course; but that was in Fort Worth. And Dr. Norris is a Baptist., and Baptists grow in the Southern states almost without cultivation. Nothwithstanding their orthodoxy, they seem to be rather indigenous to the soil." It is a fact that Baptists are perhaps the largest body of Christians in the South, and we think it is probably true that Baptist churches do multiply more rapidly in the South than in the North – that is, of course, under the ministry of ordinary men. But that explanation of the First Baptist Church, Fort Worth, will no longer hold.

For what about Detroit? Can anyone find a more difficult city on the American Continent in which to do Christian work than Detroit? It may not be more difficult than Chicago or New York, but certainly the difficulties are at least as great. And yet in the short space of three years the Temple Baptist Church of Detroit has outgrown all its buildings, and like Abraham, has dwelt "in tabernacles, with Isaac and Jacob, the heirs with him of the same promise." The story of these marvelous achievements must prove an inspiration and tonic to the faith of every true believer; and what is equally important, it will provide a spur to the Christian effort of all who read it.

## "THE YOUNG DOG THAT WAS JUMPED ON BY SEVEN OTHER DOGS"

(Still quoting from "Inside the Cup")

Regarding the Texas fight, Dr. W. B. Riley published the following story:

"I had a fine bird dog but he wouldn't fight. It was not his nature and every time a neighbor's dog would come over into his yard he would run from the house. One day I was in a car going down a steep incline and there rushed out a whole pack – seven vicious dogs, each one bigger than mine, and I feared they would tear him to pieces. Before I could stop my car and get out, they had all pounced on him, but he had backed up in a corner for protection and was snapping each one with his teeth and making the blood come, and soon they all backed away from him. From that time on, he was a new dog and every time another dog would come over or start a fight, my dog only had to show his sharp teeth and there was no further trouble.

"So it has been in this Texas Baptist fight with Frank. They all jumped on him and thought they would tear him limb from limb, but they have been cut all to pieces."

## THE VICTORY AT THE END OF A LONG WAR

Dr. R. C. Buckner was president of the Baptist General Convention of Texas for twenty-two years. He built up the greatest orphange in America.

### BUCKNER'S ORPHANS HOME

Dallas, Texas, Doc. 19, 1918.

Pastor J. Frank Norris:

I rejoice in the triumph in the late Tarrant County election, Fort Worth and all. I believe the late victory should be attributed to you more than anyone else. Truly you laid the foundation and others have budded on it, and more attention may be directed to the rattle in nailing on the last shingle over the structure, but J. Frank Norris did more work and the most effectual work as a wise master builder, heroic and untiring in everything from the bed rock all the way up till the Hall of Fame was completed. Honor to whom honor is due, and with me J. Frank Norris' stock is not tamely at par but scores a very high premium.

Accept my congratulation. You fought and bled, and instead of having died, you are today recognized as mightily alive – you are a "live wire."

Your friend all the way through,

(Signed) R. C. Buckner.

# SINCLAIR LEWIS ATTENDS FIRST BAPTIST CHURCH OCT. 31, 1937

**Says: "I Satisfied a Desire of a Great Many Years' Standing."**
**"I Never Before Have Seen So Many People at Church at Once."**

The Monday morning paper of the Fort Worth Star-Telegram has a large article occupying about one-quarter of the page, concerning the report of an interview with Sinclair Lewis who is visiting Fort Worth to lecture. Upon being asked by the Star-Telegram reporter where he spent Sunday morning he replied:

"What did I do this morning? I satisfied a desire of a great many years standing – I went to hear Dr. J. Frank Norris preach. I admire the eloquence and vigor of Dr. Norris and have wanted to hear him. I have never seen before so many people at church at once."

## THREE TREACHEROUS DEACONS

A pastor's foes are within and never without. Here's how the denominational machine would bore within.

There were three deacons, a doctor, a lawyer and a banker. They played double to Norris, like Alexander Coppersmith, and did him much harm, but they were all three exposed and turned out, and in one week the main one dropped dead.

Another example: A choir director, with a deep bass voice, that Norris trusted implicitly, played double also and worked with the machine. In Norris' absence he called the deacons together and caused Norris serious trouble. When Norris returned he not only dismissed that choir director instanter but every deacon who sided with him.

Dr. Norris received by the Lord Mayor of London in the famous "Mansion House".

# CHAPTER VI

## "WE WILL PUT YOU OUT OF BUSINESS AND NO CHURCH WILL HAVE YOU – YOU WILL HAVE NO CROWDS"

This threat occurred in the office of the pastor of the First Baptist Church at the beginning of the ill-fated $75 Million Campaign.

There were five brethren, and all good men, who came into Dr. Norris' office. The five men have all gone to their reward, and I repeat, they were very fine Christian gentlemen. Their names were Drs. L. R. Scarborough, F. S. Groner, C. V. Edwards, Forrest Smith and W. L. Whitley The latter was County Missionary and two next to the last were pastors of Broadway Baptist and College Avenue. Baptist Churches respectively. Personally, I was very fond of Dr. Scarborough and of the other four. They were sincere in their scheme to put over the $75 Million Campaign.

The plan was to apportion a certain amount to each of the states in the Southern Baptist Convention and then that was sub-divided to each Association, and then that was sub-sub-divided and apportioned to each church. (The Methodists Use "assess" and the Baptists "apportion".)

Incidentally, that choir director died of delirium tremens.

Two hundred thousand was the amount apportioned to the First Baptist Church, Fort Worth. The church was poor, struggling, in debt, trying to build, and, besides, the pastor did not believe that it was either Scriptural or Baptistic for any headquarters to apportion, to assess a sovereign church for any amount to be raised.

In vain he plead with the five brethren, and then they proceeded to pronounce the anathema that would make the Spanish Inquisition blush with shame.

Dr. Norris reached over and picked up their large envelope that had on it in red, "$75 Million Campaign" and there was a song to the tune of "Bringing In the Sheaves" with the words "When the

Millions Come Pouring In," and took that large envelope that had the apportionment of $200,000 for the First Baptist Church and tore it into many small scraps and threw it at their feet and with disdain and contempt said, "That's my answer."

They had the spirit and method of the Sanhedrin when they stoned Stephen – "When they heard these things, they were cut to the heart, and they gnashed on him with their teeth." (Acts 7:54).

And the war began.

There was a "seven-years' war" in the 18th century but this was a "seven-years war among Texas Baptists of the 20th century."

I thought at the time that Norris fought back too hard, but the more I look back at it and understand that they went in "for the kill," I became more charitable and less exacting in my judgment of his course.

It is a fact that is well known that no man who refused or for any cause failed to put up the coin, as the Roman governors demanded of the tax gatherers in the time of our Lord, that that man who failed would sooner or later be nailed to the cross, and much sooner.

Norris is the only man that I know who not only defied the conscinceless, heartless denominational machine but turned on them and fought them with everything at his command.

Incidentally, those five good men who made that demand on Norris – and I repeat they were all five good men and my personal friends – they were sincere in their demand, but Norris was sincere in rejecting it.

### Dr. Scarborough and Dr. Norris Became Good Friends

Notwithstanding the bitterest of all the bitter controversies – and they fought like two giants in the ring – the following letter tells of their happy relations before good and great Dr. Scarborough went to his reward:

"Fort Worth 2, Texas,
October 19, 1944.

"Dr. Lee Scarborough
Northwest Hospital
Amarillo, Texas

"Dear Lee:
"I just met Warren, your fine son, on the street and had a very happy talk with him. I admire him greatly. He has so conducted himself as one of the leading attorneys of the bar in this city that he has won the confidence of everybody.

"He tells me of your condition, which I had already learned through the papers. You are a heroic soul, and a long, long time ago you settled the whole question of the great crossing. Naturally, I too have thought a great deal of it though it may be many years for both of us, and yet it may come at any hour. To me one of the greatest of all scriptures is 'To die is gain.'

"Warren said a very tender thing awhile ago, 'You both are going to the same place, and you both believe the same thing.'

"I am giving lectures in the Bible Institute on the Life of Paul, and only yesterday I came to that experience where they had sharp difference over a third preacher, young John Mark. The Lord, in this case, overruled this difference and there were two great missionary journeys instead of one. How beautiful and tender Paul wrote: 'Take Mark, and bring him with thee: for he is profitable to me for the ministry.' But all of them are in glory.

"You will have, a multitude of souls to meet you that were saved through your preaching of the gospel of Blood Redemption.

"If you get there first – and I may get there first – but if you get there first I envy you the joys that await you. I am certain as I am a living man of the realities of the glories in the Father's Home, that awaits all the redeemed.

"Yours tenderly,<br>"J. FRANK NORRIS."

JFN-M

Dr. Scarborough was not able in his last illness to reply to this letter but had his daughter, Mrs. Euna Lee Foreman, to write the following letter:

«MRS. A. D. FOREMAN, JR
2010 Polk
Amarillo, Texas
Oct. 14, 1944

"Dr. J. Frank Norris,
First Baptist Church,
Fort Worth 2, Texas.

"Dear Dr. Norris:

"Your letter to daddy was so very much appreciated by all of us. It was so kind of you to write, and the nice things you said about him will linger long in our hearts.

"He is still in the hospital and very seriously ill, but we are finding God's grace sufficient for our needs.

"We have heard that Mrs. Norris is not well, and we want you to know that our hearts go out to you and her in love and sympathy, and we do pray that God will heal and bless her.

"So often I think of Lillian and the happy year we had together in Baylor. I would love to have an opportunity to renew our friendship. Please remember me to her when you write.

"Thank you again for your thoughtfulness, and continue to remember us all in your prayers.

"Sincerely,

(Sgd)   "Euna Lee Foreman."

# CHAPTER VII

## THE EVOLUTION FIGHT

It is well known that there were evolutionists on the faculty at Baylor University, Norris' Alma Mater. He got the records of eight of them and published them.

The denominational leaders who did not believe in evolution, did not stand for it, thought they had to stand for evolution because Norris was fighting it, and that's been the course throughout, the denominational controversy.

This was the real issue at the Southern Baptist Convention in St. Louis in 1947 when they reelected Louie Newton, a now confessed unquestioned Communist.

The great majority of Southern Baptists are opposed to Louie Newton and his Communism but the leaders said, "We have got to reelect him because Norris opposes him." What folly!

Instead of putting Norris of business they put themselves out of business.

Throughout this red hot fight on Evolution the First Baptist Church grew by leaps and bounds. Baptists came from every church in the city and multitudes of unsaved were won and baptized, and the Sunday School grew to be the largest in the world. And today it is one of the two largest in the world, Temple Baptist Church being the other.

Therefore, I have changed my attitude, revised my judgment on Norris' methods. I would not advise anybody else to use his methods but its the only way he could have stayed and won.

Anyway, the Lord seems to be pleased with his methods.

I have been a student of the Old and New Testaments and I have not yet understood the methods of Samson, of Gideon, of Joshua, of Samuel, of David, of Elijah, nor of great religious leaders such as Athansius, Martin Luther, John Wesley and a host of others, but the Lord seemed to understand these men whom He had called and so abundantly blessed.

### Dr. George W. Truett and Dr. J. Frank Norris

Indeed, Dr. Truett was one of the world's greatest preachers, and built, one of the truly great churches of all time.

Faithful Catholics claim infallibility for the Pope, but Bible students believe that Moses made a few mistakes. And Paul said, "Oh, wretched man that I am!"

Even Simon Peter made one or two mistakes.

When the Evolution fight started in Texas and Norris forced eight evolutionists to resign from Baylor University, Dr. Truett defended every one of them. And it is a matter of record that he made one of the most terrific addresses in the Baptist Convention on Norris and closed with the words that made everybody shudder – "damnable and despicable." Large numbers, even thousands heard him say – the greatest part of whom are living to this day – "He will soon be on the junk heap" …"He will be wrapped in his own winding sheet and cast into the bottomless abyss of oblivion." That was 25 years ago!

And the great preacher said concerning Norris' paper, "It is not fit to be printed in the bottomless pits of hell."

Such strong language did not fit the gentle and beloved Dr. Truett.

M. H. Wolfe, who was twenty years chairman of the Board of Deacons of Dallas, and read the annual report the first of every year said concerning this unfortunate controversy:

The following was published while Dr. Truett and M. H. Wolfe were living:

### "Statement of Mr. M. H. Wolfe on Texas Baptist Controversy

Mr. M. H. Wolfe, chairman of the board of deacons of the First Baptist Church, Dallas, for nearly twenty years, and who read the annual report of the church the first Sunday in each year, was the right-hand man of Dr. George W. Truett, paid his way across the Atlantic, and supported him loyally and abundantly.

Mr. Wolfe was on every important denominational board for twenty years.

He was President of the Baptist General Convention of Texas for three years. He was regarded during those days as the greatest layman among Southern Baptists.

On the night before the convention in 1921 in Dallas there was a midnight caucus held on what to do with "J. Frank Norris' remains?"

That was seventeen years ago.

The occasion of the caucus was brought about because of Norris' exposure of evolution in Baylor University. At that time G. Samuel Dow was the head professor of Sociology, in Baylor, and on page 210 of his book, "Introduction to Sociology," published by Baylor University and approved by Baylor University and approved by the President of the University, Professor Dow wrote with his own hand:

"As to his body we, have very little exact knowledge, for the skeletons left by him are fragmentary, seldom amounting to more than one or two bones. But from these, by the use of our imagination, we have come to the conclusion that he was a squat, ugly, somewhat stooped, powerful being, half human and half animal, who sought refuge from the wild beasts first in the trees and later in eaves, and that he was about half way between the anthropoid ape and modern man."

The Sanhedrin in order to cover up exposure of this anthropoid ape in Baylor University, proceeded to "hang Norris."

Dr. George W. Truett led the procession to the gallows and in his speech he said, "We will dehorn him right now and that will end it."

Many of the pastors protested and several laymen, making the plea that they should clean out evolution in Baylor University and let Norris alone.

But Pope Alexander VI was never more enraged against Savonarola, when he first hanged him and then burned him on the streets of Florence, than was the "Holy Father" that night in 1921.

Mr. M. H. Wolfe, a great layman, in the caucus following, arose and said:

"You are doing the most fateful thing – committing the greatest tragedy and blunder in the history of Texas Baptists. If Frank Norris should come to us and say, 'Gentlemen, I want you to put me out of the convention and hang me, carry out the scheme that you have determined upon, your scheme for my promotion is a thousand times better than any scheme I could devise for a greater hearing.'"

Mr. Wolfe and his pastor, Dr. Truett, broke over this controversy and Mr. Wolfe moved his membership, on account of it, from the First Baptist Church to the Gaston Avenue Baptist Church.

In view of the later connections of Dr. Truett with the Federal Council of Churches and his connection with the Modernistic World Baptist Alliance, it is not difficult to look back seventeen years and understand his ill-fated course.

M. H. Wolfe died one of the best friends Norris ever had.

### Dr. Truett and the Federal Council of Churches

Though good and great man Dr. Truett was, he compromised with the Modernistic Federal Council of Churches and toured America, speaking under their auspices. Norris had the courage to challenge Dr. Truett's compromise with the Federal Council of Churches.

### Dr. Truett Sends For Norris on His Death Bed

Dr. Truett was a long sufferer before he passed to his reward. And the great preacher called in Bob Coleman one day and said,

"Bob, I am soon to cross over, and I don't want any bitterness on my lips and I don't want any man to have bitterness against me. Call Frank Norris and tell him I want to see him."

It would be too indelicate to tell why and who interfered and persuaded Bob Coleman not to make the call. This would not be published if it were not well known.

## Dawson Joins the Communistic Banks

The "Daily Worker," published in New York is the official voice of Moscow – in its official issue of February 25th, there is a long list of Communists on the committee published, and in the list of one hundred or more, Robert Morse Lovett, Lee Simonson, Frederick L. Schuman, Evans Clark, Quincy Wright, Paul H. Douglas, Upton Sinclair, John Dewey, Arthur Garfield Hays, William H. Kilpatrick, Mazwell S. Stewart, Leroy E. Bowman, Oswald Garrison Villard, Rev. William B. Spofford, Jerome Davis, Ben Gould. There appears also,

"Rev. Joseph M. Dawson, First Baptist Church, Texas."

Therefore the Convention Baptist machine have on their hands the finished fruit of modernism – J. M. Dawson's endorsement of Fosdickism, Darwinism, Agnosticism, and now February 25, 1938, his endorsement of communism – and this in the First Baptist Church at Waco, the church of Baylor University.

One of Dr. Norris' congregations in Tyler, Texas, when he was introduced by Rev. John Rawlings.

# CHAPTER VIII

### "THE FLOP-EARED, SUCK-EGG HOUND'»

The Machine, and ungodly rich members that he put out of his church, made the pastors of the churches where they went jump on Norris.

They brought all kinds of charges against him, assailed him from their pulpits, passed resolutions against him – in short, the pot was boiling over among Baptists all the time. His enemies said, "You should take it without fighting back."

But Norris did not agree with that policy, and "Wisdom is justified of her ways," for all the crowd that fought him are gone.

One morning one of the pastors, a strong man, got up before the crowd, pointed his finger at Norris and said,

"I expect to stand down at the Union Station and tell you good-bye."

Norris called him a flop-eared, Suck-egg hound.

I confess that was a rather strong epithet to use concerning the pastor of a great church in the same city.

But it should be borne in mind that that pastor had put his arms around the enemies of Norris, the rich men whose ungodly records had been exposed, and who had tried to put Norris out of business – in short, Norris turned his guns not only on this ungodly crowd but the Balaam who covered them up.

This pastor was finally deposed, driven from the pulpit, and one day years afterwards, Dr. Norris got off the train at the Union Station; his wife met him and he saw this former pastor standing there all bedraggled, clothes worn, hat and shoes run down – Norris in the pink and prime of health, fine clothes – and he wears the finest trailored clothes that can be made from head to foot – and they are all given to him by a rich man who was redeemed from a drunkard's grave through the preaching of Norris – Norris walked up to him, called him by name and said,

"Twenty years ago you stood before your crowd, when I was fighting for my life, and said many evil things against me and closed by saying,

" 'I expect to be down at the Union Station to tell you goodbye'. I am still waiting for that engagement to be filled."

It is doubtful whether he should have told this to that deposed ex-pastor, but that is Norris, and I am not going to pass judgment on him because it seems he and the Lord have an understanding that they haven't taken me in on. But maybe Norris would like to recall what he said to that deposed pastor.

Dr. Norris has never been one of these "perfectionists" who boasts of turning the other cheek – in short, he is not a negative, spineless somebody that has been easily kicked around.

He is more like Simon Peter than any character in the Bible – brimming full of good humor, burning with zeal. He may not curse like Peter did. But he has thought about it a good deal, and I have seen him when I was afraid he was, and I can't vouch for all of his time. But I know he is like Simon Peter when he fell on his face and wept bitterly. He is always ready to forgive, generous even to a fault. I have known him to take back traitors into his bosom after they have professed repentance.

The best friend he ever had was J. T. Pemberton, president of the Farmers and Mechanics National Bank of Fort Worth. He was the only rich man that stood with him through thick and thin.

One day a group of Baptist preachers, led by Dr. L. R. Scarborough, President of Southwestern Theological Seminary, called on Mr. Pemberton and said,

"Mr. Pemberton, we simply cannot put up with Norris. Look what he says about us! He keeps things stirred up all the time."

J. T. Pemberton was a very quiet man. He and Scarborough were close friends and he said,

"Brethren, I quite sympathize with you. He says and does a lot of things I wish he wouldn't. But I came to this conclusion a long time ago. Any man the Lord can get along with as well as He does with J. Frank Norris, I have made up my mind to get along with."

# CHAPTER IX

### MOST DARING AND VENTURESOME

I am a very conservative and very quiet, mildmannered type of man. And when I was converted and quit the turpentine business, all my fighting was laid aside.

One day while we were sitting in his office a man came running in all excited and said to him and me,

"Dr. Norris, a group of men are over here at Fifth and Main Streets waiting to kill you on sight! They said they were going to and they are armed – or said they were."

Norris put on his hat and said, "Come on Entz."

Well, I didn't ask him where he was going. I was afraid not to go and I was afraid to stay. I didn't know what to do for I didn't know where he was going. At first I thought, "Well, he is going home to escape trouble."

But he walked right straight over just a couple of blocks and sure plough these men who were going to kill him were standing there. A news stand was there and Norris walked up to the news stand and bought some magazines and turned his back to this crowd that made their threats.

I was literally scared to death. He had been informed who they were and I recognized some of them. I didn't have anything to shoot with and I knew he didn't have anything – all that bunk that has been published about his "toting a gun" – and it is sometimes published that he has two guns – but being closely associated with him for years, I am in a position to say there is not a word of truth in it.

He stood there for several minutes, as I said, with his back turned. And after he bought several magazines he turned around and the whole gang had disappeared.

We walked back to the church, and my knees were as weak as water. I said:

"Now look here, next time anything happens like hat you are going to have to leave me out."

He just replied, "Well, Entz, I know this gang, and that is the only way I can handle them. If they ever got the idea that I was afraid of them they would kill me or run me out of town."

I will say here and now, after all these 34 years of trial and storm, being very closely associated with him, I have never seen him one single, solitary time lose his head.

# CHAPTER X

## HOW A RIOT WAS TURNED INTO A REVIVAL

It was in the exciting days of the sit down strikes.

At Flint, Michigan, Dr. Norris was scheduled to speak in the huge municipal Auditorium and the 10,000 capacity auditorium was packed to standing room and people standing on the outside.

The Chief of Police called him up at Detroit fifty miles away and said:

"I cannot guarantee protection. I hope you will call off the meeting. It will produde a riot."

Governor Frank Murphy, then governor of Michigan, also pled with Dr. Norris not to go to Flint.

Dr. Norris told the Chief of Police and the governor:

**"It is your business to keep order, and I am going."**

No sooner than he started to speak, there were two groups of hecklers tiled to break up the meeting. Dr. Norris stopped and said:

"I want every red-blooded American over twenty-one and under fifty who believes in God, home and native land and free speech, to stand to your feet."

They stood, and then he said:

"Remain standing. "

Then he turned and said:

"You low down, white livered, cowardly communists, now try to break up this meeting."

There was profound silence. There was a "half hour of silence in heaven," no more disturbance.

At the close of the meeting the ring leader of the hecklers came rushing up to the platform. A group of Dr. Norris' ushers tried to stop him, but Dr. Norris said:

"Let him come on up here."

And he took him to one side behind the curtain and this man said:

"I want to apologize for leading this disturbance and I want you to pray for me. I am a wrecked man. Liquor has got the best of me. I had a happy home, a wife and children and they are gone."

Dr. Norris knelt with him and he was gloriously saved. They drove fifty miles to Detroit and he baptized him into the church. This man's family came back and Dr. Norris got him a good job at Ford Motor Company and he is one of the best members of Temple Baptist Church.

That is the power of the gospel of Jesus Christ!

One of Dr. Norris' tabernacle campaigns in Fort Worth.

Welcomed home by Mayor T.J. Harrell, who greeted Dr. Norris at the airport as they got off the plane returning from their tour around the world.

# CHAPTER XI

WHY TEMPLE BAPTIST CHURCH WITHDRAWS FROM NORTHERN BAPTIST CONVENTION

(Quoting from book, "Inside the Cup")

**Northern Baptist Machine Officially Endorses Two Principal Russian, Communistic Organizations in America**

**"WE WILL NOT SERVE THY GODS"**

**SERMON BY DR. J. FRANK NORRIS, SUNDAY AFTERNOON, JUNE 30, 1935, DETROIT, MICHIGAN**

(Stenographically Reported)

**Lenin Has Won**

DR. NORRIS: There is today a worldwide propaganda, very insidious, and it is high time this country was aroused to it. The greatest brain this generation has ever witnessed was Lenin of Russia. He had the greatest scheme of propaganda, and here are some of his methods.

I have read most of his writings. First, he said to his constituents, "When you go to other countries deny you are a Communist; never admit you are a Communist." First, win them – "Then," he said, "we will attack the schools, then the pulpit." And that from the brain of a man who set in motion the propaganda and schemes that destroyed the pulpits and churches in Russia!

The first method is to honey-comb the chuches, then destroy them. Now that is the method we have in this country, the same thing. You take perhaps the most outstanding Bishop known among the Methodists – I know there are people who say they don't think we ought to deal in personalities – my answer to that is then don't let them deal in things that destroy our young men and women and their personal faith – (applause) – my answer to it is that I am opposed to Bishop Francis J. McConnell being active in the American Civil Liberties Union – in this country there are forty some odd organizations of Russian Communism. The principal one is the "American Civil Liberties Union" – get the Red Net Work and read it – everybody ought to read it. You find in there a long list of prominent citizens listed as members of this "American Civil Liberties Union" – also you will find the wife of the President of the United States. You will find the President of the Chicago University there, too, and a long list of prominent educators. It is a fulfillment of the Scriptures that while the men slept the enemies sowed tares.

During the five years of the greatest, depression – and everybody wants to relieve the depression – here is what has happened over night. The various denominational organizations have ceased to preach the Gospel of blood redemption – they have even gone so far that they say, the preachers from the pulpits, that mass evangelism is a thing of the past, and that we can't have great revivals where people are born again individually – no, now they say what we need to do is clean out the stables, clean up society – like some Baptist preachers Who met up here at Lansing, and it came out in the papers that they agreed that it Was their business to bring about a "social reconstruction."

## When Northern Baptist Convention Went Over To Communism

In 1934, at Rochester, New York, there was a meeting of the Northern Baptist Convention and they appointed and endorsed a Committee of nine, and that Committee was to be known as the "Social Action Commission." All I say is being taken down and will be published so as to get it to you.

Now here is the exact language – I quote it to you:

"That the Northern Baptist Convention desires that the churches shall have an approach" – and the words they use are "economics," "political," and 'international affairs" – and by that vote last year the Northern Baptists went into the realm of "politics," "economics" and "international questions."

Let me put before you this question: Suppose that the next day after Pentecost, where they had three thousand baptized, then the church numbered 3120 – suppose the next day after that great baptizing, Simon Peter had gotten up in church and said, "Brethren, I move that we go on record – appointing a committee to see about this church going into the realm of economics, into political and international affairs of the Roman empire."

Suppose you could read that in the New Testament!

Of course you say the very statement of it is absurd. Yet, my friends, that is exactly what the Northern Baptist machine has done. They brought that report to the Convention last week in Colorado Springs, and instead of their ending the matter, putting it on ice, they did this other more subtle thing – oh, the serpent is more subtle than any other creature – they got together and said, "Here, we will put this on the churches."

So now they have placed at the door of every church of the Northern Baptist Convention, from Maine to California, this social, economic, political and international plan of preaching the gospel of "Social Justice."

"Oh," you say "the churches won't go into it." But wait a minute – this morning three Baptist pastors of Detroit spoke on it, and they are in favor of it. I have the notes taken of what these brethren said. We had just as well make up our minds to it, a lot of the churches are going to adopt the report.

That crowd met out here the other day and they discussed what they were going to do with me. I may have to decide what I am going to do with them. (Laughter). My paper has wide circulation and I am going to publish anything about anybody, even the devil himself, when I think it ought to be done.

Here is what the Pastor of Jefferson Avenue Baptist Church said this morning. I have stenographic notes:

It was a great report on Social Action; and it was received unanimously. I didn't hear a negative vote, neither did the President of the Convention.

It was a great report – a great report of 15,000 words. The papers said that there would be terrific opposition, oh, of course there were some small eddies – it was the most forward looking expression of a mighty denomination."

Then he said further:

"This report is going far, how far we do not realize... it is the only course for sanity and safety" – and he repeated that several times.

Now, he said it was received unanimously, and he said there might be some words in it that one might desire to change here and there but that the liberalists and fundamentalists with one united voice spoke to high heaven.

Incidentally, Dr. W. B. Riley will be here July 16th, and he will bring us a first hand report. I wired him yesterday to come on. And this is just a little introduction this afternoon to what we are going to have.

The shrewdest scheme of the devil is not to deny outright – what do you think they are saying now? – that Jesus was a Communist a great social worker. My friends, the method of Jesus was to reach the individual soul as He reached Nicodemus, and changed that individual's heart – and then the redeemed individuals change human society.

You can see at once, if the devil could put over the scheme of getting the churches to be silent on blood redemption, individual salvation, of course he would have won the church to his side. Now, you Baptists have to face that situation.

I am glad to tell you the Board of Deacons of the Temple Baptist Church unanimously adopted some resolutions, and I am going to give everybody a chance this afternoon to express themselves on them, then, so nobody can raise any question, in two weeks every member will register his or her vote by private ballot, so when it is over we will have a legal record.

I think this is the largest church thus far that has made a protest – I don't say the church is unanimous – I am not interested in that. They are unanimous in the graveyard – all heads point in the same direction. (Laughter).

Now let me get the question clearly before you. The two centers today of Communism are:

First: The universities.

Second: The denominational headquarters.

I know that is shocking, but that is true. Remember what has been their platform. It has been to deny they were Communists, but to spread their doctrine in a subtle manner. To deny the name doesn't change them any – you can change the name of the rose and it won't change the sweet aroma. You can bring a skunk under this tent, and he will change this audience just as quickly with any other name. (Laughter).

To show that is their method, to show you I am not speaking idly, I want to call your attention to two things in this morning's paper – here – three columns wide, big headlines, "RADICAL PROPAGANDA AIMS AT MINISTERIAL 'ROUND-UP'."

Now you folks who live here in this city don't know what a "round-up" is. I have rounded-up, and I have been rounded-up – I went out one afternoon to round up some cattle – and I made the mistake of walking out among them, the first thing I knew they were rounding me up, and the only way of escape I could see was a Chinaberry tree a quarter of a mile away. You talk about a boy running – I ran, and I ran – those steers kept me up in that tree all day, and left a standing committee to stay there that night – I know what a round-up is. (Laughter).

But the article:

"Strenuous efforts are being made by radical propagandists to swing the clergy in behind programs ostensibly 'liberal,' but which are linked in a plan to set up some sort of Socialist republic and destroy democracy as we have known it.

"The most pretentious attempt at 'rounding up' the ministry has been made by the magazine, 'The World Tomorrow,' through the circulation of a long list of questions among ministers and divinity students. This has resulted in a declaration by Kirby Page, editorial writer, that" – This paper, "The World Tomorrow," is the official organ of the Civil Liberties Union of America – and incidentally, Kirby Page, the editor, wrote the life of Jesus Christ, and he delivered the Commencement Address to Baylor University's graduates, three years ago – I took them to a cleaning for it. Now Kirby Page says:

"Among all the trades, occupations and professions in this country few can produce as high a percentage of Socialists as the ministry."

That is what was published this morning in one of your papers, and here is the result of the questionnaire sent out:

" 'The World Tomorrow' questionnaire went to 100,000 persons. Replies came from about one-fifth, 20,870 and Editor Page writes:

"'Of the total number responding, 62 per cent recorded themselves as pacifists" – friends, there is nothing in all this "pacifism" – it is all Russian Communism. We don't want any Russian pacifism while they are arming to the teeth – We need to arm to protect our country, our homes.

"Even more encouraging" – says this official organ of Russian Sovietism in America:

"Even more encouraging are the tendencies reflected in the answers of the students in theological seminaries, 73 PER CENT OF WHOM ARE PACIFISTS, AND 48 ADVOCATES OF SOCIALISM." Now the brood of cuckoos are hatching, they are coming out in this country and are preaching in the pulpits of this land! That is what you Baptists are supporting every time you put a dime in this machine, and every time you give, you encourage this Communistic, Socialistic, unbaptistic machine. Yes, sir. Will you continue?

Crowd: "No."

Furthermore I want to show you something else – this was published in the 27th issue of one of your papers. Listen to this:

### "Red Week"

" 'Red Week' on the campus of the University of Chicago, which has just been freed by a legislative investigating committee of

Communist propaganda, shows the length to which the subversive elements will go when there is no active, aggressive opposition.

"The students were addressed, among others, by" – I wouldn't attempt to pronounce these names – I'll just spell them to you – "Trovarish Trovanovsky, Russian ambassador, and Trovarish Boyeff, of the Amtorg Trading Corporation.

"The boys and girls are being told the advantage of swapping vodka for our capitalistic-cursed machinery.

"Is the University of Chicago an American educational institution or a branch of the Moscow department of foreign trade?"

Here is something else, I want you to get it – yesterday afternoon there came out in the Evening News an interview with Dr. H. C. Gleiss in which he says that the report on this "Social Action Commission" was "epochal" – that is what Dr. Gleiss says. Dr. Gleiss is head of the Baptist machine here in Detroit – what there is left of it. (Laughter), Now, furthermore he said, that this report was not Communistic, yet he goes on and says:

"The topics touched upon in the report include peace, international relations, economic and industrial affairs, rural life and rural churches, marriage and the home, temperance and the problems of alcoholic beverages, propaganda and education and race relations."

All these questions are the very platform today of this social gospel. Not a word is said about blood redemption in the report.

Now Dr. Gleiss said there was no Communism in his report – let me show you some things – and you Methodists and you Presbyterians and Congregationalists – it is not only Baptists, but that is what all your machines have gone over to.

Now here is part of the report that was authorized by the Northern Convention's endorsement:

"1. That the N.B.C. institute a board for social action, which shall have adequate funds at its disposal to accomplish the work that may be assigned to it.

"2. That the N.B.C. adopt and work for the relization of a program of social change which shall embody in general such features as the following:

"(a) Society (the people acting through the state) shall assume control (which may involve actual ownership) of all the God given natural resources of the earth; including the land surface, mineral and oil wealth and the products of lake, sea, and river, including the water power.

"(b) Society shall control or own all natural monoplies that have to do with the necessities of modern living, such as the water supply, gas, electricity, telephone, telegraph and radio.

"(c) Society shall control or own such competitive businesses as have to do with the necessities of life (milk, bread, coal, oil, gasoline, etc.) in order to eliminate the waste in production, competition and mismanagement, and to guard against the very life of the people being made the sort of financial hocus-pocus. For the immediate future the competitive profit system should be restricted to the non-essentials of life.

"(d) Society shall take over the entire control of the money and banking function and conduct it as a non-profit producing social service.

"(e) Society shall tax incomes by a scale that will help to prevent the accumulation of great money-power in the hands of individuals or groups of individuals. * * * * * * * *

"3. That the N.B.C. through agencies already in existence or to be created for the purpose, shall adopt a definite plan (five-year, ten-year) for the education of its clergy and other teachers, in the social, business, political and industrial implications of the Gospel."

Not one word said about blood redemption – it is a social, business, political and industrial program.

## What Was the Purpose of the Northern Convention?

Ladies and gentlemen, I quote to you what was the purpose of the organization of the Northern Baptist Convention. This Convention was organized in 1907 – that would be – 7 from 35 would be 28 years ago – now there are those who say we cease to be Baptists if we withdraw from the Convention – we are going to answer this question if this church votes to adopt this resolution, and I think I know what this great people will do – the deacons have already unanimously adopted it – and I am going to give you the opportunity to express yourself – to the question that we cease to be Baptists – in the first place, Baptists were here 1900 years before you ever heard of the Northern Baptist Convention. The second answer is that the charter of the Northern Baptist Convention states specifically that the purpose of the Northern Baptist Convention is for the evangelization of the world, and not to go into politics, not to regulate society and the economic life; no, but to preach the Gospel. They put it in there 28 years ago. The Northern Baptist Convention was not organized for the purpose of taking over Henry Ford's plant, the Chrysler, or taking over the telephone companies or oil companies – I am not going to argue whether they ought to be taken over – the point I am making, that it is not the business of the churches to enter into business, to regulate society or enter into the field of economics. It is the scheme of the devil to sidetrack the Church of Jesus Christ from its one and only commission, yet the head of the Baptist machine of Detroit says this report is "epochal."

I think they are going to find themselves split from Maine to California.

Here is the answer – the third answer, instead of this church ceasing to be Baptist – the answer is it has remained Baptist – and the fourth answer is that the Convention crowd, this Socialistic, unbaptistic, modernistic, compromising crowd have gone off from Baptist doctrines. It is a fulfillment of the Scripture which says, "They went out from us because they were not of us."

### "The Evangelization of the World"

This is the chartered purpose of the Northern Baptist Convention. It is found in Section 2, of the articles of Incorporation.

"The Evangelization of the World"; Beautiful and Scriptural. If the proponents and organizers of the Northern Baptist Convention had put it in the articles of Incorporation that it is the purpose and aim of the Northern Convention "to approach or regulate the social, political, economic and international" questions of this age and generation – the Convention would have died still-born.

Therefore, the church which refuses to endorse this socialistic scheme of the Northern Baptist Convention and remain true to the one and only mission of the church; namely, "The Evangelization of the World" – it is the Convention and not the true churches which has ceased to be Baptist. The Convention machine has departed from the true faith and gone off after false gods. It is the Convention, and not the churches, that is offering "strange fire." The Convention comes with the hands of "Baptist orthodoxy", but with the voice of Russian Sovietism.

"Well, now" somebody says, "look here, I am a deacon in a church and the pastor is a modernist, what can I do?" – Well, if you haven't sense enough to know what to do I couldn't advise you. (Laughter). Suppose I give you some Scripture on that – here is what it says, II Cor. 6:14-18, "Be ye not unequally yoked together with unbelievers: for what fellowship hath righteousness with unrighteousness? and what communion hath light with darkness? And what concord hath Christ with Belial? or what part hath he that believeth with an infidel? And what agreement hath the temple of God with idols? for ye are the temple of the living God; as God hath said, I will dwell in them, and walk in them; and I will be their God, and they shall be my people. Wherefore" what does it say? Listen – "come out from among them, and be ye separate, saith the Lord, and touch not the unclean thing; and I will receive you."

I make bold to tell you here these preachers who masquerade under the livery of heaven – I don't care how many degrees they have after their names – LLDs, DDs, Asses, they are infidels when they deny the Word of God. Yes, sir – I have more respect for Tom Paine in his grave, and Bob Ingersoll – at least they had self respect enough to stay out of the church and out of the pulpits – they were not like these little modernistic, lick- the-skillet, two-by-four aping, asinine preachers who want to be in the priest's office so they can have a piece of bread, and play kite tail to the Communists.

I am not going to say anything about them this afternoon, but I plan to do so sometime soon. (Laughter).

"Oh!" some sister will say, "I don't think that's the Christian spirit" – Honey, you wouldn't know the Christian spirit, any more than a bull would know Shakespeare. (Laughter).

I'll tell you the spirit we need in this compromising milk-and-cider, neither-hot-nor-cold – you want to know the kind of spirit we need? We need the spirit of old John the Baptist when he told that Sanhedrin, "You are a generation of snakes."

We need again the spirit of the Apostle Peter when he stood before the Sanhedrin and said, "Is it right to obey men rather than God?

Talk about you Methodists, we need again the spirit of old John Wesley when he preached out of his father's church and stood on his father's slab and preached a sermon that shook the world (Applause).

We Baptists need the spirit of Roger Williams when he walked out in the snows with the Naragansett Indians rather than to stultify his conscience.

We need again the spirit of those Baptist preachers in 1767 yonder on the Court House yard in old Culpepper, Virginia, when stripped to the waist with hands tied and held up, the strap was put on their bare backs and drops of blood fell – Patrick Henry rode up and said, "What crime have these men committed?" – When they answered, "They were preaching the Gospel of the Son of God without a license." He answered one word three times: "My God, My God, My God."

Hear me, friends, you Baptists especially, the scheme today is what? To Sovietize the churches of America, to honeycomb the public schools, then the red propaganda can go on unmolested. They know if they can break down the voice of the pulpit – the greatest moral force time ever witnessed, they will have this whole country – yet you Baptists will go and put your money, your time, your presence into that sort of thing. You say, "What can I do?" "Come out from among them, and be ye separate, saith the Lord."

Friends, there is going to be a separation – all present existing denominational machines are gone – you Methodists, your machine is gone, too, and it ought to be gone – the truth of Jesus Christ will survive, but we are going to have a terrible conflict in this country and we had just as well face it – that bunch of atheistic, Communists have charge of this government, and it is high time we found it out. (Applause).

Now if that be treason, make the most of it!

If the laboring classes think they will solve their problems by going Communistic – Come with me down into the mines of Russia and see the condition there – if the farmers think it will solve their problems come with me and I will show you five million Kuluks, the owners, the highest class of farmers, driven from their homes to yonder cold Siberia never to return. If you think it will solve your problems, go yonder and see the greatest country in the world for resources – it is the devil's scheme to destroy this present civilization – But I believe old America will stand (Applause.) We will meet them at Philippi! – They snatch the new born babies from their mother's arms – They don't believe in marriage – a man may be mated a dozen times—there is no regard for sex relation. This is not hearsay. I know what I am talking about. I have seen it first hand.

What shall we do? "Wherefore come out from among them, be ye separate, saith the Lord, and touch not the unclean thing; and I will receive you."

Old Amos says, "Can two walk together, except they be agreed?"

Here is the situation we are facing – I am talking about our own upheaval – we are going to let you backslidden Methodists alone while we attend to ourselves – follow me – your machinery, your leadership, your Board, your officialdom, your Detroit Baptist Union, the head of it – they come out and say, "This is our platform" – not mine. I am not going into any social, economic, political scheme instead of blood redemption. (Applause). That is what we are facing. Now whenever we render encouragement to that bunch of modernists, when we bid them God speed, just remember what Jehu said to Jehoshaphat when he returned from battle where he had made an unholy alliance with Ahab, "And Jehoshaphat, the king of Judah returned to his home in peace to Jerusalem, And Jehu the son of Hanani the seer went out to meet him, and said to king Jehoshaphat." – Listen to this – "Shouldest thou help the ungodly, and love them that hate the Lord? therefore is wrath upon thee from before the Lord."

Listen again to the Word of God on what we should do – Rev. 18:5, "And I heard another voice from heaven, saying, Come out of her, my people, that ye be not partakers of her sins, and that ye receive not of her plagues: For her sins have reached unto heaven, and God hath remembered her iniquities."

Now you will be glad to hear this resolution recommended by unanimous vote of the Deacons – and this is what I am going to ask everybody here this afternoon to express themselves on:

WHEREAS, the Temple Baptist Church of Detroit, Michigan, has supported and co-operated with the Northern Baptist Convention and the Baptist Convention of Michigan, by sending money to their Boards and delegates to their annual meetings;

WHEREAS, June 24th, 1935, the Northern Baptist Convention at Colorado Springs forced on the churches of the Northern Baptist Convention for their consideration, adoption or rejection, the Communistic plan of Karl Marx, by the following action of the convention:

"1 – Received the report and authorized the General Council to make it available to individual churches for study.

"2 – Continued the Social Action Commission for a year with the understanding that its educational program and peace plebescite among churches be conducted only for those churches desiring them.

"3 – Stated that neither the whole 15,000 word report nor a part of it 'shall be made a test of Baptist fellowship or service'."

Let me stop here – I want to say that I can turn to fifty places in the writing of Karl Marx and find that identical expression, "Social Action Commission" – Yes, sir, and that instead of being put on the table has been forced upon the churches – that is what they propose to put over – that isn't all:

WHEREAS, the Northern Baptist Convention officially appointed the "Social Action Commission" for the avowed purpose of binding the Convention to a political and economic program which is a violation of the most fundamental doctrine held by Baptists, namely, the separation of church and state; and further the Convention by its action in receiving, authorizing and continuing the "Social Action Commission," and forcing its communistic plan upon the churches, has thereby thrust a devisive issue among the churches;

WHEREAS, the report of the "Social Action Commission" sums up, sets forth, and advocates essentially the revolutionary, communistic plan of Soviet Russia, which is better known by its American Brand of "New Dealism";

WHEREAS, the one and only business of the church and the ministry is not to enter into or regulate the economic or political affairs of the Government, but to follow the admonition of our Lord, "Render to Caesar the things that are Caesar's," and to God the things that are God's," thereby maintaining the age-long and cherished Baptist faith of separation of church and state; that the one and only mission of the church of Jesus Christ is to preach the gospel of salvation to the individual, thereby carrying out the Great Commission, "Go preach the gospel to every creature";

WHEREAS, the leadership of the Northern Baptist Convention and the State Convention of Michigan, has departed from the age-long and Scriptural position held by Baptists, by substituting a so-called social or communistic gospel instead of the gospel of salvation for the individual soul;

WHEREAS, ten years ago the Northern Convention at Seattle, Washington, adopted what is known as the "inclusive policy," sending out both modernist and fundamentalist missionaries, and at which Convention the action adopting the inclusive policy repudiated a resolution offered by the late Dr. W. B. Hinson, "requesting all the missionaries of the Northern Baptist Convention to signify their belief and acceptance of the fundamental doctrines of the Virgin Birth, the Deity of Christ, the Atonement on the Cross, the Resurrection of Christ, and the New Birth of the individual soul";

My friends, you can get the Minutes and you will find where they turned down Dr. Hinson's resolution: namely, "Requesting all the missionaries of the Northern Baptist Convention to signify their belief and acceptance of the fundamental doctrines of the Virgin Birth, the New Birth of the individual soul." – My friends, I saw that crowd of Northern Baptist modernists vote that resolution down two to one. Here is what it means: It means that the missionaries don't have any longer to believe in the Atonement on the Cross, in the New Birth, in the Deity of Christ, in the Virgin Birth, or the Resurrection of Christ – no, they are going out under a social gospel that has dictation over the churches.

Reading on, the resolution:

WHEREAS, there has rapidly developed in the Northern Baptist Convention an unscriptural and unbaptistic, ecclesiastical, centralized dictatorship over the churches, as evidenced by many definite, concrete actions through the years, the latest of which is the action of the Northern Baptist Convention at Colorado Springs when the Convention "authorized" in the report of the "General Council" to the churches what was designated by the "15,000 word report" of the "Social Action Commission";

WHEREAS, the so-called plan of designation of mission funds is a misnomer and dishonest, because when the church designates a certain amount to a mission station the Foreign Mission Board simply decreases the appropriation to that station, thereby forcing orthodox Baptists to support, in an indirect though very definite way, the unscriptural, modernistic, socialistic leadership of the Northern Baptist Convention;

WHEREAS, the Northern and Michigan Baptist Conventions belong to, and are a part of the World Baptist Alliance, which is controlled and dominated, in the main, by modernistic leadership; and

WHEREAS, the Temple Baptist Church has been on record for several years in its stand for the historic faith once for all delivered to the saints;

THEREFORE BE IT RESOLVED, by the Board of Deacons of Temple Baptist Church, and the members of the entire church, in special called session at 3:00 p. m. Sunday afternoon, June 30, 1935, that we exercise, as a church, our inalienable, sovereign right as a body of believers, in recognizing Christ only as head over all things to the church, and reaffirming our faith in the fundamentals of the Christian faith as commonly held by Baptists; and further we reaffirm and declare it our purpose to have no part or lot with the unscriptural, unbaptistic, socialistic, modernistic Convention;

RESOLVED SECOND, in separating from these bodies, from these ecclesiastical organizations which have departed from the faith held by Baptists, we call upon all true orthodox Baptists throughout the Northern Baptist Convention, to join with us in contending for the faith once for all delivered, and giving the gospel of salvation to the individual soul;

RESOLVED THIRD, that we reaffirm our faith in those foundation principles – freedom of speech, freedom of press, and freedom of worship;

RESOLVED FOURTH, that Temple Baptist Church urge every individual member to make regular contribution to worldwide missions; and that we support the Association of Baptists for Evangelism in the Orient, which Association of Baptists has adopted the identical Confession of Faith held by the Temple Baptist Church;

RESOLVED FIFTH, that copies of these resolutions be given to the denominational and secular press that the world may know of the uncompromising position and stand of the Temple Baptist Church against all the present day vagaries of modernism, socialism, communism, ecclesiasticism, and our positive stand for the faith in the whole Bible as our only rule of faith and practice.

# The Dishonesty, the Duplicity, and Insincerity of These Denominational Politicians

I know that this is strong language but we are performing a major, triple operation in order to save the patient.

You have noticed how these denominational politicians are saying that the report of the Social Action Commission is not communistic.

Here they are following the advice of their patron, Lenin. I can take the writings of Karl Marx and Lenin and put them beside the identical writings of the Social Action Commission.

Now, I am going to make a charge that the Social Action Commission and Russian Communism, especially two principal American branches are identical. Let me quote from the report:

"We are convinced that the economic system as it has been operated has also created serious obstacles to Christian living. There are multitudes of Christians in high and low positions in our economic and industrial life who desire to express their Christianity in these relations but who find it impossible within the system. The church has a responsibility to them. It is futile to bring up generations of youth in Christian ideals which they are compelled to discard when they go out to make a living. Christians owe it to themselves and to their fellows to work for an economic order in which Christian motives have freer chance for expression and in which Christian ideals have larger hope of realization.

"The possibility of change for the better must be accepted as a fact by the Christian. The economic system has been man-made and it can be changed by men. Changes must begin with the individual and an improved operation of any system rests with the individuals. 'No gain can be achieved by society that is hot supported by human wills.'

"In view of these conditions, what may be done by our denomination to effect the changes which are necessary to provide more opportunity and encouragement for men and women to live as Christians in their economic and industrial relations and to secure fundamental justice for all?

"It is clear that the denomination corporately cannot prosecute particular measures for social change. It should, however, have a constant program of education on these matters for its constituency which will enable them to act in accordance with Christian standards in these relations.

"We therefore recommend that such a program be conducted by the denomination through the local churches with the following definite objectives:

"I – To create social attitudes based on these fundamental considerations: * * *

"II – A second definite objective of such a program of education should be to keep before our constituency certain basic issues, among them being:

"(1) – Economic security for all. This would involve general education on the need of unemployment, sickness and accident insurance and old age pensions; assembling and distributing the facts relative to specific measures for economic security; making available lists of information sources and agencies; and co-operation with other denominations and agencies for the furtherance of economic security.

"(2) – Collective bargaining in industry. This would involve a program of education for a better understanding of the relative positions and problems of employers and employees in bargaining over wages, hours and conditions of work; and further the provision for a social action committee in every church, or in co-operation with other churches, to ascertain and publish the facts in the event of conflict and to encourage the exercise of moral judgment; and finally the support of whichever party in a dispute is in the right by purchasing the products of the industry or by contributions to the needs of the workers of funds, moral encouragement and places of meeting where needed.

"(3) – More adequate representation of consumer interest in the determination of economic policies. This would involve the study of how the government may safeguard the consumer and promote his welfare and how consumers themselves may be informed so as to buy for their real needs and best interests instead of being at the mercy of the producer's and seller's advertising.

"(4) – Keep open the channels of discussion of controversial economic and industrial issues. This would involve the dissemination of information about anti-sedition legislation designed to prevent the discussion and advocacy of legitimate economic changes and the organization of sentiment and effort for the defeat or repeal of any such laws as infringe upon the constitutional liberties. It would also involve giving moral and financial support to those who have been the victims of discrimination.

"III – A third definite objective of such an educational program for the denomination should be to inculcate in individuals worthy economic motives and incentives that through them the basis of the economic system may be shifted from that of acquisitiveness to that of service. * * *

"IV – A fourth definite objective should be to impress upon our individual members the importance of effecting changes in the economic order by the exercise of their three-fold citizenship, political, civic and economic.

"(1) – By political citizenship support should be given to whatever political party or candidate represents, on the whole, the most favorable disposition and opportunity to effect the desired changes. Since, however, the major political parties have not come to be in any considerable measure parties of clearly avowed and continuously held social principles, political effectiveness through them in the direction of the desired economic changes must involve support of smaller interest and pressure groups whose intelligent and persistent advocacy may lead to the espousing of social principles and programs from time to time by these major parties. Such pressure groups are numerous and range in point of view in our country from the American Liberty League to the League for industrial Democracy."

### "There Is Death in the Pot!"

Now we have the whole thing out. Two of the principal Russian Communistic organizations in this country are "The American Liberty League" and "The League for Industrial Democracy."

Just think of it, you Baptists, the free-est of the free people, the most patriotic! The Baptist machine authorized a committee of nine to bring in and report endorsing the two principal branches of Russian Communism!

What will you Baptists do?

What answer will you give?

So help me God, I will never bow the knee to Russian communism in capsule form! (Applause).

Shall we sit supinely by while Lenin's Communism plays the Trojan horse act on our Baptist churches?

### Northern Modernists Control Southern Leaders

Yes, Dr. A. W. Beaven runs and controls Dr. George Truett, who is sound in the faith personally, but he runs with modernists, especially when he comes North. He was eulogized to the skies by one of the modernist pastors of the city this morning. He is President of the modernistic World Baptist Alliance, which is no more and no less than a small self-appointed group of modernists, pussyfooting so-called fundamentalists down South to do their bidding – there is where the trouble comes.

Now friends we have crossed the Rubicon. We have come to a great hour in this country – everybody realizes it – in the realm of politics and business as well as in the realm of religion. We are facing Kadesh-Barnea, and I make bold to declare to you who believe in a supernatural Christ, who believe He had a supernatural birth, who believe He lived a supernatural life, who believe He spoke supernatural words, performed supernatural miracles, died a supernatural death, had a supernatural ascension and is coming back in supernatural glory to establish a supernatural kingdom – people who believe these things are going to get together in this country of ours! (Applause).

We are in another Reformation period like they had in the 16th century – let me say something – every century has witnessed a great awakening – the 16th century witnessed the Reformation led by Martin Luther, and other reformers; the 17th Century witnessed a great awakening led by the Puritans; the 18th Century witnessed a great awakening led by Whitfield, Wesley and others; the 19th Century witnessed what was known as the Oxford movement and the modem missionary movement; and the 20th Century is more than a third gone – Watchman what of the night ?

### "We Will Not Serve Thy Gods"

Here is what is coming, what is happening, God's people, the "Seven Thousand" who have not bowed the knee to Baal are awakening and coming to light! We are coming to a time as witnessed in the third chapter of Daniel, when there went forth the decree from Nebuchadnezzar that all the people in every province when they heard the sound of the comet, the flute, the harp, the sackbut, the psaltery, the dulcimer, and all kinds of musical instruments, that they should bow down and worship that image of gold 60 cubits high and six cubits wide, out in the plains of Dura; and every man that did not bow down and worship would be cast in the fiery furnace, and when the sound went forth, every prince, every sheriff, every secretary, every denominational leader bowed down and worshipped that statue of gold – except three that stood erect with heads up, and when the report was carried to this old king that these three Jews would not bow, he was filled with rage, and he called them before him while he sat on his throne, and said to them, "Is it true that you will not bow down as I commanded?" They said, "We are not careful to answer thee in this matter" – "We won't even bother to answer you. We will not put on your socialistic modernistic program." And they said, "If you do put us into the fiery furnace, our God whom we serve is able to deliver us from the burning fiery furnace, and he will deliver us out of thine hand" – "But if not, be it known unto thee, O king, that" – and here is my text – "We will not serve thy gods, nor worship the golden image which thou hast set up!" "We will not submit to your ecclesiastical tyranny." (Applause).

So today – America has had its Valley Forge – America has had its Gettysburg – America has had its Culpepper Court House – America has had its Concord – America has had its Alomo – and today our forefathers though they sleep in the ground, yet their spirits go marching on, and we will not bow down to the red flag, regardless of what name it comes to us under. (Prolonged applause). We still hold our allegiance to the greatest flag that was ever unfurled to the breezes. We will still hold the Bible of our fathers and mothers. We still believe Jesus Christ was born of Mary a virgin, that He lived a sinless life, died for our sins, was buried in Joseph's new made tomb, on the first day of the week He rose, bursting asunder the bars of death, and rose in triumph and victory and glory, and that He ascended back to the right hand of the Father, leading captivity captive, and giving gifts to men, and that one day He will come down the pathless skies, surrounded by a great company of angels to put down all rule, and to establish His reign on the earth! – I still believe it, friends. (Prolonged applause).

Oh, God give us a little backbone – I am praying that the preachers will wake up – here is what is going to happen among Northern Baptists, and it is true in the South.

"Oh," somebody says, "there goes Norris stirring up controversy" – Yes, and I am going to stir up some more, too. Sure. Yes, my friends, old Isaiah had some controversy. Old Jeremiah had some when he walked the streets with the ox yoke around his neck – he had some more when they put his feet in the stocks and put him up for a laughing spectacle, but it only served as a pulpit for Jeremiah, and he kept on preaching – and they put him in a pit and he spoke out of the darkness of the pit – and when Jeremiah was destroyed, Nebuchadnezzar said, "Jeremiah get in the royel chariot and go home with me." But no, Jeremiah said, "I'll stay here and preach and preach to those poor folks."

John the Baptist stirred up opposition – he had lots of it until a little old flapper dancing girl danced his head off, but he woke in heaven. Simon Peter stirred up a lot of opposition, and was crucified head downward, and today walks the streets of the New Jerusalem! Paul had controversy for thirty years, until his head fell from the block yonder in that old Roman prison – he said, "Henceforth there is laid up for me a crown of righteousness, which the Lord, the righteous judge, shall give me at that day: and not to me only, but unto all them also that love his appearing."

Yes, sir. Let me tell you something friends, if a preacher is not stirring up the devil he is dead – already sold out. (Applause). Pray for me folks. I need it.

Think I will tell you a little secret right here, and I want it clearly understood – some of these dear preachers got together the other morning and said, "We are not going to have any business meetings this summer, and we won't grant any more letters this summer, and the Norris show will be over by that time." Here is what they said, "We know that Temple Baptist Church won't take any members unless they present a letter." – See their scheme? But we beat them to it – the church voted, that any Baptist could come into the church without a letter – so if you want to get in a church that stands wholly upon the Word of God, just come on we will take you upon experience. And all you Methodists who have been dry-cleaned, come on and I will put you under so deep you will know you have been buried – with the Lord and all you Presbyterians, you won't go to heaven until I bury you. (Laughter).

The announcement I am going to make is this – friends, hear me, God is moving today as never before – a certain gentleman, I am not allowed to give his name, asked me the other day – he said, "Norris, suppose you had a big lot on which to build a brick and concrete, fireproof tabernacle that would seat six or seven thousand on one floor, would you build it?" I said, "Give me the lot." He answered, "The lot is yours." (Applause).

We could put up a big tabernacle for about twenty or twenty-five thousand dollars – folks, let's build it, what do you say? (Applause). And when the frosts and snows of winter come, and the hail comes, and the rain comes, and everything comes, the Northern Baptist Communism, and the devil himself, we will preach, and pray, and shout, and sing, "The Old Time Religion," until Jesus comes! (Applause). Let's build it. Folks, it is going to be done right here. (Applause). Give, that to that Baptist Hindquarters with my regards. (Laughter). Tell them we are going, to run on – I haven't anything against them; no, I haven't any more against them than I have against the dead. (Laughter).

Now I think we will have a new vision, a new spirit. I used to hear – Say, many of you were raised on a farm, weren't you? I was too. Well, you know the difference between. "Gee" and "Haw" – this crowd doesn't know anything about it – I am going to do my best. Oh, don't I remember when the day's work on the farm was done, the mules and horses were in the stalls eating corn, hay, and fodder, mother in the kitchen washing dishes getting ready for an early breakfast – my work was to feed the horses and milk the cows, and when I would get through, I was sleepy and tired, and I would wash my feet and crawl in bed, and I could hear my mother finishing up in the kitchen, and I could hear dear old Dad going out in the front yard with his long stem clay pipe in one hand and his "Brown Mule" in the other. After awhile he would pack that old pipe full, strike a light and lean back against a tree, out under God's stars, and as a typical Southern gentleman, he would sing with a broken voice, but a voice with music out of a soul tuned in with God – I can hear him now as it came floating out on the cool, clear summer night:

"Am I a Soldier of the Cross."

I didn't understand it then. I wondered why, but in a little way I understand it now, and the son of that old farmer today is ready to join hands with every true soldier of the cross around the world, and say, "We will go forth for our God is a Man of war, the Lord of Battle, and we are not in a losing fight, we are in a winning fight." (Applause).

**Must Take Sides**

Every time I go to San Antonio, Texas, and in many ways it is the most fascinating city in America – every time I go there, and I go often, I have held many meetings there – I never let the time go by that I don't go to that historic shrine, the Alamo – sometimes when my spirit is drooping I love to go there and walk through that old mission – I can stand there and hear again the rattle of musketry and hear the cannon balls hurled against those thick walls, while 183 Texans, brave men from every state in the union, were surrounded by 7000 well trained men under Santa Anna – at last when old Travis saw that soon they would be entirely surrounded, and all hope of escape would be cut off, he called that crowd, then only 175 who could stand, called them together and said, "Men we can yet escape, but if we wait longer we will die. What will be your answer?" "Now," he said, "others can do what they please, but I am going to stay here – I am going to stay here and die for the liberty of Texas," and he walked to the end and unsheathed his shining sword and began here at a wall, 187 feet from one wall to the other, and old Travis drew a line from one wall clear across to the other – "Now," he said, "gentlemen, I want to know how many want to die for the freedom of Texas? If you do, step over this line with me" – And every man leaped across that line. Old Bowie was there on a cot bleeding from a dozen wounds received in battle—Bowie raised up, looked and said, "Take my sword, take my hat, take my coat across" – and when they had taken them over the line, he tried to get up, but fell back, and he said to the men, "Take me across." And they grabbed his cot and moved him across, and when the battle was over in the room where he was dead, Mexicans were piled ten feet high around him. Not a man was left in that crowd – only one woman got away. Well it has been said "Thermopylae had a messenger of defeat, the Alamo had none."

As I stood there where more than a hundred years ago old Travis made the call that set the Lone Star State free, and made it the Lone Star in this glorious Union – I could hear him calling, "Every man who wants to die for this liberty of Texas come on this side of the line." Friends, today I hear another voice calling – He died on Calvary – He arose from the grave; He is coming; He is calling – How many of you Baptists, you Methodists, you Presbyterians, will cross over the line? How many will cross over this afternoon? As for me, I have already crossed over; friends, I have enlisted for war!

A few hours ago when my son, a young lawyer, 29 years old, switched in so that great crowd at Fort Worth heard me, he said, "Dad, the auditorium is packed, and people standing – and when the broadcast was over he said, "The people are weeping and shouting, they are coming and rejoicing."

Oh, my friends, I see the time when the dead in Christ shall rise, and wars will be no more – and we shall be changed in a moment in the twinkling of an eye, and we shall go sweeping through the air like Elijah in a flaming chariot surrounded by holy angels – and friends, when I look on His face, then that will be glory enough for me! (Shoutings: Amen).

Folks, I have crossed over! How many will say, "Here is my hand, preacher, we will cross over today?"

I am going to ask first of all, you Baptists that believe that the only business of the church is to preach the Gospel. How many Baptists here this afternoon will say, "That is my conviction, my platform, my faith, and I will live and die on it," stand to your feet. (Hundreds leap to their feet). Now you Methodists who want to say it stand up – you Presbyterians, stand up – all the Disciples, who want to say it, stand up – now all other Protestants who wish to stand on it, get up – yes, I will give the Roman Catholics the opportunity to stand against this bunch, you can stand too – all who want to say, "I am against this socialistic modernistic gang" stand up on your feet.

Now, how many members of Temple Baptist Church – every member of the Temple Baptist Church here this afternoon hold up your hands.

I want to say to all you Baptists, not members of the Temple Church, every time you go down and put your time and money into one of these modernistic churches you are guilty of giving them encouragement – (Voices, Amen). You should not be partakers of their sin.

(Invitation. Large number came).

# CHAPTER XII

## MEETINGS IN DETROIT BY ALL THE MAIN "PISTON RODS" TO HANG NORRIS

As soon as Norris went to Detroit all "the powers that be" concentrated to hinder his work. They even went to the papers and got them to put on a boycott and they succeeded with one of the papers but the other two gave Norris front page.

They called a meeting at the Masonic Temple with an auditorium of 5,000 capacity, and on the platform was the Secretary of the Baptist Union in Detroit, the President of the Michigan Baptist Convention, – the President of the Northern Baptist Convention, the President of the Southern Baptist Convention, the President of the World Baptist Alliance, and a score of other Baptist dignitaries.

The real purpose of the meeting was to hang Norris and he did what he has always done – when he heard he was going to be hung he always does attend his own hanging; and right in the midst of one of their meetings he perambulated down the aisle, and there were more folks on the platform than in the great auditorium.

The next Sunday night Dr. Norris took the whole Sanhedrin to a fare-thee-well cleaning.

Of course, there are those who say that Norris should not use such language or show such an "unChristly spirit." But evidently he has been a student of Isaiah, John the Baptist, Martin Luther and a few other well known protestors and defenders of the faith.

A night congregation in the leading Baptist of Edinburg Scotland in "Charlotte Chapel" where Dr. Norris preached.

# CHAPTER XIII

## NORRIS EXPOSES THE COMMUNISTIC CONNECTIONS OF DR. LOUIE D. NEWTON, PRESIDENT OF THE SOUTHERN BAPTIST CONVENTION

In the pre-convention meeting, which was equivalent to the Convention, in St. Louis, May 5th, Dr. Louie D. Newton was challenged before the whole crowd by Dr. Norris, and pandemonium broke loose. Dr. M. E. Dodd, who was presiding, refused to give Dr. Norris a hearing and the confusion was so great that Dr. Dodd had the police called.

Dr. Norris had informed the various news agencies the day before what he was going to do, namely, make a protest against Dr. Louie D. Newton's Communistic connections. He knew he would not be given a hearing but he would use the occasion as a forum to reach the whole country, and the daily papers of America front-paged the whole thing as shown by the folowing from the Chicago Daily News of May 7th, 1947:

### "Row on Communism Upsets Church Parley"

"St. Louis (AP). – A preconvention assembly of Southern Baptist pastors was thrown into brief disorder last night over an attempt of the Rev. Dr. J. Frank Norris of Fort Worth to have Dr. Louie D. Newton of Atlanta, convention president, answer 13 questions of his attitude toward Russia and Communism.

"Police, who arrived after order was restored, talked separately with the Rev. Norris and the Rev. Dr. M. E. Dodd of Shreveport, La., conference chairman, in a church hallway and left without comment.

"Rev. Newton began his report on a trip to Russia. Rev. Norris arose and laid a copy of the 13 questions on the rostrum.

"Outcries from the audience interrupted Norris when he started to read from the list.

"Newton signaled with upraised arms for the start of a hymn. The assembly of 1,000 ministers arose and sang 'How Firm a Foundation.' Norris joined in on the second verse.

"Dodd halted the singing with a wave of his hands and attempted to persuade Norris to resume his seat.

"The shouting went on for several minutes while Norris tried to be heard. Dodd and Newton likewise were unable to restore order.

"Norris' questions were based on a weekly news magazine interview with Newton Aug. 26, 1946, made after his return from Russia."

The St. Louis Globe-Democrat, the Star-Telegram of Fort Worth, and other papers published the following questions which Dr. Newton refused to answer:

"Statler Hotel,
St. Louis, Mo.
May 7, 1947

"Dr. Louie D. Newton,
President. Southern Baptist Convention,
St. Louis, Mo.
Dear Mr. Newton:

In as much as motion was made in yesterday afternoon's meeting, that you and I discuss the issues concerning Soviet Russia, and in as much as you have announced that you are going to speak on Russia again this morning for the Convention – you have already spoken three times here in St. Louis on Russia – therefore, I am submitting to you the following questions that are vital in this great crisis of America and the world:

1. In all your discussions here – why have you not said one single word in defense of President Truman's Greek-Turk aid to stop Communism?

2. You said yesterday afternoon that United States can work with Soviet Russia. How do you explain Secretary of State George Marshall's address declaring the opposite view, namely, that we can not agree, or work with Russia?

3. In all your writings, and talks about Russia, why have you not said one word to the Baptists assembled here in St. Louis condemning the atheistic-communistic tyranny of Joe Stalin and his Polit Bureau of fellow-gangsters?

4. If you are opposed to Communism, why did headquarters of Communism in Chicago and New York endorse, publish and send broadcasts their endorsement of your appeasement plea for Moscow?

5. In Time Magazine of August 26, 1946, in your interview concerning Soviet Russia, you are quoted as 'brimming with enthusiam for what you had seen and been told."

In view of Secretary of State Marshall's address last week on how Russia has blocked the peace, and aims to bring about world chaos, are you still "brimming with enthusiam for Soviet Russia"

6. (a) You stated in Time Magazine of the same date: "The Baptists stand for the same thing as the Russian Government – renouncence of, and resistance to, coercion in matters of belief."

(b) "Religiously, we should regard Russia as our great ally." Do you still hold this sympathetic attitude toward Moscow?

7. On February 22, 1947, the Associated Press published report of a 16-member committee of prominent church men, advocating the appeasement program with Russia, and with 15 others it is signed "Dr. Louie D. Newton, president of the Southern Baptist Convention, Atlanta."

Do you still hold that same attitude of appeasement with Russia?

8. The American Russian Institute, 58 Park Avenue, New York 16, N. Y., the Communistic headquarters of Moscow in America, sponsored your endorsement of Moscow with the title, "An American Churchman in the Soviet Union."

Do you think the president of Southern Baptist Convention should be sponsored by this Communistic headquarters?

9. On April 7, this year, the United Press published "an assault on President Truman's plan to bolster Greece and Turkey against

Communism," and this assault was signed by 200 clergymen from 30 states. This is the crowd you associate with and endorse.

Do you still hold to the view of these 200 clergymen, and are you in sympathy with this assault on President Truman?

10. On January 20, 1947, you gave to the Atlanta Journal a letter from the head of the propaganda department of Moscow, one V. Kemenov, president of the U.S.S.R. Society for Cultural Relations, you gave to the Atlanta Journal how that you were thanked by Moscow for your defense of Moscow.

Do you still accept and enjoy the commendation of the head of the department of propaganda in Moscow.

11. Quoting you from Time Magazine of August 26, 1946, you give an account of your personal visit and conversation with Joe Stalin and that you gave him personally a Bible with an inscription "From one Georgian to another Georgian."

Did you actually have this conversation with Joe Stalin? (Dr. Ralph Sockman of New York City, one of your fellow-travelers to Moscow, says you did not see Stalin nor any of your party.)

12. You said in your published statement upon your return from Russia that there was religious freedom.

Is it not a fact that all church properties are owned and controlled by the Soviet Government? How then can there be religious freedom?

13. Are the ministers of religion in Russia permitted to criticize the government? If not, how can there be religious freedom?

14. Is it not a fact that the Secret Police are in every religious service to check on and report on all that is said and done? How then can there be religious freedom?

15. There are four well-known Latvian ministers attending this convention and Latvia is a part of Russia and they report that their churches are confiscated, members of their family – brother and father, were murdered and others sent into Siberia. Then how can you claim there is religious freedom in Russia?

16. You state: "The future of religion is as bright in Russia as anywhere in the world." In view of the recent exposure of the spy-ring in Canada, where ten Russian spies were convicted and sent to prison, and this spy-ring reached into the United States – how can you say that the future of religion is bright in Russia?

17. Is not your campaign for "better relations with Russia," an appeasement program with Southern Baptists, more hurtful to the cause of freedom than Henry Wallace's campaign in the political world for appeasement?

I am giving this letter and questions to the press.

Yours very truly,<br>J. PRANK NORRIS."

On the red hot controversy the following comment is typical of Baptist pastors all over the country:

"Elizabethton, Tenn.<br>Box 707,<br>May 20, 1947,

"Dr. J. Frank Norris,
Fort Worth, Texas.
Dear Dr. Norris.

It was good to see you and hear you again at St. Louis. The Southern Baptist Convention came and went, as usual, a little closer toward the camp of Modernism, and helped to further the work of Communism, not only in America, but throughout the world. Our hearts were made sad to see this awful trend. More and more they are cutting off their own heads just because of their hatred for you. God pity them!

All the large denominations are going more and more into apostasy, and since there is never any redemption offered for apostasy, God is making provisions through the great Fundamental movement to take care of the multitudes who do not want it.

The people may be slow to open their eyes and for a long, long time will hold on, hoping all is well or will be, but after while they will break away, and especially so when they fully realize they have been betrayed by their leaders. There are multitudes who will say they are glad you are making the fight and are doing what you are, though they may not come out in the open. They feel so helpless with no radio, large paper, churches backing them as you have, and with but little experience. They know too well their heads would be out off by the machine and many would be out of a place to preach.

The machine is merciless, without reason, heart or soul. They would grind any man to the earth.

Dr. Norris, I have never ceased to thank God that this Fundamental movement and work you are in has come to the kingdom for just such a time as this. May God give added strength and cause this work to prosper in a great way. I am positive it will. It must. It is our only hope.

The minute the Southern Baptist Convention unites with Northern Baptist Convention, and thereby with the Federal Council of Churches, true Baptists will be through with them. Many are already through; they are just waiting.

My heart is sad. Many have loved Southern Baptists; they have, in times past done a mighty work for God. They have been the last of the great Denominations to surrender to Modernism, and to see them go is so painful. Any one familiar with the whole affair can easily see the awful drift. The most painful of all is to see great Fundamental men and leaders swept away with it all, as we did at St. Louis. Why can't men see!

We must have a great revival, but it will never come through any compromising Denomination; it will come at the hands of the faithful. "O Lord, I have heard thy speech and was afraid: O Lord, revive thy work in the midst of the years, in the midst of the years make known; in wrath remember mercy."

Yours for the Master,<br>
W. CLAY WILSON, Evangelist."

Overflow crowd when Dr. Norris held protest meetings in Kiel Auditorium at the Southern Baptist Convention, May, 1947, against the Modernism, Communism of Louie D. Newton, et al, and he held these meetings for four nights.

One of the four night crowds that Dr. Norris had at Kiel Auditorium in St. Louis. Multiply this crowd by four and the reader will have an idea of the large numbers reached during the Southern Baptist Convention.

# CHAPTER XIV

## "HOW NORRIS RUNS THE BAPTIST CONVENTION"

When the Texas Baptist Convention 25 years ago got hot and furious, Dr. J. C. Hardy, then President of Baylor at Belton, got up before the whole crowd and said:

"I am tired of J. Frank Norris running this Convention. Here's how he does it. He is smart enough to know the course we should pursue and will name the two courses before us, and will say:

" 'Brethren, one of these roads leads to defeat and destruction, and the other road leads to peace and victory, and my advice is to take the latter road and avoid the road to damnation and the bow-wows. Stop before it is too late or you're going over the precipice of destruction.'

"Then we'll met together and bow our necks and determine that Frank Norris is not going to run this convention and we'll show him we'll not take his advice and we'll go on over the precipice of destruction.

"Then the rascal will stand there and look over the wreck and ruin, and laugh at us and say,

" 'Now, brethren, that's what I knew you would do, what I wanted you to do, and advised you to go the other way to peace and victory.'

"When, oh, when, are we going to have sense enough to do the wise thing regardless of what Frank Norris advises us or does?"

And he is running the convention today as never before.

Take for example that infidel book by Erskine that was endorsed by the Sunday School Board and J. M. Dawson, the book that denied the Virgin Birth of Christ and makes Mary a scarlet woman – Norris exposed it and sent a copy of his exposure to every Baptist preacher in the South just before the Southern Baptist Convention met at Miami. (That is one of his chief methods, to turn loose a carload of dynamite just before the Convention meets, but it is a free country.)

That endorsement of this infidel book by J. M. Dawson closed with the words:

"To sum up: Erskine has probably taken the track that leads to the view of Jesus that may dominate the future judgment of mankind."

This attack and exposure by Norris of this infidel book forced the Sunday School Board through its secretary Dr. T. L. Holcomb to make an apology before the whole Southern Baptist Convention in which he said, "It was a mistake to send out that book, and we are withdrawing it from the market."

I don't know of any other man, in or out of the Convention, that could have forced the great conservative Southern Baptist Convention to follow this course, and applaud the apology of the Secretary of the Sunday School Board.

He certainly ran the Convention at St. Louis, for at the pre-Convention meeting before all the pastors present he made the protest publicly against Louie Newton, the president of the Convention's endorsement of Moscow, and it took front page in the daily papers of America. And Southern Baptists have been shaken to their depths, from center to circumference by this exposure.

Incidentally, not only in a corrective manner does he run the Convention, but also in an affirmative and constructive manner. Having given many years of my life to Sunday School and church building, I am in a position to say that the whole Southern Baptist Convention – as for that matter, churches of all denominations, north and south, have adopted his methods. Of course they cuss him out for it, but it is like it was with old man Henry Ford the greatest industrialist of his age.

# CHAPTER XV

NORRIS' SURVIVAL OF THE CONSPIRACY OF THE DENOMINATIONAL LEADERS TO DESTROY HIM AND HIS MINISTRY – A LETTER

Some time ago I received a letter from one of the dearest friends I have ever had. I shall not mention his name. That is not necessary.

In that letter he was displeased at something I had written in the Fundamentalist about another brother who was excluded from the Convention because he wouldn't support the 75-Million Campaign. This dear friend took me to task for "The constant bickering and attacks on the Convention."

I am reproducing in this brief chapter a part of my reply to that letter to this dear friend:

"As to my leaving the Convention, I had good scriptural grounds, according to my best judgment, for doing so. And I did not leave because I had fallen out or had a fuss with anybody. Neither is there any "bickering and strife" so far as I am concerned now.

"So far as I know I have had no fights with any of the brethren in the Convention. We are still on most friendly and cordial terms.

"But then so far as I know they have never tried to ruin me and destroy my ministry, which according to my own intimate knowledge and experience they have done for my co-laborer and brother beloved, J. Frank Norris. If a man could have absolutely been ruined forever, the leaders of the Southern Baptist Convention would certainly have put him out of business a long time ago.

"He and I are as different as two men could possibly be. I have been associated with him more or less now for thirty-four years. I have read the history of Christianity, and written a good bit on some things and I know of no man in Christian history that has done a greater job of winning souls and preaching the gospel of the grace of God, and to more people, than J. Frank Norris.

"This whole city was against him when I came here. Now the department stores will close up and invite him in to preach to their clerks and workers – I mean big department stores where hundreds of people work. And even the courts where he was once persecuted will now stop long enough to have him preach to the judge, jurors and people.

"The daily papers, when he was fighting the liquor crowd, wouldn't even publish a paid ad. I know what I am talking about – they now write profuse editorials on his incomparable accomplishments as a Baptist preacher. If you knew him as I do, my candid judgment is that you wouldn't feel like you do about him. But he needs no defense from me.

"I still believe that in the main Southern Baptists are orthodox. But just why as many great men as there are in the Southern Baptist Convention, they would dishonor themselves by putting an appeaser of Joe Stalin in as president, who will have around him two or three modernists, – men I know are modernists, like Joe Dawson, Jim Dillard, et al – and having read Christian history as much as I have, I know that these great ecclesiastical bodies are never reformed on the inside. They drift further and further away from the old landmarks.

"I am happy with the group in which I work. We believe in the old faith, including the glorious hope of the return of our Lord. There is not a postmillennialist in our number.

So you and I are both happy in our connection and we both believe in the old Book and the blood and grace of God. We have both lived, I suppose, our allotted time, and if by reason of strength we have a few years left here, all praise and glory to Him who sustains us and keeps us by his grace."

I might add this word, that Norris and the First Baptist Church were excluded from the Tarrant County Baptist Association and also from the Texas General Assembly for no greater crime than exposing evolution in Baylor University, refusing to subscribe $200,000 to the 75-Million Campaign – he did give $20,000 cash, however – and for putting the Sunday School Board Literature out of the Sunday School and adopting the Bible only as a textbook.

He was even tried and excluded from the Tarrant County Association while he was 1,000 or 1,500 miles away in a revival meeting and not even given the privilege of defending himself or his church.

His messengers to the Association begged to be heard but were refused a hearing.

In addition to that, thousands of pages of slanderous literature in the form of tracts were circulated all over the land by these denominational leaders.

I am amazed at the thousand and one things I have been told, things reported about Norris. I am amazed at the reliable and responsible people who say these things about Norris when there isn't a word of truth in them. It is amazing how good men because of prejudice will say and report things that are not in a thousand miles of the truth."

I could have written my friend many other things that might enlighten him about Norris.

But I remember the old proverb I used to hear in my boyhood days:

"Man convinced against his will is of the same opinion still."

A part of one of Dr. Norris' great crowds in Dallas.

# SECTION IV

# CHAPTER I

DR. NORRIS DOES MUCH PERSONAL VISITATION

**From Sermon Dec. 26, 1937**

Since I was here a great soul went home to God. I shall never forget one morning – the office was right over yonder – she came in a morning ahead of time, before we were expecting her. Someone knocked on the door and I said, "Come in."

The door opened and there stood a slender girl. She said, "This is Kate Tarlton."

I rose and said, "Why Miss Kate you have come ahead of time. I was going to meet you this afternoon."

I looked at her. She looked at me. That was nearly a quarter of a century ago that happened, and not until the leaves of the judgment book unfold will this church know some of the things she and others went through. Do you know when our greatest crisis was? It was when our property was destroyed, with the depression following. Some of you wondered why we didn't tell you our real financial condition. We knew you couldn't stand it. The congregation was scattered and we had no central place in which the church could meet. We met in tabernacles on the North Side, East Side and South Side. The bookkeeper sitting over there will tell you I never got one check for salary during those three years. Business went to pieces and one insurance company after another crashed and went into receivership. We had to take what was left. Indeed, it was very dark.

There were only five persons on earth knew the actual condition of the finances. A. L. Jackson knew it, Jane Hartwell knew it, Kate Tarlton knew it, and Harry Keeton knew it, and I knew it.

And so we decided to take all the blame. We were criticized.

When I saw the conditions, people losing their jobs, and I walked around this pile of smouldering ruins – at first in the weakness of the flesh I was tempted to give up. But I called Kate Tarlton and said, "Kate, we are facing the greatest crisis. Our flock is like a flock of sheep scattered abroad. We can't get one central place. There is no such place. Without saying a word about it I am going into the homes of these people. You get the membership list up to date and be at my command."

And morning, afternoon and night the girl and I drove and held meetings all that spring and summer and fall for the next year. And many of you can testify to it, even in the hottest of the summer – many of you are saved today because of those visits.

I remember one night way out here in Arlington Heights. The address wasn't on the street but around at the side. They had dug a basement and had a concrete foundation. She sat in the car until I would find them and then we would get out and come in. A man says, "They live around on the back side of that lot." And so I tore out, walk pretty fast as you know, and I hit that concrete foundation. And when the undertaker lays me out he will see two chipped places on both shins. I turned forty somersoults down into that basement. I thought the judgment day had come. After while when I got up I was so disfigured and my wife never saw me until I had gone by the hospital. –

We drove and drove and drove. And oftentimes at the close of the day when the battle was hard she and I would join together and we would sing together when I would come and put her out at her home on West Second. And the other day I saw Miss Jane at my daughter's home – her hair is almost white. I said, "Yes, the First Baptist Church put those gray hairs there." She will be back soon. And when my wife phoned me Kate had passed away I immediately called up the airport. There was a terrible snow storm in the West and all the planes were grounded and it was impossible for me to make it.

I wrote her mother and wired her too, and I received the most wonderful letter from Mrs. Tarlton. She said, "I am so grateful for her life. I am so grateful that that night when she called me to her bed she knew that she was crossing and said 'Mother, hold my hand. Hold it close. Hold it tight. Hold it, mother, I am nearing the crossing.' And then she said, 'Mother, go and lie down and go to sleep. Please do, for my sake'."

And when the nurse took her mother to the room and came back Kate had turned over on her side. She touched her and said, "It is time to take your medicine" and she did not respond. She shook her – she too had gone to sleep.

And this mother says, "It is worth everything in the world that I was permitted at the last moment to hold my child's hand when she crossed over."

At the funeral she says, "The whole earth was covered with snow and the sun shining so bright. It is all a beautiful picture of her white life. We buried her body in the cold earth, but her great soul has gone to be with God, and it won't be long until I too will hold that hand again."

Abilene, Nov. 27th and 28th, 1941

# CHAPTER II

INSIDE HISTORY OF THE TWO CHURCHES, FIRST BAPTIST CHURCH, FORT WORTH, TEXAS, TEMPLE BAPTIST CHURCH, DETROIT, MICHIGAN

The two largest congregations in the South and North, respectively, largest in membership, largest in Sunday School, greater attendance upon their regular services, and most important of all, people being saved in large numbers "daily" in New Testament fashion – These brief chapters on the inside history are given with the hope that some discouraged pastor or defeated layman may "Thank God and take courage."

If the reader thinks the language is often too plain and blunt let him remember that David did not go against Goliath with a bottle of perfume nor did John the Baptist answer the Sadduces and Pharisees with a pearl handled pen knife, "But wisdom is justified of all her children." And remember "That a notable miracle hath been done... is manfiest... we cannot deny."

With churches as with individuals, "do men gather grapes of thorns, or figs of thistles?"

In this day of defeatism, downgradism, modernism, communism, and atheism, there is but one need, and that need is to come back to the God of our fathers.

## "The World's Work" of New York in Its Two Issues, September and October, 1923, Published the Following; "The Fundamentalist War Among the Churches"

"I hear the Fundamental Movement 'lacks a leader,' and so it does – at present. Fundamentalism has only started. No one man started it. It is a result of simultaneous uprising all over the country. Organization, with accredited leadership, will come later. Potential leaders abound, and among the strongest, shrewdest, and most romantically adventurous is J. Frank Norris, of Fort Worth, Texas. But he denies he is a leader.

"In Fort Worth opinion regarding Norris is divided. Several years ago his enemies got him tried 'for burning up his church.' He was acquitted. Later on, a mass-meeting ordered him out of town. Legend recounts that he and his merry men prepared to defend themselves with a machine-gun. I asked him about that. 'No,' he replied, 'I had nothing – that gun business is just newspaper headlines. Never carried one since I entered the ministry.'

"Many of 'Frank's' former foes adore him, as does half the community. Buildings covering a block and more attest his success, and his auditorium, when alterations are complete, will hold five thousand applausive adherents, with a choir of seven hundred.

"Recently his paper – circulation 55,000 (I saw the affidavit) – proclaimed in red headlines, 'WAR IS DECLARED – SECOND COMING OF CHRIST ISSUE!' Nailed to the door of his church, meanwhile, was a huge poster announcing his 'World Convention of Fundamentalists.' The array of celebrated speakers included William Jennings Bryan.

"Prince of crowd gatherers, paragon of advertisers, Norris has created a new profession, that of the church-efficiency expert, and is its most brilliant practitioner. Heralded as 'the Texas Cyclone,' he will enter any city you choose to name, lay hold of some doddering, deader-than-alive downtown church, draw crowds into it, galvanize them, get the gloriously revivified institution financed, and erect a living, lasting monument to his abilities. After witnessing his performance in Cleveland, Dr. W. W. Bustard declared that in the service of a business corporation Norris' genius would be worth $50,000 a year. He understated the case.

"It is true that Norris' belief in 'the literal, personal, bodily, visible, imminent return of the Lord to this earth as King' somewhat limits his leadership.

"It was Norris who said to me at the very start of the first talk I had with him, 'There is going to be a new denomination.' He named the three distinguished Fundamentalists who are about to organize it.

"The champion college-baiter, so far, is Rev. J. Frank Norris, who has transformed his church bulletin into a weekly newspaper, the Searchlight (Now The Fundamentalist). In an upper corner of its front page, we behold Norris grasping a Bible in one hand, while the other directs the glare of a searchlight. In the corner opposite, revealed by the glare, cowers Satan. Red headlines complete the effect. Week by week Norris flays the evolutionists in his adventurous journal, and mails it far and wide.

"A year or so ago, hearing that evolution was tolerated at Wake Forest University, near Raleigh, he raged against Wake Forest and mailed Searchlights to all the North Carolina ministers. Uproar followed. A local religious paper attacked President Wm. L. Poteat, and all over North Carolina anti-evolutionists demanded his resignation.

"In his warfare upon his Alma-Mater – Baylor University at Waco, Texas – Norris is succeeding. Professor G. Samuel Dow, author of 'Society and Its Problems,' and an 'Introduction to the Principles of Sociology,' stood his ground until flesh and blood could endure no more, then resigned. Professor O. C. Bradbury has done the same. Encouraged by these triumphs, Norris is not only assailing Professor Pace, a lady, but insisting that President Samuel Palmer Brooks must go."

The Lord Mayor of Losdon showing Dr. Norris the ruins of London in 1941. The Mayor took him in his privet car after giving him a reception in the "Mansion House".

# CHAPTER III

## THE METHODS USED IN BUILDING THE WORLD'S TWO GREATEST SUNDAY SCHOOLS AND CHURCHES

Dr. Norris boldly challenged unscriptural and outworn customs and traditions by calling the two churches, both First Baptist and Temple Baptist, back to the scriptural method as set forth in Acts 20:28 –

"Take heed therefore unto yourselves, and to all the flock, over the which the Holy Ghost hath made you overseers, to feed the church of God, which he hath purchased with his own blood."

In both churches he found the "Board of Deacons" in absolute charge and they ran everything, including the pastor."

He used the illustration that instead of the pastor being the head and God's appointed leader, he was like the farmer boy riding the coupling-pole. Not that the pastor should lord it over God's heritage, but that as the spiritual leader he asked his churches to "be imitators of me as I also imitate or follow Christ."

He preached often on the church at Antioch – Acts 13:1-5:

"Now there were in the church that was at Antioch certain prophets and teachers; as Barnabas, and Simeon that was called Niger, and Lucius of Cyrene, and Manaen, which had been brought up with Herod the tetarch, and Saul.

"As they ministered to the Lord and fasted, the Holy Ghost said, Separate me Barnabas and Saul for the work whereunto I have called them.

"And when they had fasted and prayed, and laid their hands on them, they sent them away.

"So they, being sent forth by the Holy Ghost, departed unto Selucia; and from thence they sailed to Cyprus.

"And when they were at Salamis, they preached the word of God in the synagogues of the Jews; and they had also John to their minister."

The pastor riding on a coupling pole.

He took the position that all that we need to know of "organization," "methods," "plans," "messages" – all these fundamental truths and methods are clearly set forth in the New Testament churches.

Of course, he ran head-on into sharp conflict with the powers that be.

He used the illustration of the June bug – he said: "When I became pastor of the great First Baptist Church I was like the June bug, a beautiful bug and absolutely harmless. Tie a string on the leg of a June bug and it just junes around like a gee-whiz church soloist. I had a dozen strings on every leg and limb and the denominational headquarters had a rope around my neck. One day I decided to sever all such unscriptural connections, and denominational bishops, secretaries and other piston rods called on me and told me I could not do that, but I answered, "gentlemen, its already done," and the fight was on within and without.

And everybody knows, every pastor knows, that he is not a free man but lives under constant dread for his life. There is little difference between the tyranny of a Pharaoh, a Hitler or a Stalin and the tyranny of the denominational bishop or machine. I am not sure but that it is more merciful to stand them up before the firing squad at midnight than to persecute, hound and murder pastors and yet let them live. The world is full of "ex-pastors" who have been driven from their pulpits by the little worldly clique on the inside, and always the denominational headquarters will support that worldly clique against the pastor.

Norris would not have any deacon, teacher, or any other officer unless they knew how and actually did invite people to hear him preach or win them to Christ.

## But the Pastor Set the Example

Having been very closely and vitally associated with J. Frank Norris for more than a third of a century, God is my witness, I have never seen a man that could do as much in one day's time.

Personally, I have known of him making many calls at six o'clock in the morning or at breakfast time, for, be said then he knew he could find people at home. And we would go until midnight and pull people out of bed.

Today he is doing more personal work, more visitation, seeking the lost, than I have ever witnessed in his whole career.

He arrives at his office early, keeps three stenographers busy for an hour, then on the radio, then lectures to the Seminary student body.

After that he has an hour to receive callers – and unsaved people come to his office every day – and he will listen to anybody's troubles, regardless of how poor.

Then when noon arrives he eats a light lunch, emphasis on the light, usually a bowl of soup or some fruit juice, and then will lie down and sleep an hour, maybe more, during which time nobody can disturb him and no telephone calls, unless from his wife.

Then he will dictate to his stenographers for another hour and by three or four o'clock is ready for several hours visitation until bed time, and bed time, with him, is midnight.

He lives out on Eagle Mountain Lake, eighteen miles from Fort Worth, in a $25,000 house that was given to his wife by a man who had been redeemed from a drunkard's grave under his preaching, a man who made millions in oil after he was saved.

At daylight he is working in his garden, and he has a most beautiful garden the year around, and then he goes down to the pier in front of his house and takes a plunge in the clear, cool waters of Eagle Mountain Lake.

Both his energy and good humor have been a constant surprise to me and to all associated with him. He is always pulling off pranks and jokes on his workers. For instance, not long ago his whole fine crowd of young men went out early one morning to take a plunge in the lake and he came out first and gathered up all their clothes, put them in the car and drove off. But he came on up to his house and had four dozen eggs scrambled, five pounds of bacon broiled crisp and plenty of toast and coffee and then he sent back the clothes and had the boys, about a dozen, to come up and enjoy a good breakfast out in the open in his back yard – something after the fashion –

"As soon then as they were come to land, they saw a fire of coals there, and fish laid thereon, and bread.

"Jesus saith unto them, Come and dine. And none of the disciples durst ask him, Who art thou? knowing that it was the Lord.

"Jesus then cometh, and taketh bread, and giveth them, and fish likewise." (Jno. 21:9,12-13).

His associates do not regard him as a "boss," for he is intensely human and is, indeed, one of them and they can approach him and do approach him with all of their problems and sorrows.

Contrary to what some of his critics have said, he is the easiest man in the world to get along with if you "get along." He is more severe on himself than any one else so far as doing a job is concerned. He has no patience with laziness and often says that laziness is the greatest curse of the ministry.

Speaking of his crowded duties, he has plenty of time for every student to come into his office and listens to them patiently and helps them, as hundreds of them can testify.

25,000 hear J. Frank Norris, Forth Worth Baseball Park, June 7, 1942. The panoramic picture was so large it had to be cut in three parts to get on the page.

# CHAPTER IV

THE HOW – METHODS OF ENLISTING MEMBERS

**By G. B. Vick, Superintendent Temple Baptist Church**

(Quoting from book "Inside the Cup")

As clearly, as concisely and as unadorned as possible, I desire to set forth in this chapter, a few of the methods which have been used to build and maintain these two churches, which are said to be the largest congregations in the North and South respectively.

Having been associated with Dr. Norris at the First Baptist Church in Fort Worth for nearly nine years, and having worked with him in Detroit nearly two years, I have had the opportunity of observing the inside workings and the methods in personal work, in house-to-house visitation, in Bible study, and in finances. For those of you who have not had a like opportunity I pass this on.

## The Bible Only

One of the most startling departures from the ordinary church methods was made by the First Baptist Church more than sixteen years ago, when it pioneered in discarding the International Sunday School lesson series, all quarterlies, leaflets and man-made literature, and announced that henceforth the Word of God itself would be the only text book in the Sunday School, as well as the only rule of faith and practice in the church.

Wide publicity was given to this far reaching step and soon around the world this church, which had already built the largest Sunday School in the world, now came to be known as "The Church that studies the Bible only."

There were several reasons why this step was taken:

1: Because we believed that it was better to study the Word of God than to study merely what some man had written about the Word of God.

2: Because the International Sunday School lessons, as used by churches all over the world, never covered or even touched upon three-fourths of the Bible. A survey was made of the lessons for sixteen years past, and this was found to be true.

3: The hop, skip and jump method of taking a few verses out of one chapter this Sunday and next Sunday studying an entirely different portion of the Scriptures, was not giving our teachers, much less our Sunday School pupils, a clear, coherent grasp of the Bible as a whole.

4: Another fact that no one will deny is that the Quarterlies and literature of all denominations are written from the post-millennial viewpoint and either misapply, or, as is usually the case, omit entirely, most of the great prophetic Scriptures.

Immediately many happy results were noted. Many of our teachers who, at first, had entered into the proposition with fear and trembling, were surprised at their own rapid growth as real Bible teachers.

Another immediate result noted was a large increase in attendance throughout the whole Sunday School. Within a few short weeks after we started teaching the "Bible only" the Sunday School attendance showed an increase of over 900 above what the attendance had been running.

Most important of all, our experience showed indisputably that more souls are saved when we teach the "Bible only" than when we used the quarterlies.

One of the by-products of our new method was the greater spirit of reverence and better deportment, particularly with Juniors and Intermediates. We found that there was a deeper spirit of reverence when every pupil opened his Bible than when they turned, in their quarterlies, to the lesson text:

Another thing, it is easier to get people to bring their Bibles when we study the "Bible only" than when we merely give them 10 per cent for bringing their Bibles, according to the old denominational "Standard of excellence."

One of the results that we did not foresee was the increased attendance at our mid-week teachers' meeting. We realized that no Sunday School could do its best work without a well-attended, regular weekly teachers meeting. That is where plans for the next Sunday are set forth by the Superintendent, where the weak places in the various classes and departments are strengthened and where due acknowledgement is made and encouragement given for extraordinary accomplishments.

We found that after discarding helps and literature that the teachers were anxious to hear the next Sunday's lesson as it would be taught by the Pastor or Superintendent on Wednesday night. Therefore, every Wednesday night from 7:30 to 8:00 the teachers and workers of each department meet and discuss those problems and plans which are peculiar to their own age group. Then at 8 o'clock all departments come together in a general meeting where the Pastor or Superintendent gives the lesson for the next Sunday.

We have found that it is impossible for a teacher and indeed his entire class to keep step with the rest of the Sunday School and Church if the Wednesday night teachers' meeting is neglected.

### Visitation – "Daily... in Every House"

Besides the study of the "Bible Only," another distinguishing feature of the First Baptist Church at Fort Worth and the Temple Baptist Church at Detroit, is their constant, persistent Scriptural house-to-house visitation.

From the human standpoint the secret of the growth of these churches may be summed up in one word "Visitation." It is impossible to have a church-going people without you have first a people-going church. In other words, the average unsaved, unregenerate man of the street is not going to anybody's church if that church doesn't first go to him. Jesus knew this to be true, and therefore, said:

"Go out into the highways and hedges, and compel (constrain) them to come in, that my house may be filled." Luke 14:23.

The secret of the phenomenal growth of the First Church in Jerusalem is found in Acts 5:42:

"And daily in the temple, and in every house, they ceased not to teach and preach Jesus Christ."

That is the New Testament method, and God's method of building a great church and Sunday School. Certainly we cannot improve upon it.

In the 9th and 10th chapters of Acts, we also have two splendid examples of the far reaching results of two personal visits made in two homes.

In the ninth chapter God told Ananias (who as far as we know was not a preacher but an ordinary layman who loved the Lord) to make a personal visit. God gave him the name and address and said, "Go to the street which is called Straight, to the house of a man named Judas and there call for Saul of Tarsus. He is a good prospect and needs your visit just now."

But Ananias argued with the Lord and said: "Lord, I don't believe it would do any good for me to call on him. I have heard a lot about that fellow. He is bitter against the church, He persecutes believers unto prison and even unto death, and besides that, he is well educated and possibly knows more about the Old Testament Scriptures than I do, and I am not gifted or qualified to make a visit to such a man. Someone else could do it much better. Besides all that, Lord, I have had a hard day at the office or shop, and I am tired, and don't have an automobile so I don't feel like making that call tonight." Or perhaps Ananias said: "We have some friends or relatives coming to our house tonight and I have a very important social engagement, and I just can't make that visit at this time, and anyway I don't believe it would do any good."

But God said: "Ananias, you do what I told you, for he is a chosen vessel to bear my name before the Gentiles and kings and the children of Israel. I am going to give the world a demonstration of what God can do with a transformed life."

Speaking from the human standpoint suppose Ananias had not made that visit. The scales would never have fallen from Paul's eyes. He could never have preached in the power of the Holy Spirit and would never have become the greatest preacher, evangelist and soul winner of all time; thousands of souls whom Paul personally won to Christ would have been lost, and we would not have thirteen books in the New Testament today, written by the great Apostle to the Gentiles.

On the other hand because Ananias obeyed God and made that particular visit, Ananias has some part in all the souls that Paul won to Christ, and every soul that has been saved by reading any part of Paul's epistles.

If today you or I can be used of God in making one visit whereby we will win one soul that will turn many to righteousness, then let us rejoice in the opportunity and not neglect it. It is still God's plan for men and women who love Him to go into the homes daily to teach and preach Jesus Christ.

In the 10th chapter of Acts we have another wonderful example of a visit that Peter made to the home of a man called Cornelius. Here too God had to almost compel Peter to make this call. When God told Peter to go to Caesarea to the home of Simon the tanner who lived on a street near the seashore Peter also argued with the Lord. He said: "Lord, it is an unlawful thing for a man that is a Jew to keep company or come unto a man of another nation," but God said, "Peter, if I can visit that home with a special visitation of my divine power, certainly you can afford to visit there."

And as a result of Peter's visit in that home Cornelius and all his household were saved, and the door of salvation was opened to the Gentiles.

## Plan of Visitation

On Monday night of each week our men meet at the church at 6 o'clock, coming directly from their work. There they are served a good warm supper, which has been prepared by the good women of the church. At 6:30 the men are handed a group of cards (usually not more than five or six) and go out into the homes two by two. These cards contain the name, address, church affiliation, a word about the spiritual condition, or any other helpful information that we have concerning that individual. The cards have been copied in advance by a secretary who always retains the original card for every prospect in a permanent prospect file, which is kept in the church office. A duplicate card has been made out in advance and all of those living in different sections of the city have been grouped, so that as little time as possible will be lost in going from one house to another.

The men go into the homes and make a good spiritual visit, not merely a polite social call. We urge them always to have prayer in every home before leaving it. The men get all the information possible concerning every member of that household, who is not a regular attendant of some church or Sunday School. They write the names and ages of every individual on the back of the card, together with a brief report or summary of what they have found in the home.

At 9 o'clock they meet back at the church to give their reports and it is a rare thing that a Monday night passes without good news of several conversions in the homes that night.

Of course, that does not mean that we win somebody to Christ in every home that we visit. Often times the workers find that the best thing to do in some homes is to tell them how God is blessing our work and merely give them a warm cordial invitation to attend our Sunday School and church the next Sunday, and if that is not sufficient, to make arrangements to go by for them and bring them to Sunday School the next Sunday morning. That usually gets results.

When the men's reports are concluded, they all hand in their cards with the written reports on the back. These cards are carefully gone over by the Visitation Secretary and she puts the results of each visit on the back of her permanent card in the prospect file. In that way every one who follows up that visit has the benefit of the information found by the first visitor and each succeeding one.

The Visitation Secretary also makes out individual prospect cards for every new prospect found in that night's visitation, and distributes them to the class in whose age-group they belong.

The ladies' work is carried on in a similar manner each Thursday as they gather at the church at 9:30, receive their cards and visit in the homes until 12:30, when they meet back at the church for lunch and fellowship, which is followed by their reports and a short, practical Scriptural message by the pastor.

The ladies bring their own lunches and spread them all together.

In addition to these periods of special visitation, every class and department carries on a constant visitation of their absentees, sick members and prospects.

I have before me last week's report, which shows that there were 56 present at the men's Monday night visitation, and 73 present for the women's visitation on Thursday. The total number of visits reported for the week was 948.

The numbers of visits made and the visitors in the homes varies, of course, from week to week. Sometimes the women have as many as 125 present and the men about 75, with 1100 or more visits made some weeks.

In taking the verbal reports of visits made from the men and women Monday nights and Thursdays, we try to emphasize two things about the reports:

1st. Be brief, stating only the important things, and 2nd, be enthusiastic. In other words, we urge every worker to talk only about the good things and not sound a discouraging note. If the people of one particular home visited are not interested or if they are antagonistic, we tell our workers to write the report of that upon the card, but not to talk about it in the group meetings. We want them to bring back **good news** – "As cold waters to a thirsty soul, so is good news."

That is very important because if two men who are perhaps naturally pessimistic get up and begin to tell about all the hard times that they had and all the discouraging obstacles they met, they will soon have everybody in the meeting crying on each other's shoulder – or at least feeling like it.

The good King David once had a messenger put to death because he was the bearer of bad news. In some ways it wasn't such a bad law, at that.

## God's Plan of Financing His Church

We believe that God's plan of financing His work through His church is set forth in His word.

We do not believe that it is God's plan that His work should be financed by suppers, ice cream socials, rummage sales, neither by lotteries, other gambling schemes nor dances as some of the churches here in the North put on to raise money. We are convinced as a matter of conviction and as a matter of experience that when Christian people hear what God's Word teaches as to our financial responsibility in carrying on His work, a good proportion will respond.

Here at the Temple Baptist Church for the past year we have not even asked anyone to pledge any certain amount per week. We merely ask them to sign a card, covenanting with God to obey Him and bring all their tithes and offerings into His storehouse at this church. The only pledge card that we use, reads as folows:

"The Tithe is the Lord's... it is holy unto the Lord." – Lev. 27:30.

In obedience to the Saviour's command, and in gratitude for His many blessings, I will gladly bring my Tithe into the Lord's store house at the Temple Baptist Church during the year 1938.

Name _____

Address_____

Dept: _____ Class _____

"Bring ye all the Tithes into the store house." – Mal. 3:10.

When born-again people sign such a card in goodly numbers the church finances are solved. Thus we place upon every teacher the responsibility of properly teaching and properly enlisting the members of his class in weekly Scriptural giving.

May I say in this respect that we have a Finance Committee of seven men who O. K. every check that is given out. This Finance Committee has a weekly meeting preceding the Wednesday night services and a financial report is made to the church every

Wednesday night. Every check has to be signed by two individuals selected by the deacons.

## Church Architecture

Even on the matter of church architecture the First Baptist Church at Fort Worth and the Temple Baptist Church of Detroit have decided convictions. Instead of cloud-reaching spires, and churches patterned after ancient cathedrals, we believe that the church building should be a modern lighthouse, a work shop for the Lord. We believe it ought to be practical and simple.

One reason why many poor people do not go to church today is that they feel ill at ease and not at home in a church with stained glass windows, a fine carpet on the floor and mahogany pews. We want our churches to be simple but comfortable, attractive but not extravagant, inviting to people of all classes and conditions; not too shoddy for the wealthiest and not too fine for the humblest and poorest. For instance we believe it is very desirable that a church shall not have any steps on the outside. Stores, business houses and places of amusement have found that such are not conducive to getting the greatest number of people on the inside and people are what we are after. Some preachers and churches say there is nothing in numbers. But we believe that to get people saved we must get them under the sound of the Gospel.

THURSDAY, SEPTEMBER 11, 1942.

# Churchill, Norris Confer

*By International News Service.*

LONDON, Sept. 11. — A great worldwide "moral and spirtual re-awakening" as a result of the war was predicted by Prime Minister Churchill Thursday.

The leader of Britain at war stated his beliefs regarding religion in a 45-minute interview with Rev. J. Frank Norris, pastor of the Temple Baptist Church of Detroit and the First Baptist Church of Fort Worth.

Rev. Mr. Norris, who arrived in London with a letter of introduction to Churchill from Secretary of State Hull, quoted the Prime Minister as saying:

"The whole issue is one of God or no God, faith or no faith, soul or no soul.

"One result of the war will be a great moral and spiritual reawakening of the world . . . Religion is th hope of the world."

Churchill added that he had "clung to the same faith of my devoted American mother."

Norris will preach in English churches during a two-week tour of England. He is sending autographed photographs of Churchill to his churches in Detroit and Fort Worth.

# CHAPTER V

### WHY THE FIRST BAPTIST CHURCH CONTINUES WITH INCREASING CROWDS AND REVIVALS AFTER 38 YEARS UNDER THE SAME PASTORATE

Through all the storms, without exception the morning has always come.

One of the favorite texts of the pastor has been: "Now when the morning was come."

The First Baptist Church has been like a healthy beehive. It has swarmed many times and sent out a large number of churches.

More than twenty thriving, growing churches in and around Fort Worth have gone out of the First Baptist Church.

The great Travis Avenue Baptist Church of Fort Worth, of which C. E. Matthews was pastor – that pastor was saved, baptized and married in the First Baptist Church. He learned his methods from the First Church. He was working for Swift Packing Company when he was converted. He was superintendent of the First Baptist Sunday School for a while.

Large numbers of the members of that church happily acknowledge their debt and love to their mother church, the First Baptist Church.

Maddox Avenue Baptist Church is a great church. Its pastor, George Crittenden, came to the First Baptist Church one night – well, he had imbibed too much, but he was converted and baptized in the First Baptist Church and he has built one of the great churches of the whole country.

Ross Avenue Baptist Church, of which Lloyd Adams is pastor, he, too, was converted and baptized in the First Baptist Church, as well as a large number of his members.

The Gideon Church, of which George Norris is pastor. He was converted, baptized, educated and trained in the First Baptist

Church. He was co-pastor with his father for a while, and he has built a great church some three or four miles from the First Baptist Church. He is a successful evangelist as well as pastor.

There are many other churches that have gone out from the First Baptist Church and instead of weakening the First Church, it has grown stronger.

Of course, some times, as to be expected, they go out with bitterness and strife but they get over it, and as the Apostle Paul wrote the church at Philippi – "What then? notwithstanding, every way, whether in pretence, or in truth, Christ is preached; and I therein do rejoice, yea and will rejoice." (Phil. 1:18).

The same thing has been true of the Temple Baptist Church. Many have , gone out and organized new churches, and it is natural, like it is even with children and their parents – some times the children get mad at the father and mother who gave them life and educated them.

Nevertheless, the work, the influence of these two great churches is manifest.

But the greatest mission work of the First Baptist Church has been throughout the Baptist denomination and religious world. Dr. Victor I, Masters, long-time editor of the Western Recorder, said – "Frank Norris saved Southern Baptists from evolution and modernism."

The Sunday School Board at Nashville adopted many of the plans and methods of the First Baptist Church which pioneered them.

The two largest Sunday Schools in the world, the First Baptist and Temple Baptist, have furnished hundreds of workers to the whole religious world.

# CHAPTER VI

## THE GREAT TENT CAMPAIGN IN DETROIT

Norris went to Detroit in 1934 and held a meeting for E. J. Rollings. The Temple Baptist Church was without a pastor and they called him to be pastor.

It was a typical city church of some eight hundred to a thousand members. It was a mixed breed. The majority were Fundamentalists, but a strong modernistic minority, and they were in the machine and of the machine.

Norris had no notion of leaving Fort Worth. He had been called to the largest cities of the east several times and always declined.

The Temple Church made the proposition for Norris to divide his time between Fort Worth and Detroit. The First Church agreed also.

It was, humanly speaking, an impossible task for a man to be pastor of two churches thirteen hundred miles apart. But he came to the conclusion that if God wanted him to do it he would undertake it. Many of his strongest friends begged and pled with him not to try it.

For instance, Dr. W. B. Riley and he were very close friends at that time, and he came to Detroit and told Norris,

"You will fail. You will break in two in the middle. You will lose your church in Fort Worth and will not be able to build here. And besides, you can't build a Baptist Church in the North like you do down South. It will have to be on interdenominational lines."

But Norris came, and soon after he went to Detroit the church asked me to be joint pastor with him. Talk about opposition! We had it within and without!

All the ecclesiastical powers, not only of Baptists, but the Detroit Council of Churches, the Federal Council of Churches – it was fulfillment of Acts 4:27,

"For of a truth against thy holy child Jesus, whom thou hast anointed, both Herod, and Pontius Pilate, with the Gentiles, and the people of Israel, were gathered together."

Frankly, I was scared of the whole proposition. But such venturesome faith I never saw. He got a big parcel of land of several acres on Oakman Boulevard and Grand River. Colonel Robert Oakman owned it, and he was living at that time. He had been mayor of the city. In fact he had been a very decided factor in the life of Detroit for many years. He was regarded as hard to approach, but Norris approached him and secured the lot without charge.

He got the big circus tent that Henry Ford had used at the World's Fair, and for three months and two weeks we ran that meeting, Norris doing the preaching.

And there was not a single service that people were not saved and came into the church.

The very hugeness of the tent challenged the attention of the whole city. Multitudes driving by thought a circus had come to town – and it had!

There was a circus nearby, a short distance away on the same plot of ground, and it greatly disturbed the meeting. And a storm came up and lightning hit that circus tent and tore it to pieces, and our tent was untouched.

Time Magazine published that Norris prayed for God to strike the circus tent with lightning, and he was severely criticized for such an imprecatory prayer.

I was present and no such prayer was prayed. If he did pray it, he certainly got the answer.

This is just one of the ten thousand examples of the many falsehoods that have gone out concerning this man, which he never answers. He takes as his motto I Peter 2:15,

"For so is the will of God that with well doing ye may put to silence the ignorance of foolish men."

I never saw a meeting of such power. Three different Sundays more than a hundred people were saved and came into the church.

Of the more than a thousand new members that came into the church 85% of them came by baptism, and the Temple Baptist Church in the new and larger life was born.

And this joint-pastorate is now 13 years duration. Last year, 1946, there were 3126 additions to both churches, and total cash raised $443,000, and he has the ablest company of helpers.

A part of the crowd attending revival led be Dr. J. Frank Norris in five-pole tent Oakman Boulevard and Grand River Avenue, Detroit, Michigan. The tent covered 45,000 square feet and seats over 8,000.

Dr. Norris preaching in the famous Spurgeon's Church, London.

# CHAPTER VII

### THE TRIPLE MAJOR OPERATION IN DETROIT

**(Two hour ten minute address of Dr. J. Frank Norris at the Temple Baptist Church, 14th and Marquette, Detroit, Michigan, Sunday, January 13, 1935, at 3 P. M.)**

(Only brief summary of address given)

DR. NORRIS: There are many Scriptures which I could read to you clearly setting forth the absolute necessity of a separated church life. Second Corinthians 6:14-18 is an unequivocal command for a separated church life. "What concord hath Christ with Belial" – or "What communion hath light with darkness?" And Revelation 18:4 says for us to come out from among them and "be not partakers of her sins."

It is all right for the boat to be in the water, but when the water gets in the boat, you had better get out. We are in Babylon but we should not be of Babylon.

Next Sunday this church is going to adopt a one hundred per cent fundamentalist Confession of Faith. It is not enough to affirm certain things, but we must deny some things. For instance, every great truth in the Scriptures first denies error and then affirms truth.

To illustrate the New Birth, negatively, "Which were born, not of blood, nor of the will of the flesh, nor of the will of man," – "But – affirmatively – "But of God." "Being born again," – negatively – "not of corruptible seed, but" – affirmatively – "but of incorruptible by the word of God, which liveth and abideth forever."

Take the method of inspiration of the Scriptures, first, negatively, a denial of error, "For the prophecy came not in old time by the will of man:" – now affirmatively – "but holy men of God spake as they were moved by the Holy Ghost."

Take baptism, "The like figure whereunto even baptism doth also now save us" – How? First, negatively – "(not the putting away of the filth of the flesh,"—not the forgiveness of sins, and now affirmatively – "but the answer of a good conscience toward God) by the resurrection of Jesus Christ."

In this proposed Confession of Faith which the Temple Church will adopt next Sunday morning, notice how carefully the great doctrines are stated; first, negatively; second, affirmatively – following the twofold Scriptural method.

Take for example the article on the inspiration of the Scriptures, here it is both negatively and affirmatively stated.

And we have both negative and positive statement of the doctrine of creation.

"We believe in the Genesis account of creation, and that it is to be accepted literally, and not allegorically or figuratively; that man was created directly in God's own image and after His own likeness; that man's creation was not a matter of evolution or evolutionary change of species, or development through interminable periods of time from lower to higher forms; that all animal and vegetable life was made directly, and God's established law was they should bring forth only 'after their kind'."

No Modernist will sign that. If he does he will join the Ananias Club the day he signs it.

Of the Virgin Birth, we say:

"We believe that Jesus Christ was begotten of the Holy Ghost in a miraculous manner; born of Mary, a virgin, as no other man was ever born or can ever be born of woman, and that he is both the Son of God and God the Son."

No Modernist will sign that.

The point I am making is that error must be defined and repudiated. A simple affirmation is not sufficient. Modernists, dishonest as they are, will sign any affirmative statement, with mental reservations, then give their own interpretation.

This is the Scriptural method of all the inspired writers.

Why do we have the letter to the Galatians? First, to deny Judaistic legalism on the one hand, and affirm justification by faith on the other. Why do we have the letter to the Colossians? First, to deny the false philosophy of the Gnostics on the one hand, and affirm the fullness and preeminence of Christ on the other.

Thus I might illustrate with all the books of the Bible.

I want to talk this afternoon particularly about this 13th Article.

"We believe that a church of Christ is a congregation of baptized believers associated by a covenant of faith and fellowship of the gospel; observing the ordinances of Christ; governed by His laws, and exercising the gifts, rights and privileges invested in them by His Word; that its officers of ordination are pastors or elders and deacons, whose qualifications, claims and duties are clearly defined in the Scriptures; we believe the true mission of the church is found in the Great Commission; First, to make individual disciples; Second, to build up the church; Third, to teach and instruct, as He has commanded. We do not believe in the reversal of this order; we hold that the local church has the absolute right of self government, free from the interference of any hierarchy of individuals or organizations; and that the one and only superintendent is Christ through the Holy Spirit; that it is Scriptural for true churches to cooperate with each other in contending for the faith and for the furtherance of the gospel; that every church is the sole and only judge of the measure and method of its cooperation; on all matters of membership, of policy, of government, of discipline, of benevolence, the will of the local church is final."

By this time next Sunday afternoon the will of this church is going to be one of love and unanimous membership; we are going to adopt that article!

(Applause.)

If anybody doubts this, let them come and see. Our authority is supreme and it can be in all things affirmed by the people of this church, and cannot be controlled by the Michigan Baptist

Convention. But they claim to judge everything. We come today to discuss that question. They are not final on all matters. A Baptist church has the right to run its own affairs. I am going to tell you, my friends, that is the biggest issue today among Baptists. It is the issue in the South, in the West, the issue in the North; the issue in Michigan. It is the issue in Detroit. It is the issue in the Temple Baptist Church right here this afternoon!

(Congregation: Amen!)

To show you that is the issue in Michigan, you, Brother Pease, from Jackson, stand up, please.

My friends, this is Dr. J. J. Pease, pastor of the Loomis Park Baptist Church of Jackson.

DR. PEASE. I was born in Michigan, and most of my 27 years in the ministry has been in this state, and during the last six years I have been pastor of the Loomis Park Baptist Church in Jackson.

The Baptist Association where my church is located is composed of 26 churches. Without and boasting, but that you may know the character of my work during this six years, our church had a larger increase than ony other church in the Association. In one years we took in more than all the other churches in the Association.

I have spent most of my ministry trying to coperate with the Michigan Baptist Convention. But a long time ago I saw the drift of things, and more and more as a matter of conscience I could not cooperate with what I considered unscriptural practices.

The issue came up in our churchy and the church stood by three-fourths majority with me in my contention for the Truth against error, in my stand for old time Baptist beliefs and practices.

But this minority went to the Convention headquarters to get aid and support in seeking to overthrow and set aside the will of three to one majority. They received that aid, and caused much trouble in the church.

The Convention officials in control started whole trouble, and requested a meeting with the Jackson Association. The officials did this with the announced purpose of getting the Jackson

Association to recognize the minority group of our church; and if the minority should be recognized, the majority would be repudiated, and that would mean that the minority would control the Loomis Park Baptist Church. Their plans were to lay a predicate for court action, showing that the majority was not regular, but that the minority was regular because recognized by the Convention headquarters.

We had a Board of twelve members, and it was unanimous. The Chairman is here with me on the platform. There was a Committee of five appointed, and two members of that Committee reported to me what took place. They told me that the State Secretary, Dr. Andem, labored for more than two hours with that Committee. The whole purpose was to turn the property over to the minority by going through the courts. Here is where the Convention officials did everything in their power to defeat the will of the local church.

And this forced the church to take drastic action on certain leaders of this minority troublesome group who were in official position.

The property and land contracts were in the hands of this minority, and we were forced to hire a lawyer to protect the rights of the church and force the property to be turned over to the church, the rightful owners. We had to come to Detroit and hire a good lawyer, for we were afraid to trust a Jackson attorney. (Laughter.) (The name of the Detroit lawyer is Hon. John C. Winter.) This lawyer sent several notices to these people, yet they refused to turn the property back to the Trustees, and when the Convention officials saw what was about to take place, the officials backed down, and in two or three days the property was in the hands of the Trustees of the church. But they kept up the fight.

DR. NORRIS: Where is the Chairman of the Board? This is Brother Kent. I am not going to call on you to speak. This is the Chairman of the Board of Trustees. What is your occupation?

MR. KENT: I am a dentist.

DR. NORRIS: Then I don't want to have anything to do with you.

(Laughter.)

DR. NORRIS: This is S. E. Kent, Chairman of the Board. Has Dr. Pease stated this correctly?

MR. KENT: Yes, only he hasn't told half.

(Laughter and applause.)

DR. NORRIS: Here is Brother E. Roloff Jackson. He has had a similar experience. I just want him to say whether or not they have been interfering with his church and trying to regulate them.

REV. E. ROLOFF JACKSON: Well, our experience was something similar to Brother Pease's, except that the Convention was successful in removing us from the Wall Street Baptist Church. They had a secret session. An active member was Judge Hate –

DR. NORRIS: What is his name? (Laughter.)

REV. JACKSON: Judge Hate, of the Michigan Baptist Convention was in the city. They were successful in getting us out. With the pastor of the church, 75% of the active members went out, the whole Board of Deacons, half of the Trustees, the whole Sunday School staff of the church, and one Sunday School teacher, and the Church Treasurer and the Financial Secretary. 75% of the active church membership remained loyal to the pastor and to the Lord Jesus Christ, and we have stepped out now, and, as in Romans 8:28, we are all doing work. We are happy in our work, and have no bones to pick with the Michigan Baptist Convention. We are just glad we are rid of them.

(Applause.)

DR. NORRIS: My purpose in calling attention to these two churches is that they are right here under our door, right in front of us. What you have heard this afternoon has been going on from one end of this land to the other, and in Heaven's name, it is time for it to stop!

(Congregation: Amen!)

(Applause.)

That is what is going on right here in Temple Baptist Church, and we are going to stop it!

(Applause.)

We have already stopped a part of it, and we are going to take care of the rest of their hides, beginning with a Mr. Tanner, and not Simon the tanner. (Applause.)

Let me tell you something. This thing called Modernism – I have ten thousand times more respect for any Catholic that is faithful to Roman Cotholicism than I have for Modernism, because they do believe in God and in Christ and in immortality, and these modern infidels don't believe in anything! It is high time that the Christian world was waking up to the fact that Modernism comes like Absalom stealing the hearts of Israel and at the same time stealing the crown of our Lord. It comes like Judas Iscariot with "Hail, Master!", and with a sardonic smile with the price of blood in its hand. "Come out from among them," is the Word of God, "and be ye separate."

That is what Modernism does. They are doing that everywhere. They "cuckooed" the Congregationalists when the Unitarians took charge of the Congregationalists of America, and they have been "cuckooing" the Methodists, and they are trying to "cuckoo" the Baptists, but bless God we have got that old cuckoo bird by the neck, and they are not going to cuckoo the Baptists and break them down!

(Applause.)

Somebody says, "Well, we have just a few modernists in our church." You get a barrel of apples. You put three rotten apples in the barrel and which will change? You put a pole cat in this room and which will change? (Laughter,)

Let me tell you what has been going on, no matter what anybody says. In 1925, the Northern Baptists held a convention in Seattle. Dr. W. B. Hinson submitted a resolution requesting our foreign missionaries to say they believed, first, in the Inspiration of the Bible; second, in the Virgin Birth of Christ; third, in the Atonement of Christ on the cross; fourth, in the Resurrection of Christ; and fifth, in the New Birth of the soul. You would have thought any Baptist on earth would have signed that, but the Northern Baptist

Convention turned it down two to one, and said, "We will send out both modernist and fundamentalist missionaries." That is what they said.

Send out missionaries that don't believe in the inspiration of the Bible! Send out missionaries that deny the atonement of Christ! Send out missionaries that deny the Virgin Birth of Christ! Send out missionaries that deny the resurrection of Christ! In Heaven's name, what are they going to preach? They cannot walk together except they be agreed. "What accord hath Christ with Belial," or "What communion hath light with darkness?" That is what is going on.

**The Modernism of the World Baptist Alliance**

The World Baptist Alliance is run by a bunch of modernists – and as proof of the rank modernism go back to the Stockholm meeting when the late Dr. A. C. Dixon offered a simple resolution that the World Baptist Alliance give to the world a platform of principles. The resolution stated:

We believe,

1. In the Divine inspiration of the Scriptures.
2. In the Virgin Birth of Christ.
3. In the Deity of Christ.
4. In the Atonement of Christ.
5. In the Resurrection of Christ.

And the World Baptist Alliance turned it down overwhelmingly, and instead thereof adopted a platform of "internationalism," "fraternalism," et cetera.

And let me say here the World Baptist Alliance is the biggest cuckoo frame-up ever known among Baptists. Dr. J. H. Rushbrook is a rank modernist, and when he comes South he preaches orthodox sermons – he is the Secretary of the World Baptist Alliance.

Dr. A. W. Beaven of Rochester University is one of the smoothest modernists, and he too when he goes South speaks oily words of orthodoxy. His is the hidden hand of the North American Continent that is directing this modernistic World Baptist Alliance, and he reached down South and got Dr. George W. Truett, and uses him as a wall-flower, and their next meeting is scheduled to be held among Southern Baptists, but the great majority of Southern Baptists are not in sympathy with it, for they have long since learned to "beware of the Greeks when they bring their gifts." And this modernistic machine has got Dr. George W. Truett going up and down the land speaking in behalf of their scheme; although he extends the hand of orthodoxy, yet the hidden voice is that of modernism.

By the way, do you know who Dr. George Truett has as a pulpit supply? Dean Shailer Mathews of Chicago University! (Groans from the audience.)

No wonder you are surprised. But he is the best defender or representative the modernists of the North have in the South. Oh, he is orthodox, he plays the part, of Jehoshaphat.

Mr. Chairman, would you allow Shailer Mathews, the arch modernist of Chicago University, to preach in this pulpit?

CHAIRMAN: No, sir.

DR. NORRIS: That's what happened to the First Baptist Church at Dallas. That is the hidden hand behind all this upheaval.

We have had a great many upheavals in Texas and in the South, over Modernism.

### The Texas Fight

There have been all kinds of falsehoods sent broadcast throughout the Northland.

But what are the facts? Some fifteen years ago I exposed the first evolutionist in my Alma Mater, Baylor University, This evolutionist was one of the head professors, and wrote with his own hand that man came from the anthropoid ape, and this book was published by the Baylor University Press. I didn't believe it then, and I don't believe it now, and I protested against it, and I made no apology for it then, and I do not now, denying that man came from the ape.

(Applause.)

Before we were through there were eight anthropoid apes twisted out of the faculty of Baylor University.

But the interesting thing about it all was that "the powers that be," and the Board of Trustees, and the President of the University stood for the last one of these apes, and they only resigned when the aroused sentiment of the denomination forced them to resign.

And Dr. George W. Truett, instead of standing against these materialistic evolutionists, defended every last one of them, on the one hand and lost his temper, and denounced in a public address the man who had the courage to expose the evolution. He called him "damnable and despicable."

All these things are matters of record.

### Talk About Ecclesiastical Dictation

In the beginning of the Seventy-five Million Campaign, put on at the same time you had your One-hundred Million Dollar Promotion Drive in the North, a group of denominational despots called on me in my office, and demanded I take their apportionment of $100,000.00. I quietly informed them I did not believe in that method, and my conviction was then, and is now, that every church has the right and the sole right of naming how, what, when, and the method of its liberality, and that no set of men on the face of the earth has a right to even suggest what the local church will do, much less dictate to it. But this group of political, ecclesiastical dictators, headed by Dr. L. R. Scarborough, the head of the Southwestern Baptist Theological Seminary, said to me:

"Now, Norris, if you don't cooperate and put on this drive, we will brand you to the ends of the earth as a noncooperating Baptist, and you will lose out; you will not have any crowds to hear you, your church will disintegrate."

That was fifteen years ago!

You can look around this afternoon and judge whether or not they were false prophets. (Laughter and applause.)

Just think of it, a Baptist Church excluded from the Convention for the two following reasons:

First, because the church decided to exercise its sovereign right and throw the literature overboard and use the Bible only, plus nothing and minus nothing.

Second, because the church decided it had the inalienable right to order and run its own affairs, rather than take the dictation of the unscriptural Seventy-Five Million Dollar Campaign Committee.

But the interesting and amusing thing, this ill fated action on the part of the machine cost the Convention – well, they were out of debt, and now they owe over six million dollars. Then they had three thousand churches cooperating with the headquarters, now they have only about six hundred that send in contributions each month. The records speak for themselves. Then they had a great army of laymen, now they have practically all quit.

The machine must be congratulated, however, in finally waking up to the terrible consequence of their course toward the First Baptist Church. Instead of it putting the church out of business it put it in business. They gave it hearing around the world, and thousands upon thousands have been saved at home and abroad through the ministry of the First Baptist Church. How true is Philippians 1:12: "But I would ye should understand, brethren, that the things which happened unto me have fallen out rather unto the furtherance of the gospel."

Then the church had no radio, and it now has a radio that covers the great Southwest and part of the East.

The church had no paper then, now it has a paper four times the size of the average denominational paper.

But that is not all. Last fall at the State Convention at San Antonio the Convention repealed the Article in its constitution that put the First Baptist Church out of the Convention, and now they want the church to come back, but sooner would we break into a graveyard or crawl through a jail door – we are free!

We are happy; we are united – "For that a notable miracle hath been done by them is manifest to all them that dwell in Jerusalem; and we cannot deny it."

They sent out this unscriptural demand, dictating to the churches how much money they should raise, in a large envelope that had on the outside in crescent shape red letters these words:

"Seventy-five Million Campaign."

I had received that letter some few days before the excathedra demand of the coterie of these ecclesiastical dictators. I reached over on my desk and took the envelope with this demand and tore it to pieces without saying a word, and then crumpled the pieces in my right hand and cast the pieces at the feet of these dictators, and said: "That's my answer to your papal demands."

(Prolonged applause.)

And, ladies and gentlemen, I would not have had any self respect if I had done otherwise. (Applause.)

They proceeded at once to carry out their threats, and they went after me hot and strong, and believe me, we had a merry-go-round for many years in the Lone Star State.

I didn't have any paper or radio at that time. I told them they had the advantage of me. They circularized the whole country. They published article after article in all their machine papers. They misrepresented my church. They sent out hundreds of thousands of tracts – one series of six – and the President of the Seminary, Dr. L. R. Scarborough, sent out one hundred thousand tracts, paid for by the corrupt mayor of Fort Worth, because I exposed his crookedness. The tracts were entitled, "The Fruits of Norrisism." They even hired time for seven nights on the radio and called me everything on earth – the most blistering and vitriolic terms that ever fell from the lips of man. It is doubtful if even John Dillinger would have used the language that they used.

### Great Revival Followed Hate-Feet

What an indictment of the Texas Baptist Machine from the pen of Dr. W. B, Riley as published in his magazine, "the Pilot"!

And this was the prevailing opinion among all fair people East and West, North and South. While they were on the air I thought of the old adage, "Whom the gods destroy they first make mad."

I went on the radio immediately when they signed off, preached the Gospel of salvation.

There was something coming back through the darkness of the night – it was between 10:30 and 11:30 P. M. Everybody could feel the hush! Presently a telephone rang and a call for me. The girl at the telephone said: "He is on the radio and cannot talk to you," but a woman in tears said: "I must talk to him. My husband is saved!"

And a note was put on the desk in front of me while I was talking and I called the quartette to the radio and said to the listeners, "Excuse me, I have an important call at the telephone."

The first I heard was the shoutings of this good woman, and she said: "My husband is saved, and he wants to tell you about it."

He came to the phone and said:

"This is J. R. Thompson, Greenville, and I listened to the bitterness and vilification with joy and delight. I have been your bitter enemy – I have hated you. I have cursed you, but I realized a few minutes ago that I was going to the judgment, and I fell on my knees and called on God for mercy and my wife prayed for me and I am saved, and I wish you would tell the brethren and all the world that I know I am saved."

I went back and reported it over the radio. A mother phoned from Tyler, Texas, saying: "My boy was at his filling station tonight and heard what they said against you and then listened to your Gospel message and came running home and is here and I will let him tell you how he was saved."

And all the way through the eight nights and on the Sunday following 142 people united with the church, most of them for baptism. Perhaps the most remarkable case of conversion through the radio hate-fest was Mrs. A Ellig. She had a large party in her home with liquor on the table and while they were drinking and gambling they wrung their hands with glee at the cussing and abuse that was heaped upon the head of J. Frank Norris by the denominational leaders.

But when the next hour, the message of salvation, of sin and judgment, went into that same drinking, wicked company, tins woman fell on her face and cried out before them all, "I am lost, I am lost!" And she was most gloriously saved.

And it ended that drinking party!

The next Sunday she stood before the great audience and told the whole story and she and her dear husband are two of the most active soul winners in the First Baptist Church today.

If there was ever an occasion where the Scriptures were vindicated it was during these eight nights of the hate-fest, "But I would ye should understand, brethren, that the things which happened unto me have fallen out rather unto the furtherance of the gospel;" – Philippians 1:12.

### The Master Mind Behind the Radio Hate Feet

As is now well known, and has been known for many years – it is no longer a secret as to the master mind back of the radio hate feet. In truth there was no secret at the time. His highness, the chief priest of that year, called several secret councils and all for one purpose – "This man" – "This man" – "This man" – "This man must be eliminated."

Some who have passed to their reward protested in the council, and among those who protested was Dr. S. P. Brooks, President of Baylor University, even though he was pulled into the debate and against his will.

Immediately after the debate started the first morning, this high priest that had pushed everybody into it sent out an S. O. S. call and said,

"Scarborough fumbled the ball last night. Norris went rings around him. It is a regular tom cat fight. He is conducting a revival meeting. My telephone has been ringing all night long. Telegrams are pouring in Just one week of this will ruin everything."

Dr. Scarborough was not present and they called him by long distance and told him that the radio hate fest must be called off. And Scarborough was consistent and said,

"What we have begun we must finish" – and it was finished.

Dr. F. S. Groner at that time was superintendent of missions. He was also pushed off into it by the same high priest, and after this high priest cut Groner's throat, and he did it after he had entered into solemn agreement that "We will stand together to the last ditch" – Groner and the high priest had one final meeting at a restaurant in Dallas when he told the high priest,

"Your course and conduct in my affairs is the most diabolical and cowardly that was ever known."

For full particulars of this whole mad radio hate fest, communicate with Dr. F. S. Groner, President Marshall College, Marshall, Texas. And for further information communicate with Dr. E. C. Routh, Editor of the Baptist Messenger, Oklahoma City. Dr. Groner has since passed to his reward. He was a great man.

### Ecclesiastical Hate When Born of Deep and Long Standing Conspiracy Goes to Any Length to Accomplish Its Purpose

That the Sanhedrin would bribe one of the twelve, is characteristic of the Ecclesiastical Sanhedrins of all ages. As was to be expected there were many who were unstable, others who were untrue and some who played the part of Judas Iscariot.

More than once it was found that the First Baptist Church was actually paying the salaries of tools of the enemies of the church but this is a characteristic of the nations when they go to war, and the First Baptist Church was in a greater war than with flesh and blood, than when the nations of the earth go to battle with each other. "For we wrestle not against flesh and blood, but against principalities, against powers, against the rulers of the darkness of this world, against spiritual wickedness in high places." – Eph. 6:12.

### Statement of H. M. Harris, One of Fort Worth's Best Known Citizens

There was a young man converted and baptized into the First Baptist Church and was in its office force as bookkeeper and then as superintendent and later entered the ministry. He did not have the courage to resist the inducements of the Sanhedrin and he went on the radio. Here is the statement of one of the best known business men in the city of Fort Worth which tells the true story of the pitiful treachery of the former employee of the First Baptist Church:

"In the fall of 1927 I was listening to a red hot debate between a group of Baptist preachers on one side and Dr. J. Frank Norris on the other, and I heard one of these Baptist preachers state substantially as follows:

" 'That you may know what kind of a man Dr. J. Frank Norris is, the First Baptist Church sold certain properties and he, Dr. Norris, charged the church with $7,500 commission and charged it to the name of a firm called Harris and Hyde. I was bookkeeper of the church at that time, and there was no such firm of Harris and Hyde, and Dr. Norris used this name as a fake to collect from this sale $7,500 for himself.'

"When I heard this my amazement knew no bounds because I and my partner, Mr. Hyde, did make the sale, and we did receive the $7,500 commission. And Dr. J. Frank Norris did not receive one cent of it.

"And while the radio discussion was going on I called up and made this statement and it was given to the public. And the preacher who made the false charge never had the decency to make the retraction and apology." (Signed) H. M. Harris.

Mr. H. M. Harris' address is 1415 Petroleum building, Sixth and Throckmorton, Fort Worth, Texas, and his telephone is 3-1997.

The above answer to the $7,500 false charge could have been published to the world, but the policy was never to answer and let the God that answers by fire – let Him be God. Thousands heard this slander by this preacher over the radio. He was forced to tell it.

A pitiful thing is that this preacher afterwards sold his influence to the gamblers of Fort Worth and in return his son received a small mess of pottage. All the lawyers and citizens of Fort Worth know of this deal.

This information is public property, therefore privileged to repeat. Only the most pitiful attitude should be held for this twice sold preacher.

The mantle of charity should be pulled down over the conduct of the preacher who made this false statement over the radio. He came into the office of the pastor of the First Baptist Church and wept and said he was forced to do things against his will. He told how one of the high priests called him into his office, and this was in the beginning of the denominational controversy. The high priest scared the young preacher out of his wits and convinced him that they were going to "ruin Norris."

This is in keeping with the methods that the Sanhedrin followed, for instance, they sent another young fellow out to see an old man by the name of P. P. Pierce. The old man had been in the asylum and went again afterwards, and this representative of the Sanhedrin got him to sign a statement that he could not read, and said afterwards he never did read it, and the statement read as follows:

"This is to certify J. Frank Norris stole $50,000 from me and still has it." (Signed) P. P. Pierce.

Honorable R. V. Patterson, a great lawyer at Decatur, Texas, and who was with the machine, made a thorough investigation of the Pierce Affidavit.

Dr. J. L. Ward, President of Decatur College, had the dear old man at Decatur and was going to give out the affidavit to a huge crowd, but Mr. Pierce told Judge Patterson,

"I did not know I signed it and J. Frank Norris never stole any money from me."

But Dr. Ward went on the radio and read the above affidavit and the Sanhedrin photographed and sent it throughout the Southern Baptist Convention.

That it was proved to be a fake did not lessen the circulation of it, and even after they found it out they never had the courage to confess their sins.

But the $7,500 false statement and the $50,000 fake affidavit were just samples of the floods of propaganda over the radio and in the denominational press.

The pitiful situation is that the same former employee of the First Baptist Church was the same tool that was used by the Sanhedrin before the young preachers at the Seminary, giving the false testimony that Norris owned the property of the First Baptist Church. Also he gave circulation to the fake $50,000 affidavit as well as numerous other slanderous reports.

But he probably should not be blamed, for it may be an inherited weakness. And when the young priests are tempted by the high priests with promotion – things have not changed since Samuel's day – I Sam. 2:36, "And it shall come to pass, that every one that is left in thine house shall come and crouch to him for a piece of silver and a morsel of bread, and shall say, Put me, I pray thee, into one of the priests' offices, that I may eat a piece of bread."

## Norris Owns the First Baptist Church

It was amusing as well as pitiful the volumes and volumes of propaganda that the denominational leaders broadcast through the land. It was, indeed, the serpent casting out of his mouth tracts, leaflets, publications "as a flood."

A typical example of their propaganda was "NORRIS OWNS THE PROPERTY OF THE FIRST BAPTIST CHURCH." Young preachers were called together in the Seminaries and denominational colleges and instructed to tell this to their people.

And they did!

The young preachers believed it and so did other people!

And it did not matter with the leaders that the deed of records were open to the public and showed that the property, every bit of it, was owned by the First Baptist Church, and Norris did not own one square inch of it.

But the mischief was done!

Anything to destroy Norris!

"And there were above forty in this conspiracy."

### Tracts Circulated Ahead of Norris

There was a series of six tracts, telling the world who Norris was, and in addition, "The fruits of Norrisism" by the President of the Seminary. Everywhere I went for a meeting these tracts were sent on ahead.

Take for example, the Euclid Avenue Baptist Church in Cleveland, Dr. W. W. Bustard was then living and the pastor. This great church wired me to come and hold a meeting for them and the week before I arrived every member of the church received these tracts.

Of course, tracts from the leaders of the denomination greatly disturbed many good people. The pastor and the deacons met and discussed it but decided for me to come on, and again: "But I would ye should understand, brethren, that the things which happened unto me have fallen out rather unto the furtherance of the gospel."

Everybody came – some out of curosity, some out of sympathy, some out of contempt, but the Lord came also and more than two hundred new members came into the church, and at the close of the meeting over $500,000.00 was raised to build a new building and one woman who was converted and baptized into the church, led the offering with $55,000.00.

### Tracts on Door-Steps of People of Fort Worth

On Saturday nights these tracts would be distributed on the door-steps of the homes of the people of Fort Worth. While they prejudiced a great many, yet they interested a large number and they came to hear the Gospel and were saved.

## "Norris Refused to Pay for Literature and Was Cut Off"

This is the statement that the Secretary of the Sunday School Board, Dr. I. J. Van Ness, told his field men to circulate throughout the South and they did. Something had to be done to counteract the rapid decrease of the literature of the Board by churches that were throwing it out of the window and putting the Bible only, plus nothing and minus nothing, as their only text book.

This was far from the truth because the First Baptist Church paid cash on delivery for all literature that it received from the Board, but the mischief was done.

Incidentally there was an audit of Dr. Van Ness' books and for ten years or more it was found that he had been giving huge contracts of printing to a printing company without competitive bids, and he had connection, with this company.

There was an estimated over-pay of more than $300,000.00.

Dr. Van Ness "resigned."

This is just a simple statement of the inside facts with malice toward none and love for all.

"So they hanged Haman on the gallows that he had prepared for Mordecai."

Baptizing at Lake Worth, Fort Worth, Texas.

# CHAPTER VIII

## NORRIS AN OLD-TIME AND ELOQUENT PREACHER OF THE GOSPEL

I shall never forget how he lifted a great audience to the third heaven when lie said – and I quote from one of his sermons:

"Now the first, the unspeakable, glorious truth that the Holy Spirit does come into the life or soul and body of the believer. The same divine Spirit which, in creation's morning, when darkness Covered the face of the deep and there was disorder and chaos and death, the Spirit of God moved upon the face of the deep and out of that brooding, that vital impact of the Spirit of God with matter, there came light out of darkness and order out of disorder and life out of death. Even so, the soul that is in disorder, in sin and in rebellion against God hath he quickened and raised up together with Christ and made him a child of God...

"We either have or we have not the Holy Spirit dwelling in us. If we are not filled with Him, let's go to the tap root of it, and find out what is the cause. Paul gives an X-ray picture of the soul in the greatest chapter in the Bible on the Holy Spirit, which is the eighth chapter of Romans:

" 'For they that are after the flesh do mind the things of the flesh; but they that are after the Spirit the things of the Spirit.

" 'For to be carnally minded,' fleshly minded, worldly minded, 'is death.'

"He is not talking about the death after this life. He is talking about the believer who is spiritually dead. He is talking about the fig tree with nothing but leaves. He is talking about clouds without water. He is talking about the born-agains who have lost their first love...

"That brings me then to our second proposition, that the believer is not his own but is bought with a price. I will not take time to dwell on it, but I do pray that some day I may have the gift of speech to expound so great a truth. I have the burden of soul, my soul set on fire that I can in some measure tell you what was that price.

"Oh, we can not fathom its depths; we cannot scale its heights; we cannot measure its breadths; we have no measure of its lengths, but I believe in that cry which David prophesied a thousand years before the cross when he said, 'My God, my God, why hast thou forsaken me!' It is God asking God! It is not man, it is God in man, but here are two persons. The world is shut out; the Son of God face to face with God, and the first time in all eternity was He forsaken of God...

"I am forsaken of all men. Friends have forsaken me. Dippest thou in the dish with me? Oh, Simon, thou who deniest me, oh, Judas who planted the kiss on my cheek, I was betrayed in the house of my friends, but, 'My God, why, why?' I can sum up all the wealth of the world – I could get the twenty-nine billions of gold and pile it up as high as Pike's Peak, but that was not the prise. I could get all the silver of the silver mines of the world and pile that silver higher than the dome of the Capitol at Washington, but that was not the price. I could take all the animals that were ever slain from the first lamb slain by Abel to the last sacrifice before the temple was destroyed, but that was not the price.

"I could take all the men that you can call great, all the philosophers and sages and statesmen, all together, and let them die, but that is not the price. But the Son of God who made yonder Stars and sun with His own hands, He said, 'I will give the price – Greater love hath no man than this, that he lay down his life for his friends.'

"He was offered by God the Father; He was offered by the Gentile world; a Gentile judge pronounced the sentence of death on Him; He was offered by His own people, Israel; He was offered by the eternal Spirit of God, and yet He said, 'I lay down my life.'

" 'Who for the joy that was set before him endured the cross despising the shame...' Why ? Because He shall see the travail of His soul. He was numbered with the transgressors; He poured out His soul unto death.

" 'How rich the depths of love divine!
Of bliss, a boundless store!
Dear Saviour, let me call thee mine;
I cannot wish for more.

" 'On thee alone my hope relies;
Beneath thy cross I fall,
My Lord, my life, my sacrifice,
My Saviour, and my all'."

"Listen, it is not the gambler and it is not the out breaking sins; 'but grieve not the Holy Spirit of God whereby ye are sealed unto the day of redemption. Let all bitterness, and wrath, and anger, and clamour, and evil speaking be put away from you with all malice.'

"The word drunkenness doesn't occur there. Isn't that an awful sin? The word 'adultery' doesn't occur there though that is a terrible, terrible sin. The word 'gambling' doesn't occur there, though that is a dishonest, terrible sin. But these are sins that there is no law in the State of Texas against. They are sins of the Amen corner, the Awomen corner. They are sins in the class, they are sins in the choir, they are sins in the pulpit.

### Why No Power

Then last, how there can be no prayer, and no power, no soul-winning if sin dwells in us instead of the Holy Spirit. I am not talking about energy of the flesh. Let me say this to you. I have been doing a lot of thinking of late. I have been reading and studying afresh, all the great revivals of history, and I want to make you an astounding statement this morning. I have not yet found one single great revival where there was any prayer for that revival. That shocks you. I want to emphasize that. There was never a great revival in history from Pentecost until now where they prayed for the revival.

"You say, 'What did they pray for?'

"Let me show you. Before Pentecost, you read in vain, where they were praying for the coming of the Holy Spirit. No, no. They were there and praying and having a surrendered life for those ten days getting ready for His coming.

"Why, Jesus said, 'I am going to send you the Holy Spirit. 'Then, it would be nonsense to pray for something that is certain to happen. But we are praying, not for more of Him, but that He might have more of us.

"This is nothing sudden with me. I have been going through with it for a long time, particularly for the last two years. I told you of the prayer of the old preacher when he baptized me. 'Take him, break him, and make him.' I am willing for the 'taking' and the 'making,' but I have never been willing for the 'breaking.' I come this morning and stand before my whole congregation, this huge auditorium filled, and to the radio listeners, with my heart open to you. If I could roll back all these years, oh, I would pray more, I would study my Bible more, I would win more souls; and I want to take you into the fullest confidence. God spoke this message. It is very definite. I am certain about it. This is the first time that I have given expression to it.

"What I have been through! My life is no secret; you know it. I have been through a great many tragedies and sorrows, and you know what has occurred to me, and I have done a lot of thinking about it. In the nighttime I hear it; in the daytime I hear it; when I am on a train or a plane I hear it. And I have been thinking deeply on this question!

"What, oh God speaking to my soul, What if you just once, once, fully, wholly, absolutely say 'Yes.' 'Yes, I will.' God says, 'I would like to show the world what I can do with a man that every mean thing on earth that ever could have been said or published or circulated for thirty years – I would like to show the world what I can do with that man, if you will let me. If you will let me! If you will let me! If you will let me.'

" 'Which dwelleth in you.'

"What would it mean? I want to close by saying that you will have the revival in this dark age whenever a group of people who are absolutely, with all self out, covetousness out, all sin of every kind out, and nailed to the cross with Him, then God says, I am ready, now, to use you.'

"I have tried to get from under my several responsibilities. One church is enough for any man and two is too many. The building of a great Seminary takes more time, blood and tears than administering one that is already built.

"I am not tired but I don't want to get tired, I have been through two serious operations the last year and the Lord healed both completely.

"I have thought much of the experience of Hezekiah when he was told to put his house in order –

" 'In those days was Hezekiah sick unto death. And Isaiah the prophet the son of Amoz came unto him, and said unto him, Thus saith the Lord, Set thine house in order: for thou shalt die, and not live.

" 'Then Hezekiah turned his face toward the wall, and prayed unto the Lord,

" 'And said, Remember now, O Lord, I beseech thee, how I have walked before thee in truth and with a perfect heart, and have done that which is good in thy sight, And Hezekiah wept sore.

" 'Then came the word of the Lord to Isaiah, saying,

" 'Go, and say to Hezekiah, Thus saith the Lord, the God of David thy father, I have heard thy prayer, I have seen thy tears: behold, I will add unto thy days fifteen years.' (Isa. 38:1-5).

"So, old stubborn me, I have had to take a new growth and the Lord has definitely assured me of many, many and more useful years, and I am ready to organize a Century Club. I am going day by day with John Henry Newman –

" 'Lead, kindly Light, amid th' encircling gloom, Lead Thou me on!

The night is dark, and I am far from home; Lead Thou me on!

Keep thou my feet; I do not ask to see...

The distant scene; one step enough for me

" 'I was not ever thus, nor prayed that Thou shouldst lead me on;

I loved to choose and see my path; but now Lead Thou me on!

I loved the garish day, in spite of fears,

Pride ruled my will. Remember not past years!"

"I hope I am ready this morning. I have been two years in coming to this. I have been longer than that. I am ready to say this morning, I don't care anything about my little success. Two preachers came the other morning and said, 'You should be a happy man, pastor of the two greatest churches in the world.' That doesn't appeal to me any more.

"Preaching to the largest crowds of any preacher on earth – but that doesn't appeal to me any more. I am not concerned about that. I am not interested in that.

"I want this great audience to join with me in prayer, then after the prayer, we will quietly file out. We will sing, 'Holy Ghost with Light Divine,' which will be our benediction."

# CHAPTER IX

## "BUT GOD" – THE GREATEST SERVICE IN THE HISTORY OP THE FIRST BAPTIST CHURCH

**Sermon by Dr. J. Frank Norris, First Baptist Church, Fort Worth, Texas**

(Stenographically Reported)

(A great crisis was on in the church. Much misunderstanding and many false rumors and reports were published in the papers. Dr. Norris was absent from the city in an evangelistic campaign. His office force called him by long distance phone when the crisis broke and newspapers headlined it. He refused to come back to issue a statement, and a week later there was read to the congregation this telegram:

"Regarding the matters that have been widely published I will return in two weeks and give an answer."

A great crowd was present. It was a scorching hot Sunday in July. People were not only packed around the wall but standing on the outside looking in. There was intense anxiety. Dr. Norris rose and said,

"Regarding the matter that has been so widely published I did it. I assume the entire responsibility. I did it for you. My text this morning is just two words, 'But God'."

That was the only explanation he gave and the whole incident that had caused so much discussion immediately became past history. His method through the years of meeting great crisis is to leave the whole thing in the hands of the great God of the universe.)

DR. NORRIS: I invite your attention to four Scriptures:

The first is found in Ephesians second chapter, fourth verse, "But God, who is rich in mercy, for his great love wherewith he loved us."

The second is found in the last chapter of Genesis – the words of Joseph to his eleven brethren, Genesis 50:20 "But as for you, ye thought evil against me; but God meant it unto good, to bring to pass, as it is this day, to save much people alive. Now therefore fear ye not."

The third Scripture is found in I Cor. 15th chapter and 38th verse, "But God giveth it a body as it hath pleased him, and to every seed his own body."

The fourth Scripture is found in the book of Daniel on the momentous occasion when Daniel stood before Nebuchadnezzar and interpreted his dream, that the wise men of Babylon could neither tell nor understand, "But there is a God in heaven that revealeth secrets, and maketh known to the king Nebuchadnezzar what shall be in the latter days."

A very interesting thing happened last week, two of the best women in this church, neither knowing what the other said, said to me, "You preached a sermon many years ago on two words that linger in my soul, I wish you would preach that sermon on those two words again." Unfortunately I did not make any notes on the sermon, and when I had the sermon looked up – it was gone – I guess it's all right.

Those two words – I counted them at one time – and they occur 252 times in the whole Bible – there may be more than that number.

The two words are found in the four Scriptures which I read to you.

First, found in Ephesians 2:4.

Second, found in Gen. 50;20.

Third, found in I Cor. 15:38.

Fourth, found in Daniel 2:28.

Around these four statements can be summed up all the destiny of the soul of man.

There are four things that a man needs:

1. He needs salvation.
2. He needs comfort and grace in the struggles of life.
3. He needs to have an answer to the question of what is beyond this life.
4. He needs to understand what is going on in this present turbulent world.

If you answer those four questions you will have a true philosophy of life.

I repeat them.

1st. A man must know that he is saved – saved from something to something. Saved from sin to righteousness. Saved from hell to heaven. Saved from death to life; and

2nd. After he is saved he must have the answer to the problems of suffering in this world; in other words, a daily supply for his needs as he journeys through this pilgrimage here below; and

3rd. When he looks into the open grave he must have an answer to, "Is there a life beyond this life?"

4th. When he sees that all civilization is going down, governments crashing right and left, he must understand that there is the Hand that guides it all.

The first of these expressions is found in Ephesians 2:4, "But God" – as I said before I counted them once, and they occur 252 times, I marked them in my Bible, but it was lost in the fire.

There is our salvation – as I said to a dearly beloved friend a while ago, when we walk through the pearly gates wondering angels will say, "How did you get here, you so great a sinner?", our answer will be, "By the grace of God" – "By grace are ye saved through faith; and that not of yourselves: it is the gift of God." – and in a world that shall never see the setting sun, we will join the innumerable throng in singing,

> "When we've been there ten thousand years,
> Bright shining as the sun,
> We've no less days to sing His praise,
> Than when we first begun."

Then we will know the breadth and length, the height and the depth of the exceeding riches of His grace, and the meaning of the language of Paul when he said, "That in the ages to come he might shew the exceeding riches of his grace in his kindness toward us through Christ Jesus."

Then this glorious sunlit text of Scripture, after it describes the darkness of death, "Wherein in time past ye walked according to the course of this world, according to the prince of the power of the air, the spirit that now worketh in the children of disobedience; Among whom also we all had our conversation in times past in the lusts of our flesh, fulfilling the desires of the flesh and of the mind; and were by nature the children of wrath, even as others" – born in sin, doomed to die – helpless – then like an over-arching rainbow on the bosom of the storm, these words: "But God."

"But God"!

Over the guiltiest sinner that ever stumbled and fell arches the word of grace:

"But God"!

"But God," in contrast, not the work our puny hands can do, not the rivers of briny tears that might come unbidden from our anxious souls, "But God," the Man, the Omnipotent, the Everlasting One has a listening ear, a forgiving heart, He who is rich in mercy, forgives and makes us His.

That is the first thing we need – Our salvation.

> "With broken heart and contrite sigh,
> A trembling sinner, Lord, I cry:
> Thy pardoning grace is rich and free:
> God, be merciful to me.
>
> I smite upon my troubled breast,
> With deep and conscious guilt oppressed;
> Christ and His cross my only plea:
> O God, be merciful to me.

> Far off I stand with tearful eyes,
> Nor dare uplift them to the skies;
> But Thou dost all my anguish see:
> O God, be merciful to me.
>
> Nor alms, nor deeds that I have done,
> Can for a single sin atone;
> To Calvary alone I flee:
> O God, be merciful to me.
>
> And when, redeemed from sin and hell,
> With all the ransomed throng I dwell,
> My raptured song shall ever be,
> God has been merciful to me."

Second: Having been saved we are on our wilderness journey – with many troubles we do not understand – the problems of suffering never will be understood.

Some sorrows come because of our own misdeeds. Only a few minutes ago I saw the quivering, trembling, broken, weeping form of a little wife and mother. The worst thing that could happen to a wife is to have a drunken husband; he not only breaks her heart, but he takes the stars out of her sky. This particular case, like millions of others, has been of long standing through the years. Tell me not her sufferings are for any wrong she has done; it is because of another. Therefore, we have to come and plant our feet on the Rock in the midst of the storms of life.

Here is a most outstanding case: Joseph, loved by his father, envied, and hated by his brothers – and that is a sure way to turn the hate of some of the people (and preachers) – if you are especially blessed or have a little more success, there are some people who will never forgive you for it. You recall the tragic story of how they took him and put him in the pit; how they brought him down to the Egyptian slave market; how Potiphar's wife conspired and schemed to wreck and ruin him, and preferred false indictment against him for which he was put behind prison bars for two years, "But God!" –

"But God" was with him when the hour came for him to interpret Pharaoh's dream of seven years of plenty followed by seven years of famine – Oh, to God that somebody in Washington had as much sense as Joseph! Now some of you are not going to like that, but if you knew how little I care what somebody says – well, you wouldn't say them – you just say what you please and I will say what I please, that is the way to get along – Oh, that somebody instead of destroying the crops of America had had the sense of Joseph, we would have plenty during this time of drought! (Applause.)

I will show you tonight how the judgment of God is on America because of it.

At last when the famine drove the brothers of Joseph to his throne and old Jacob died – the brothers came together and they said – their guilty conscience was at work – "he will kill us now that our father is dead," and when they came and stood before him, and asked forgiveness, Joseph said, "But as for you, ye thought evil against me; but God!" – "Ye meant to do me evil when you put me in that pit – I cried all night; and when those iron bars clanked behind me and left me alone – ye meant to do me evil. 'But God!' You didn't reckon with God, but I did. Let me tell you something, brothers, God was with me that first night in that old dark pit – He whispered, 'Don't be uneasy, Joseph.' When you told me, God said, 'Don't be afraid" – Oh, brothers, God and I have a special understanding you didn't know anything about. Ye meant to do me harm, but I am the head of the empire now; I forgive you – ye meant to do me evil, but God."

I am going to give you a very interesting story that happened since I was last here – the next time I come to the pulpit I am going to bring me a towel. (Mopping perspiration.) Last year when I went to Detroit – there are three great daily papers there, either one of which has a larger circulation than all the daily papers here put together. The church editor of one of these papers went to see the other two and said, "Let's put a boycott on Frank Norris. He stirs up trouble everywhere he goes, and the only way to stop him is to put a boycott on him. Boycott him and he won't be here long. He won't get any crowds and he will have to leave, but let him get loose here, give him publicity, and he will stir up trouble."

One of the papers, instead of putting on a boycott went back and published a lot of things that had happened here for the past 25 years – well I didn't say anything about it – then there came out another story about me – well I went to see the head of that paper who is a Roman Catholic, but he is very big hearted. I said, "Now if you are making anything by that, all right."

He said, "I pay very little attention to the news department, but I think you are right about it."

And the next Sunday morning there came out, in double column, a very flattering write-up about me. From then on up to last Saturday there were fine reports made in the Detroit Times, and soon the other papers began to do likewise. The Detroit Free Press, one of the great dailies, is owned by one man, Mr. Ed Stair. He and I had a very happy visit afterward. About a month ago our annual report was carried to the Free Press and they didn't publish it. I said, "Well, that's funny." – and two or three things like that happened – so Mr. Entzminger carried my address down to the paper. He thought it would be a good piece of news, and the reporter lit in and said some severe things about me. Mr. Entzminger told me what he said.

I said, "That accounts for some things."

The next morning I went into Mr. Ed Stair's office on the 13th floor of the Free Press Building – a newspaper that has 300,000 circulation.

I said, "I have come here to take up a matter with you, that I don't believe you know about. There has been a certain amount of prejudice."

He said, "I know all about it, and I am not going to stand for it. Anything you send down here, mark it personal to me."

And now the three papers come out with news and headlines – "Ye meant it for evil, but God."

That's what happened; nothing to boast of, but the God of Joseph lives today as of old! That is just a commentary on Romans 8:28 "And we know that all things work together for good to them that love God, to them who are the called according to his purpose." – Sometimes we may not understand, but just await God's purpose.

Third, after we have been saved, after we have gone through this life, we hear the breakers roar, and we wonder about the crossing ahead – we would like to know – I Cor. 15:38, "But God giveth it a body as it hath pleased him, and to every seed his own body."

Two illustrations are sufficient. Years ago when crossing the old Coosa River in Alabama, as a boy only eleven years old, – another boy and I were driving two mule teams. As we went down on the old ferry boat I was afraid I would drive off of it – I was scared of the water. When we were on, the old ferryman unhitched a chain from a big tree on the bank, threw it on the flat bottom ferry and out we started – First thing I knew the old boat began to move and soon began to turn around. I was scared. The mules were scared – you know a mule gets scared when he gets out of place – the first thing I knew instead of crossing the river as I thought we should, we were going down the river – down and down we went, the trees were passing on either side – I said to myself, now that old ferryman has taken a drink, and he doesn't know where we are going – I could hear the roar of the falls a short distance below – I thought, I can't swim, but I will unhitch one of the mules and hold on to him – I was scared. That old ferryman let the boat drift – and after a while he put out an oar and began to paddle, first on one side, then stroke on the other side – and the first thing I knew we came right up to the bank on the other side where there was a graveled road, and the ferryman walked off and threw that chain around a big tree, and we drove off, safe and sound.

Oh, I have seen that a million times – sometimes I wonder whether or not my little boat will make the landing – sometimes it begins to whirl around and drift down, and sometimes there is a dreadful load – sometimes I begin to cry – sometimes I feel God himself has forsaken – sometimes I can't see the ferryman – sometimes darkness overtakes. "But God!" is on board, and my little ferry boat will land safe on the other side! (Shoutings.)

"Children of the heav'nly King,
As ye journey, sweetly sing;
Sing your Savior's worthy praise,
Glorious in His works and ways.

We are trav'ling home to God,
In the way the fathers trod:
They are happy now and we
Soon their happiness shall see.

Fear not, brethren, joyful stand
On the borders of your land;
Jesus Christ, your Father's son,
Bids you undismayed go on.

Lord, obediently we go,
Gladly leaving all below;
Only Thou our Leader be,
And we still will follow Thee."

A few days ago a very great tragedy happened – a four year old boy was on the Boulevard where there are two streets, with a strip of grass and trees which separate them – this little boy was playing with some children and they would run up and down and across – this four year old child ran behind one of the cars, just in time to be crushed to death by a powerful truck. His little body was so mangled they could not open the casket. He was the only child of this father and mother. The mother was a devout Christian, the father an unbeliever.

He said, "It's a new world, what shall I do? – When I go home in the evening and he doesn't stand on the porch to meet me, what shall I do? – When I leave in the morning and don't feel his embrace, tell me will I ever see him again?"

Thanks be unto God, Jesus will raise him up in the morning of the resurrection!

**"But There Is a God"**

This last word – There was a terrible condition, all the world was going to pieces, the king was in distress, Babylon was in confusion, all the wise men couldn't tell what was going on. Daniel was in bed, but God revealed the secret to Daniel and when he stood before that old pagan king here is the word, "But there is a God in heaven that reveals the secrets, and maketh Known to the king Nebuchadnezzar what shall be in the latter days."

So today beloved, I tell you there is a God – I don't understand the things that come, none of us can, but I believe profoundly that God, the God of our Lord Jesus Christ, has called me to do a specific work.

I stood the other day, yonder in upper New York State, when the thermometer was 104 degrees, and spoke to a great crowd of preachers who came from a long distance – when the afternoon session was over every thread on my body was wringing wet – a preacher whose hair was white – looked like he was past sixty, but he was just a little past forty, came to me and said, "I know you are tired, but I would like to have five minutes with you."

I said, "You can have more." I was rooming in Mrs. Miller's home next to the church, and I said to him, "Come on and go with me to my room while I bathe and change clothes and we can talk."

He did, and when he sat down in that room he bowed his head in his hands and poured out his soul, and said, "Oh God! Oh, God! I wish I had heard that message ten years ago."

What had happened? He had come into a great tragedy, the devil had defeated him, and (as is the trouble so often) the deacons who ought to have stood by him stabbed him in the back. He was a heart-broken man. His wife's health was gone; his children had lost their faith in God because of what the church had done to him. I crossed over, put my arm around him and said, "God still lives."

He said, "I know He does, but He has turned His face forever from me."

I said, "He has not turned His face from you – He never did turn from one of His, when he gets down in the depths and cries out

'Lord help, help, help!' – That is what He has been wanting to hear." And we had a season of prayer.

I received a letter from him and a good church he never thought of called him to be the pastor. He is one of the happiest men in the country. He says, "Come on and help me celebrate,"

God has called me to do that kind of thing. I want you to understand I am not going to forsake you. No. But God has prepared me to do that kind of thing.

I believe one of two things is going to happen – we are going to have a great revival, or Jesus Christ is soon coming again. There isn't any doubt about it.

That thing in Spain may be the spark that will set off the conflagration – you read in the papers where France is ready to go to the help of the Communists. If they do Italy and Germany will go to the help of the other crowd.

I sent George, who as you know is aboard the Battleship Oklahoma which has been ordered to the rescue of American citizens in Spain – I sent a cablegram out of an anxious father's heart, and asked him to cable at my expense – the answer was that I couldn't send him a cablegram and he couldn't send me one.

The condition, my friends, is terrible, but there is a God in heaven, and God knows what is going on, and God is going to take care of George. (Voices: Amen.)

Four things we need to know.

1. "But God," reaches down and saves us.
2. "But God" overrules everything to His glory and for our good.
3. "But God," in the morning of the resurrection gives us a new body, robs death of its sting, and the grave of its victory.
4. "But God" even knows the workings of evil men and will bring their counsel to naught.

Oh, to God we knew how to sing those words our fathers and mothers used to sing, that martyrs inscribed on prison cells, and indelibly traced with their rich red blood:

"God moves in a mysterious way
His wonders to perform;
He plants His footsteps in the sea,
And rides upon the storm.

Deep in unfathomable mines
Of never-failing skills,
He treasures up His bright designs,
And works his sovereign will.

Ye fearful saints, fresh courage take;
The clouds ye so much dread
Are big with mercy, and shall break
In blessings on your head.

Judge not the Lord by feeble sense,
But trust Him for His grace;
Behind a frowning providence
He hides a smiling face.

His purposes will ripen fast,
Unfolding every hour;
The bud may have a bitter taste,
But sweet will be the flower.

Blind unbelief is sure to err,
And scan his work in vain:
God is His own interpreter,
And He will make it plain."

Speaking of George, I would rather have this reward than anything I know. I had a letter from George the other day, and he said:

"I am on the other side, but I want you to know that I believe in the Bible I learned at home, and in the First Baptist Church, and when I come back I want to tell them that I have still that faith, and I want you to know, although far away, every night when I read the Bible and kneel and pray, my last word is 'Oh God, bless dear old

Dad as he works so hard, give him strength, and may I – when he is broken down – may I be a joy and a comfort to him'."

But God lives!

Let us stand.

(Large numbers were saved and came into the church. The whole congregation broke and came to the platform and there were shoutings and rejoicings and streaming tears. Mr. John Hope stepped to the microphone and reported to the outside world what was going on. It was one o'clock when that scene, the greatest ever witnessed in the First Baptist Church, was over.)

# CHAPTER X

THE CLOSE OF MESSAGE BY DR. NORRIS ON THE TEXT: "WAGES OF SIN" IN WHICH HUNDREDS WERE SAVED

What is soul-death?

I wish I knew how to define it. But I can only approach it – "Depart from me ye workers of iniquity."

What is soul-death? – "Where their worm dieth not, and the fire is not quenched." – "And the smoke of their torment ascendeth up for ever and ever: and they have no rest day nor night."

"Oh," you say, "I don't believe that."

I have no argument for you. You tell God about it. But listen to me. If I had never seen a Bible, never heard a Scripture, never heard a sermon, song, or prayer, never heard of the name of Christianity, I would be compelled to tell you according to the rules of providence, there is such a place as hell. I have held the hands of saloon keepers, I have held the hands of officers; I have held the hands of cattlemen; I have held the hands of paupers and millionaires while they died. I have seen those men as they came to the hour – men who while in life said there is no God, no judgment, no hell, no heaven. They scoffed and laughed at religion, had no time for God, no time for the church. But when they came to die I have seen it take half a dozen men to hold them on the bed. I have heard them shriek and scream, I have heard their cries – "Don't let them take me out of here!"

I can hear old Buck Cooper – Buck owned two saloons. He knew he couldn't live long. He sent for me. When I walked in he stared with his big eyes; he had a big frame, over two hundred pounds. I walked in, bent over the bed. His breath was short, but he was still conscious and in his right mind.

He said, "Preacher, they tell me I have got to cash in – they tell me I have got to cash in." He was tearing at his clothes, ripping the cover. Friends would put it back and he would throw it off.

He said, "I can't stand it. I can't stand it! They tell me I have got to cash in. Let me live! Pray for me! If I live to get up I will go to church and become a Christian. I will quit the saloon business. I can't stand it!"

Then he dropped back.

Then he said, "Look at them! There they are! There they are! Look at them!"

I said, "What?"

He said, "That long line of boys, drunkards. They have come! I sent them to hell!"

And that went on – two – three – four – five o'clock in the morning. And "Oh!" and he fell back dead!

What did he see? What did he see?

Come on, Mr. Infidel, what did he see? What did he see? – "The wages of sin is death!"

When I was a boy about the size of one of these boys here, Dad and I were walking through the woods one day in North Alabama – we were walking out through the woods and Dad had an axe and I had an axe. We were going to cut down some wood. After a while we came to a big old black gum tree.

That old black gum tree had fallen full length and smashed the small trees right and left. There had been no storm, so I walked up to see why it had fallen. That big black gum tree was green all 'round on the outsides, but it had decayed all the way through on the inside, and it was rotten and had broken off at the stump. Here is what happened. It grew while it rotted within, until at last it came crashing down, of its own weight, to the ground.

Oh, I have seen that thing happen ten thousand times! I have seen men who were classed as Successes, men who held high positions, men who had the greatest banks, men head of factories – I have seen the common every day laborer, strong on the outside, but dead on the inside, rotten through and through.

Oh, my friends, the wages of sin is death! Don't you tremble with the thought of it? Oh, you say, "I will wait a while." That is the devil's shrewdest lie.

I saw a picture of a character in Victor Hugo's "Lee Miserables." And as he looked out across the white sands, all was well and the sand was firm and white. After a while about half way across suddenly he finds his steps heavy. He is down to his ankles – going down! – to his shoe tops! Then horrified he finds he is in that terrible quicksand. He turns to go back but he is down to his knees. With an awful force it snatches down everything that touches it. Soon he is down to his waistline! He calls for help but his calls are not heard. He looks! But there is no one in sight. The white sands are sweeping around him. The little whirling white clouds only mock him. The birds fly over but none can help and their song is only a funeral dirge. Soon he is engulfed to his shoulders, soon to his chin, soon the blood is bursting from his temples, streaming from his nose, his ears, his eyes, and then the quicksands become his tomb.

Oh, my friends, "There is a way which seemeth right unto a man, but the end thereof are the ways of death."

So tonight I plead with you – I have no other interest but your soul. "Death!" – "The wages of sin is death!"

Oh, for the call to repentance! That is your only need; your past is made, the record is fixed, you are in rags and naked. Without the garment of righteousness, without the covenant ring. What can you do? Listen to the call of God to repentance. I wish I knew how to quote it; "Seek ye the Lord while he may be found, call ye upon him while he is near; let the wicked forsake his way, and the unrighteous man his thoughts: and let hint return unto the Lord, and he will have mercy upon him: and to our God, for he will abundantly pardon." God is waiting, He is calling.

> Sinner, the voice of God regard;
> His mercy speaks today;
> He calls you, by His sovereign Word
> From sin's destructive way.

Like the rough sea, that cannot rest,
You live devoid of peace;
A thousand strings within your breast
Deprive your soul of ease.

Why will you in the crooked ways
Of sin and folly go?
In pain you travel all your days,
To reap immortal woe.

But he who turns to God shall live,
Through His abounding grace;
His mercy will the guilt forgive
Of those who seek His face.

\* \* \* \* \* \* \*

The greatest peroration in any sermon was the last message by Dr. Norris in the famous Norris-Wallace Debate in which they discussed the following questions:

(1) Christ will establish a literal throne in Jerusalem, and reign over the whole earth for a period of one thousand years.

Dr. J. Frank Norris, Affirming; Rev. Foy E. Wallace, Denying.

(2) Jews, as a nation, will return to Palestine when Christ returns to the earth, and will then be converted to Christ.

Dr. J. Frank Norris, Affirming;

Rev. Foy E. Wallace, Denying.

(3) Baptism, to the penitent believer, is essential to his salvation from past, or alien sins.

Rev. Foy E. Wallace, Affirming;

Dr. J. Frank Norris, Denying.

(4) A child of God, one who has been saved by the blood of Christ, can so sin as to be finally lost.

Rev. Foy E. Wallace, Affirming;

Dr. J. Frank Norris, Denying.

The conclusion of Dr. Norris, the last message:

There is, in conclusion, therefore, not one single solitary Scripture that supports the proposition that the believer that has been saved by the blood of Christ, can fall away so as to be lost. He may fall, but he cannot fall away so as to be lost. Now, therefore, it is our duty to interpret certain Scriptures, and give warning. Certainly it is no encouragement to sin, since we know we are saved. Does a son break his father's heart because he is already his son?

God has given me, in my humble judgment, three very fine boys – they err a lot of times, but they are sons of their father – but my, friends, don't I remember when one of my boys was leaving home to go off to a distant state school – I took him in his room, and we got down together and I put my arms around him, and I said, "Son, you are going out into a strange world" – and when he lifted his eyes, they were filled with tears, and he said, "Papa, Papa, there is one thing I wish to say." I said, "What is it J?" He said, "I wish that I could start over again as a baby, and never break your heart again." Now he didn't say that in order to be my son, but because he is my son. And I answer to Mr. Wallace's charge that it is a dangerous doctrine, I answer back and say, it is the most glorious doctrine, for it impels, and constrains, and inspires us! (Voices, Amen)

Therefore, the positive teaching of the Scripture is overwhelming, showing that a child of God, once saved, cannot fall away and be lost, and the security of the believer, his eternal salvation, is guaranteed:

1. Because of the election of the Father.
2. Because of the death, burial, and resurrection of Christ.
3. Because of the combined work of the Trinity in redemption.
4. Because the believer partakes of the Divine nature in the new birth.
5. Because the believer is the Son of God and the Son can never be lost.
6. Because the believer receives everlasting life once for all eternity.
7. Because salvation is by grace, unconditioned on works, past, present or future.

8. Because the believer is kept by the power of God.
9. Because of the intercession of Christ that never fails.
10. Because the believer has been forever translated out of the kingdom of darkness into the kingdom of His dear Son.
11. Because the Security of the believer is based on imputed righteousness of God.
12. Because the security of the believer is guaranteed by his union with Christ.
13. Because the security of the believer is guaranteed by the full atonement on the cross.
14. Because the security of the believer is based wholly on justification by faith.
15. Because the security of the believer is guaranteed by his adoption into the family of God.
16. Because the security of the believer is guaranteed because he is an heir of God and a joint heir with Christ.
17. Because the security of the believer is guaranteed by the covenant of grace made before time began.
18. Because of the all things of God's eternal purpose.

Therefore, we sing:

> "My name from the palms of His hands
> Eternity will not erase;
> Impressed on His heart it remains,
> In marks of indelible grace;
> Yes, I to the end shall endure,
> As sure as the earnest is given;
> More happy, but not more secure,
> The glorified spirits in heaven."

Years ago when an old Union Pacific train pulled by two powerful mogul engines – there were 16 cars, including baggage and Pullman cars – went winding through curves and climbing mountains, as they crossed over the great divide – soon they were going faster and faster as they gathered momentum, as they swept rapidly down the steep road on the west side – suddenly as they turned a sharp curve, two little children were seen on the track – the engineer signalled and threw on the brakes, reversed the engine, but the momentum was too great, as they rolled on, the old veteran engineer shouted to his fireman, "Great heaven, I have run over two children." Soon the train was brought to a standstill, the word flashed back, and all the passengers heard, "We have killed two children" – the engineer and fireman, brakeman and conductor and some of the passengers started back up the track – their hearts melted within them, women fainted before they got there – but as they approached the place they heard the little eight-year-old girl shouting at the top of her voice to her little brother:

"HOLD TO THE ROCK, BROTHER – HOLD TO THE ROCK—HOLD TO THE ROCK."

What had she done? When she saw death was on them, with that peculiar intuition womenkind are endowed with, she snatched that little six-year-old brother and threw him in a crevice of the rocks, and held him tight in the broken rock, and saved their lives.

Oh, my friends, this world is in the midst of a terrible tragedy; the war clouds are hanging low; thirty million men are marching to battle – God grant tonight that you my unsaved friend, and all of us who believe in the name of Christ, shall together hold to the Rock, the eternal Rock of Ages, and when this little life is over, and we have fought our last fight, delivered our last address, then together we will see the "Pure river of water of life, clear as crystal, proceeding out of the throne of God and the Lamb. In the midst of the street of it, and on either side of the river, was there the tree of life, which bare twelve manner of fruits" – and then we shall see God face to face, coming down to dwell with us, and as we look on His face, with His own tender hands He will wipe away all tears from every weeping eye. And there we shall meet the innumerable hosts from Abel and Enoch, on down, including old John, Martin Luther, Alexander Campbell, and every humble country preacher of whatever denomination whose names are written in the Lamb's Book of Life, and all the blood-washed throng who have gone through life's weeping way, who are kept by the power of God, saved by His grace, sealed by His Spirit, shall rest forever and forever on Emmanuel's shores.

When Dr. Norris held meetings in Shanghai, China

# CHAPTER XI

## SOME VERY EFFECTIVE, PROFITABLE AND TRUE ILLUSTRATIONS USED BY DR. NORRIS

### At Close of Sermon on Text: "Ye Must Be Born Again"

Dr. Norris' strongest forte is a gospel appeal to the unsaved and he never closes a sermon without a concrete example – he used the following illustration:

This word, and I am through. I think one of the greatest experiences I ever had was some years ago, the second meeting that I held in a northern city – some five years ago. There was a young man that had been converted and joined the church in the first meeting. He was manager of one of the stores there. He had been a wild, gambling, drinking, carousing young fellow, but he was saved. You let a dead-game sport get a good case of religion and he makes a fine church member. Let me tell you something. I want to stop right here and give you a word – don't misunderstand me. There are a whole lot of folks who go around and say, "I never took a drink in my life. I don't know one card from another. I never swore an oath in my life. I never even fished on Sunday." Bud, you are not going to enjoy heaven when you get there. Don't misunderstand me. On this second meeting with this young fellow, above 30 years old, one night in the meeting, the power of the Lord came upon us in a great way and many were being saved, and I asked everybody to pray, especially for their unsaved friends and loved ones. That young man went home that night and as the midnight hour came he found his heart heavy for his lost and wrecked and ruined brother who lived 200 miles away in Detroit. He said, "I believe I will write that brother a letter," and he lay, and rolled, and tossed, sleeplessly. After a while he said, "Lord, I believe I will call him up over the telephone." He got up and put in a long distance telephone call and got that brother on the line and said: "Say, I want you to catch the next train and come to Cleveland. I have got the biggest business proposition you ever heard of – a great big deal, and we can put it over together." And the brother says, "What is it? Tell me what it is. Give me some idea what it is," And this man says," I can't do it. Get on the train and come over. It's the biggest deal you ever heard of, and it will go through and we can clean up on it. Get on the train and come over – I will look for you in the morning. Goodbye."

The next morning this brother showed up. The man called me up and said, "Say, you know that lost brother I was telling you about? He is here in my house now downstairs. You have got to help me out, I got him over here and you have got to do something with him." "All right," I said, "you bring him down and we will do something with him." He said, "Listen, we are not going to let him get away until we have put this thing over." I said, "If you go at it that way, it will go over all right." That night both of them came to the meeting. I preached on the Prodigal's Return and used as my text, "I shall arise and go to my Father." This lost brother had separated from his wife and three children, and they were living with her mother in Philadelphia. This man had been the manager of another store, but through drink and prodigality he had lost his position. I preached the best I could. When I gave the invitation he came to the front and gave his hand and said, "Pray for me. I don't think there is any chance or any hope." When he did that he fell on his knees and cried. He said, "My sins are too great, I have sinned away my day of grace. Good people, there is no use for you to pray for me, I have committed every sin in the category. The door of mercy is closed – there is no use." When he started to leave the meeting that night his brother, who had him by the arm, said, "Don't go, let's make an appointment with these preachers," and so an appointment was made. At exactly ten o'clock the next morning, in the office of the Euclid Avenue Baptist Church, they came in and when a fellow comes in on you like that you have got to do something. I just reached over and took the Bible and said, "Gentlemen, we are here for a very serious business. Suppose the first thing we do is to let God speak to us," and took the Bible and I read. "Him that cometh unto me, I will in no wise cast out." And then I read and repeated the story I have just given you. And then I read, " Where sin abounds, grace doth much more abound." Then after we had finished talking about how God saved us, turning from every known sin, coming to Him by faith, just like a hungry child comes for bread, I said to him, "Is that clear?" And he looked at me and says, "Mr. Norris, it is clear. My trouble is not to understand. I undersand you and I understood you last night. I know perfectly well what has got to be done. I know God will save a man if he comes to Him, but you don't understand the guilty distance there is between God and me. If you knew my life as my brother knows my life, you would understand. Do you know what I have done in my domestic affairs? I broke my wife's heart and marred her life. God gave us three of the most precious girls you ever saw. I am not fit at all to be their father. I have got the best mother and father on earth. I stood high in the business world and plunged down and lost everything. Did you know there isn't a man in the world that would trust me with a dollar?" I said, "I didn't know that, but I do know that you cannot be too big a sinner for God to save. Are you willing to try it? Let's get down here and pray." Both preachers and both brothers got right down on our knees. I said, "Brother Pastor, your prayer first." And then I prayed the best that I could, and then I said to his saved brother, "You lead us in prayer." And I shall never forget how he prayed. He said, "Oh, God, you know what my brother needs. I wish you would do for him what you did for me. You know how mean he has been. You know how he has treated that little wife and those three beautiful children." And he just went on and told every mean thing his brother had done, and then he says, "Lord, I don't know how to pray. I wish you would save him. If you will save him I will just make you the best Christian I can. If you will save him, Lord, it will make that little woman the happiest woman in the world, and Lord, save him for his sake. Sin got hold of him and the devil has ruined him. Lord, is it asking too much? If you will just save him Lord, I will show you what I will do." And then I said to the seeking brother, "Now, you pray." "Oh," he said, "I can't pray." "Yes you can." "No, I can't." And I said, "You must, you know what you need, tell God what you need." And he commenced and he said, "Oh, God, I don't know how to pray, but Mr. Norris says I've got to pray. You know what I need, and if you will give it to me I will be much obliged."

My friends, listen, when he said that he broke down and stopped and couldn't say another word, and cried and cried, and we all cried. Dr. Bustard, the pastor, cried, and I cried, and the brother cried, and then we prayed again. After that I felt like something had happened. He got up, great big tears streaming down his sin-stained face, and he turned and said, "Come on, let's go," and he walked down to the Western Union and sent a message and then he went to the ticket office and bought a ticket. His brother and he were exactly the same size, weight, height, – he said, "I want two of the best suits of clothes you have in your house. I want to dress up."

He put on one of his brother's suits of clothes and he came by the hotel. He says, "Good-by, but you will hear from me again. I'm going to Philadelphia." And the next morning he walked into his wife's mother's home and he says, "Wife, you have got a new husband. Wife, the old things are gone. I don't ask you to take me back. All I ask you to do is this – give me a chance and you will see what a man can do." What did she do? She threw her arms around his neck and said, "I have prayed for this hour." And then the three little girls came in and he gathered them in his arms, and then the mother-in-law came in and took them all in her arms.

What happened? Next Sunday morning he walked down the main aisle of Grace Temple Baptist Church, wife, husband, children, all, and took their stand for Jesus Christ.

Listen! Sometimes when I am tired, some times when these old legs won't carry me, some times when this old head is about to burst, some times when these nerves are ready to give way, I just reach up in the drawer of my desk and pull out a letter he wrote. He says, "I am the happiest man in the world because God's grace has made me what I am."

How many of you can say: "I know what the Father's house is and I'm going back to it?"

Who will come? Who will say tonight, "Others may do as they will, sink or swim, survive or perish; I will arise and go to "Jesus, I will go back to the Father's house?"

\* \* \* \* \* \* \*

At the close of sermon on "The Unpardonable Sin" he used the following illustration and large numbers were saved by this message:

Listen, friends, when in San Antonio years ago, when the Spirit of God came on multitudes of people and they were being saved – a lot of people came through curiosity, just like they do here and everywhere and God gets hold of them. I have had that criticism of my meetings – they say, "People just come out of curiosity." Well, the rest of them had better get some curiosity. If I can reach some mother's boy or save some home from a living hell by that means – well, just let them go and talk. That's all I have to say.

So, this high-society woman said to a group of her friends. "Let's go over and hear Norris at the tabernacle." I didn't know anything about who they were – they came and they stayed throughout the services. When this woman and her husband drove up to their home she got out in the drive and he drove, on down to the garage, and as she took out her night key to unlick the door, she said, "There was a voice said, 'Don't unlock that door.' " She stopped, looked around – she said, "I was amazed, I didn't know what on earth had happened," then she said, "I am crazy," and started to put the key in the lock, but a voice said, "Don't unlock that door." She stepped back. She was amazed at herself, she wondered if she had gone crazy, and she said, "I will open the door, it is my door and my house," and she started to put the key in again and a voice said, "Stop, don't unlock that door, go back to the tabernacle."

She turned and screamed, "Oh, husband, husband, bring the car back quick." He said, "What on earth is the matter?" She said, "Don't ask me, bring the car back and take me back to the tabernacle just as quick as you can." He backed the car out, she got in and he began to ask her what was the matter, and she said, "Oh, husband, don't ask me, don't say a word, hat drive as fast as you can." And they came back as fast as he could drive and they reached there just as the after service had been dismissed. A group of us were standing there and we saw this woman as she came running in – she was beautifully dressed—and as she rushed up she said, "Am I too late?" I spoke and said, "What is it?" "Oh, men!" she said, "Listen! pardon me if I am intruding, but something awful has happened to me tonight and she told that story, how she started to go into the house and something told her three times not to go in – she said, "I am afraid, what on earth is it?" I looked at her and said, "Let us pray." I didn't have to say to that woman, "get down on your knees" – she just fell full length right there in the sawdust, and she started to praying and confessing her sins, and it wasn't long until she was gloriously saved, and she said, "I know now that was the voice of God. "

The next day she resigned every connection with every worldly club she belonged to, and that night she stood on the platform of that big tabernacle and told that story, and she said, "This is the last thing on earth I ever thought I would do. I came out here out of curiosity," anti she said, "at first I made fun of the singing and I criticized Mr. Norris when he started to preach, and said, 'there is nothing in it,' and she said, "I know what did it, my mother's prayers followed me and God reached down His hand and wouldn't let me open that door, but God opened the door of salvation."

* * * * * * *

At the close of the sermon "To Die Is Gain" Dr. Norris used the following illustration:

One morning many years ago, my telephone rang – a long distance call.

"Brother?"

"Yes. Is that you, sister?"

"Brother, if you expect to see mother alive, you better hurry."

I looked at my watch – only bad a few minutes to catch the southbound Katy, but I said, "I will get there." When, they rushed me down to the station I saw the train backing out, and the best I could, do was jump on the blind baggage. I said "I will ride this to the next station," and when I got to the next station I got on the coach, and when I reached the place they met me, and I said, "Is she still alive?"

" Yes, and calling for you."

I was the oldest and, the first born, and there is a peculiar tenderness that every mother has for her first born child, and for the baby, too, and when I walked in she was sitting propped up-in a big armchair – her breath was short, the only way she could breathe – her sight was gone; death had closed her eyes forever to this world, but her hearing was still good and her speech, though faint, was still clear. I rushed up and said, "Mother!" and she said, "Frank, Frank, my boy, you got here." And I said, "Yes," and I fell down by the side of her chair and she reached out her hand and found my head and rested her hand upon it. Oh, I had felt the touch of that hand a thousand times! It felt familiar. It had touched my brow when I was racked with pain, tossing with fever – it had been the best friend that I had ever had, and now it was on my head for the last time. I looked at her, and I said, "Mother, do you see me? Do you know me." And she says, "My boy, I can not see you but I can feel your face," and she put her thin, emaciated hand all over my face and said, "Yes, I have felt of that face when you were a baby; I felt of it all through the years, but, son, I am going home this morning, they have come for me. Do you hear that music?" And I said, "Mother, I don't hear it," and she said, "My son, don't you hear, that music?" and I said, "No, I don't hear it," and she said, "Oh, I wish you could hear it, I never heard such music in this world." I said, "Why is it, mother, I can't hear it?" and she says, "Oh, I hear it and they have come for me and I will have to go. Good-by son, preach the old gospel on. It is just like I taught it to you. It is good in life; it is better in death. Preach it on until you come home to mother and God," and she fell asleep in Jesus, and as I looked at the little silent form, still and cold in death and planted the kiss of my love on her brow – what a heart, what a soul, what character! Oh, God, give us women like that – I said, "She has gone home and some of these days I shall go to be with my Lord and then I will see mother just like I used to see her, without her sorrow, without her weakness, without her affliction, but in Glory with all that have gone on before.

Let us pray.

(There were 97 professions and additions to the church).

\* \* \* \* \* \* \*

At the close of the sermon "Lord Thou Knowest All Things" Dr. Norris used the following example:

He knows all about us. He knows us in the depth of poverty. He knows us in the darkness of night. He knows us in the keenest pangs of disappointment. Don't you know He was in company with Enoch all the time that he walked with God? Don't you know He was with Noah when he built the ark? Don't you know He was with old Abraham and Sarah when they left the land of their nativity and went to the land which they had never seen? Don't you know He was with Jacob, the first night he was away from home, and then He was with him when he returned and divided his cattle and family because of the wrath of Esau? Wasn't He with Joseph in Egypt? Wasn't He with him when his brothers stripped his bright colored robe from him and put him in a pit and sold him to the Midianites, and the Word says, "The Lord was with Joseph in prison." He was with Moses alone in the land of Midian. He was with the people when they walked down through the divided sea. And David! Who is better qualified to testify, "Lord, thou knowest all things?" In singing of the immeasurable mercies – the everlasting mercies – mercies to the third and fourth generation of them that love Him— who but David, out of the depths of tragedy – he was brought up out of an horrible pit, out of the miry clay and set upon a rock, the eternal Rock of Ages – I say, who but David could shout down through the ages, "He knoweth our frame, he remembereth that we are dust" – "He hath not dealt with us after our sins, nor rewarded us according to our iniquities

He was with the three Hebrew children, Shadrach, Meshach, and Abednego, when they were cast into the fiery furnace and old Nebuchadnezzar asked if they didn't cast only three in the furnace and they said yes, and he shouted, "Lo, I see four men loose, walking in the midst of the fire, and they have no hurt ,and the form of the fourth is like the Son of God (Shoutings.)

He went with Daniel into the lion's den and sat with him and closed the mouths of the lions and he came up next morning.

He went to prison with Simon Peter when they said they were going to cut his head off, and the Lord who made the earth and the universe, who knew "all things" and who knew that Simon Peter still loved Him, sent down his angel who opened the door of the prison and let Simon Peter out into the streets.

My friends, He was with old Paul and Silas in the jail at Philippi at midnight, and He sent the earthquake and shook the doors and loosed their feet from the stocks, and they had a revival meeting.

He was with Paul yonder in Rome when he wrote, "At my first answer no man stood with me, but all men forsook me: I pray God that it may not be laid to their charge." What else Paul? "Notwithstanding the Lord stood with me, and strengthened me; that by me the preaching might be fully known, and that all the Gentiles might hear: and I was delivered out of the mouth of the lion."

\* \* \* \* \* \* \*

In the sermon "Lord Thou Knowest All Things" Dr. Norris used the following:

### Jesus Cooks Breakfast And Serves His Disciples

What is the conclusion? "Why, Peter, I know you love me. Now prove it to me." "How, Lord?" "Feed my sheep; give them the gospel, feed my lambs."

The highest honor in the world is to feed the sheep; the highest honor is to do service for the Lord Jesus Christ. I just call your attention to it briefly.

I am glad this 21st chapter is here. What an appeal it makes to us. What happens? Jesus makes the fire, broils the fish, toasts the bread, cooks the breakfast before daylight so when the tired disciples come ashore He says, "Come and sit down and I will serve you breakfast." Listen! "As soon then as they were come to land, they saw a fire of coals there" – who made that fire? – "and fish laid thereon, and bread" Who did that? Here is who did it – "Jesus said unto them come and dine. And none of the disciples durst ask him, Who art thou? knowing that it was the Lord. Jesus then cometh, and taketh bread, and giveth them, and fish likewise."

Oh, mothers, sometimes the burdens seem heavy and you think you can't bear them, but just remember that when you are tired, that is exactly what Jesus did one morning before daylight; Isn't that a beautiful picture? Peter didn't say a thing, and it must have been a strain for him to not say anything. John didn't say anything! Nobody said anything. Jesus just walked around and He gave Peter a piece of fish and then John a piece, and then Nathaniel, and then Thomas a piece, and then He gave them all some bread and He just stood there and said, "Can't you have something more?"

Listen, folks, when I walk in a hotel or restaurant I don't think of the girl who waits on me as some people do – I think, "One morning my Lord served breakfast to His disciples." (Shoutings.)

This is a type of the great supper when up there we can all sit down together, for, did not our Lord say, "Blessed are those servants, whom the Lord when he cometh shall find watching; verily I say unto you, that he shall gird himself, and make them to sit down to meat and will come forth and serve them." That is why old David said, "Thou preparest a table before me." That is why he said, "we will come from the east, and from the west, and from the north, and from the south" and we will sit down with Abraham, like old Abraham sat down with the two angels under the oaks of Mamre, and we will sit down with old Isaac and with Jacob and with Joseph and Moses and Joshua and Caleb, with Samual, (shoutings) with Gideon, David, Elijah and Elisha, and John the Baptist, with Paul, and old Simon Peter will be there, and all our fathers, mothers, grandfathers and grandmothers, all of them will come and sit down at the table of the Lord. It is the Lord's feast, it is the Lord's table, it is the Lord's people – they are tired and hungry; they have some up from the resurrection hour, they have come from far-off battle field – their crowns are waiting for them – the angels will arise, too, but they won't be eating with us. No, sir, they will join with the Lord in waiting on us.

Talk about happy renunions! We will gorget the grief of this hour, we will forget the funeral processions, we will forget the sad faces, we will forget the sorrow of parting with loved ones. Then we will shout and sing and we'll never grow old and we will die no more! (Shoutings.)

Photostatic copy of front cover page of greatest religious weekly in Britain.

● DR. J. FRANK NORRIS VISITS BRITAIN (see page 227)

# The CHRISTIAN HERALD
## SIGNS OF OUR TIMES AND RADIANT YOUTH

Price Twopence.    THURSDAY, OCTOBER 9, 1941.    75th Year No. 42.

(The page referred to in the above)

OCTOBER 9, 1941.   THE CHRISTIAN HERALD AND SIGNS OF OUR TIMES   227

# FAMOUS AMERICAN PREACHER VISITS BRITAIN

DR. J. FRANK NORRIS returned to the U.S.A. last week, but at a special interview granted us at the Savoy Hotel, I learned that at the express desire of the Prime Minister and the Minister of

*In a Special Interview with our Representative*

ping magnates and so on at a luncheon, I said: 'My Lord, what do you want me to discuss?' He said: 'Bring us a Gospel message.' And he is a Roman Catholic. I said: 'Well now, I can do

---

## Dr. J. FRANK NORRIS
### records his impressions

has toured London's bomb damage with the Lord Mayor. But this is not all. He said to me: "Conditions are a good deal worse than I thought. I shall take back a story that will break the hearts of the women of America. The numbers of people killed or wounded or maimed for life is terrible; but, worse still, I learn that many of the old people have become mentally unbalanced.

"Even worse, I am told this very delicate thing. The Health Authorities are terribly alarmed about children born in these times. The awful thing is that many children have come prematurely, and even for those that are not, there is grave concern for their future. Think of those innocent babes! Who knows what will develop in them twenty, thirty years hence? Criminologists now tell us that in most criminals there is some pre-natal influence. I believe that prophecy has more than one fulfilment, and I quoted to the Authority concerned Matthew 24 : 19 : 'Woe unto them that are with child, and to them that give suck in those days.'"

Dr. Norris said: "Four years ago, when I was over in Germany, I saw this thing coming. I went back and warned our people, 'We are heading for war.' But they shrugged their shoulders. I heard Hitler speak. I told them, 'That fellow is Satan incarnate.' I never saw such a dynamic personality in my life. There were 140,000 people, and he had absolute hypnotic influence over that whole crowd. But Hitler's epitaph is written: '*I will make thy grave; for thou art vile*' (Nahum 1: 14).

"The other day when I got to Glasgow, the Lord Provost had a large group of military men, ship-

---

Information, he hopes to return to Great Britain shortly for a further period of three months.

The purpose of this return trip is to tour the principal cities of this country by arrangement with the Lord Mayors, and to preach the Gospel, pure and simple. Reports would go to the American Press, and thus the hearts of these two great democracies would be linked in a unique and vital way.

Those who have come in contact with Dr. Norris' Spirit-filled personality will know that his messages will be delivered with dynamic power. In speaking of the Prime Minister, Dr. Norris said he found him "intensely human." This man of God from the States, who is Pastor of two churches 1,500 miles apart, with a combined membership of 17,000, is just that—intensely human. He can laugh, and he can cry; and he sways his audiences with the same emotions.

During his morning sermon delivered in the ruined building of Spurgeon's Tabernacle, Dr. Norris told his congregation: "The other day I had an interview with your Prime Minister, whom we regard as one of the greatest statesmen of all time, and I said, 'Mr. Churchill, my wife has your picture on the wall of her bedroom, and every night she prays "God bless Winston Churchill".'

"Mr. Churchill bowed his head and closed his eyes, and then, with tears in his eyes, he said, 'Tell Mrs. Norris I thank her; and *keep on praying*. I have the same faith that I received from my devoted mother.'

"When I left him I said, 'I think this will be a suitable epitaph for the arch-enemy of this hour: Nahum 1: 14, "I will make thy grave; for thou art vile".' And your Prime Minister said, 'It can't be written too soon to suit me.'"

Dr. Norris feels for the women and the children, the babies and the old folk, in this war-stricken land, and he goes back to the other side to tell the people of America that there has never been such courage since the world began as is now manifest in this little island.

Those of us who have seen and heard Dr. Norris will be able to conjure up in imagination the electrically-charged atmosphere as he addresses the listening multitudes, with fire blazing in his deep-set blue-grey eyes, and punching the truth home with that powerful fist

---

last." And the whole crowd of them were in tears in a few moments, and admitted that that is what is needed.

"I have seen several Cabinet Ministers, among others, Mr. A. V. Alexander, a cold, taciturn man, the most important man right now, I suppose, next to the Prime Minister. I said to Mr. Alexander: 'Do you believe that out of this will come a great spiritual awakening?' He said: 'When we look that way, and feel that way, I believe it will.' Point No. 1. I said: 'I am going to preach in Spurgeon's Church on Sunday.' He replied: 'I wish I were not tied up. I cannot go to church on the Lord's Day in this position like I once did. I must be on the job every minute.' Point No. 2. He said 'on the Lord's Day.' The third thing, he quoted from memory verses 19 to 31 of the 107th Psalm, and I never heard it quite in the same way; he made it a new song to me. I said to him, I am both amazed and pleased.

"When he finished his eyes were filled with tears, and I said, 'I thank you; it was worth a trip over the Atlantic to hear the First Lord of the Admiralty quote that Psalm.'

"I said to Lord Reith, your Minister for Reconstruction, who has the colossal task of planning not only the rebuilding of the ruins of London, but of all Britain: 'It is a very strange experience, Lord Reith.' He looked at me, and he said: 'I don't think so. I believe profoundly that for Britain and America this war is a judgment of Almighty God.'"

Speaking of his own work in America, Dr. Norris said: "Detroit is the biggest industrial place in the world, and the hardest place for preaching the Gospel. When I went there I was told I had made a mistake. I said: 'I am going to put up the biggest tent ever.' I was told: 'You can't hold tent meetings here. People won't come. You just can't do it.'

"But I did. I put up a tent 272 feet long and 166 feet wide, and 1,012 people were converted and joined that church in three months. I preached there every night, sometimes we were cold and oftimes shivering, but there was not a single service when people were not saved, for over three months.

"I don't put in a great deal of time there. Both the churches, the one at Forth Worth and the one at

Dr. Norris in the privet office of the Grand Mufti at Jerusalem.

# CHAPTER XII

## DR. NORRIS' CONNECTION WITH THE OUT STANDING MEN IN BUSINESS AND GOVERNMENT

### By BEAUCHAMP VICK

One of Dr. Norris' favorite texts: is "The king's heart is in the hand of the Lord, as the rivers of water: he turneth it whithersoever he will."

I have seen this demonstrated times, without number.

For instance, when the Temple Church wanted the big lot on Oakman Boulevard for the famous tent meeting in 1935, it was already rented to a circus, but Dr. Norris made his appeal to Colonel Robert Oakman who had been three times Mayor of the City, and was one of Detroit's outstanding citizens, and he granted this lot free for the entire summer.

Another example was the famous Cadillac lot, where the old Cadillac factory had been located, owned by General Motors, and the church wanted this vacant square for a temporary tabernacle. General motors turned down the request, but Dr. Norris secured an interview with the head of General Motors and rented the lot for five hundred dollars a month for fifteen months, and at the end of the fifteen months, the church owed General Motors $7,500.00, and Dr. Norris took it up with Mr. William Knudsen, president, and said, "Mr. Knudsen, you don't need that money, and Temple Church is now carrying a heavy burden in building its buildings."

Mr. Knudsen took the contract and wrote across the front of it, "P-A-I-D."

Perhaps the most remarkable example was when Dr. Norris first came to Detroit and found a city ordinance that forbad the erection of any tent or tabernacle except by the consent of the Council of Churches and it would have been like feeding raw meat to wild animals for Dr. Norris to ask this modernistic Detroit Council of Churches for permission to put up a tent or tabernacle.

He made application for the above-mentioned tent on Oakman Boulevard and immediately the then-secretary of the Detroit Council of Churches filed an objection and when the matter came before the Common Council, strange to say, the Council chamber was packed full, and when the request of the Temple Church was read, there was an immediate objection by the Secretary of the Detroit Council of Churches and their lawyer.

Dr. Norris had already been to the several members of the Common Council, the Honorable John Lodge, Eugene Van Antwerp, and others. Mr. Van Antwerp is one of the leading Roman Catholics of the city and after the objection had been filed against the Temple Church securing the permit, Mr. Van Antwerp rose and said, "I know that there is a law that permission should be obtained through the ministerial alliance or the Detroit Council of Churches, but this Council is the law, and what Detroit needs is a great revival, as a Roman Catholic and not a Baptist – I move that we suspend this law and give Dr. Norris his permit."

Dr. Norris rose and thanked the Council and led the whole crowd singing, "Old Time Religion."

### Church Office Building

Another example in the building of our three-story office building, the law required that there be cement floors, expensive roof and other fire-proof construction which we could not afford at that time. Two inspectors came out and condemned the building and threatened to lock the doors unless we tore up the floors and put an entire new construction in the roof, which would have cost us thirty or forty thousand dollars.

Again, Dr. Norris went before the Common Council and that was the last of that trouble.

And only recently another example. How the Lord uses the powers that be to His own glory!

The above picture was the speaker's stand at the Economic Club where fifteen hundred industrialists gathered to hear Hon. Sam Rayburn, Speaker of the House of representatives. Reading from left to right, the are: Dr. J. Frank Norris, Malcom W. Bingay, Editor of the Detroit Free Press; Hon Sam Ryaburn, Speaker of the House of Representatives, and Mr. B.E. Hutchinson, Execitive Vice-President and Finance Committee Chairman of the Chrysler Corporation.

## Our Magnificent Four and One Third Acres in the Ten Thousand Block, Grand River Avenue, For Which We Paid $45,000 And For Which We Have Been Offered Much Higher Price

The Department of Parks and Recreation gave notice that they were going to condemn half of that magnificent property and were going to take it away from us, because the city needed this strategically-located property as a public park or play-ground. That would mean an absolute defeat of our larger plans. Again, Dr. Morris and I went before the Common Council and the result is, the Temple Baptist Church retains the entire property.

### Transportation Provided

On Dr. Norris' several trips abroad, he never asked the automobile, corporations for any favors, and never has asked them for any favors. The truth is, one of them sent a handsome check as a donation to him personally and he very promptly wrote a letter of thanks and returned it, stating that he could not accept any gifts personally, and they made the donation to the church.

On, one of his trips to Palestine, General Motors furnished a Buick car, chauffeur and interpreter for the entire time.

On three pf his other trips, the Ford Motor Company offered, and he accepted their kindness of transportation.

Just recently, on our latest trip, we were facing the question of getting plane reservations for the last leg of our journey from London to Palestine on account of the Italian Government holding priority. We were stymied at this end, but Dr. Norris had a warm friend in Sir Stanford Cooper, head of the Ford Motor Company in Great Britain and Europe. He had furnished Dr. Norris transportation in England and had met Dr. and Mrs. Norris several times at the pier and airport when they landed. The Preacher called him over long distance trans-Atlantic phone and stated our dilema. Sir Stanford said, "Cable me what you want and I will present it to the minister of transportation." We had immediate results, as the following cable well shows:

When Hon. Sam Rayburnm Speaker of the House of Representatives of the American Congress, was the guest of Mr. K.T. Keller, President of the Chrysler Corporation, and Dr. J. Frank Norris, they went through the largest tank factory in the world, The Chrysler Tank Factory.

From right to left, Hon. Sam Rayburn, President K.T. Keller and Dr. J. Frank Norris.

WESTERN UNION

"NLT Dr. Frank Norris Temple Baptist Church
" '4th and Marquette Sts Det.

"Thanks for cable Mr. Bowers of our traffic department will try to arrange as you desire and will keep you informed AAA Understand your arrival date London airport will be August 20 AAA Have confirmed the booking at Savoy Hotel for three persons AAA Will your party be three or four in England AAA Glad to speak to you last night.

Stanford Cooper."

In his connections with high officials at Washington and the governors of several states, if doesn't make any difference whether they are Republicans or Democrats, as the Apostle Paul said, "I am become all things to all men, that I might by all means..." get to Palestine... or wherever else he wants to go.

**Secretary of State**

Former Secretary of State Cordell Hull, I know, rendered him several special favors.

For instance, when I went to the Orient, I did not know I was going until Thursday night before I left on Sunday night. I had no passport, I had made no preparation. Dr. Norris said, "You're going to China and Japan." I appreciated his enthusiasm but deplored his judgment, as I knew it was impossible. But, to my surprise, Friday morning he called up the Secretary of State and though I had not made any application, he told the Secretary of State he had to have the passport by the following Sunday morning, two days afterwards. The Secretary of State said, "You get the application in, and I will get the passport back to you." That was only two days before. I filed the necessary application and early Sunday morning a Special-Delivery registered letter came, and it was my Passport to China, Japan, Manchuria and Korea. That was really cutting the Washington red-tape in a hurry.

Then there remained the question of transportation, and Dr. Norris was a great personal friend of Mr. C. R. Smith, President of American Airlines, and he called him and secured my round-trip ticket from Detroit to Seattle and upon my return from the Orient the proper plane reservation from San Francisco to Los Angeles and then to Fort Worth and on back to Detroit. Then he had another friend who was agent for the biggest shipping company and secured steamer passage without delay on that trip.

Everything went according to clockwork and I got back to Detroit within two minutes of my scheduled time, after going half way around the world and back.

I mention these things not to boast, but to prove that the Scriptures are true, "The king's heart is in the hand of the Lord, as the rivers of water: he turneth it whithersoever he will" (Prov. 21:1).

Take another case; as everybody knows, we have been up against it to get cars. The Temple office force and the First Baptist Church and the Seminary were without cars and one Monday morning he and I went over to see the Chrysler people. The top executives were in a meeting and he called out of that meeting, Mr. Vanderzee, Vice-President and general Sales Manager of that great corporation, and told him what we wanted. We asked for three cars, but got four instead. This also has been true of both Ford and General Motors. These great corporations believe in the work that the Temple Baptist Church, the First Baptist Church and the Bible Baptist Seminary are doing.

I HAVE KNOWN DR. NORRIS FOR TWENTY- SEVEN YEARS, AND UP TO THIS HOUR I HAVE NEVER SEEN HIM FEAR TO FACE ANY UNOPENED SEA OR ANY BURNING SANDS OR ANY WALLED CITY OF THE ENEMY.

ONE OF THE MOST UNUSUAL THINGS ABOUT THIS UNUSUAL MAN IS THAT NEITHER PUBLICLY NOR PRIVATELY – AND I SUPPOSE THAT I HAVE BEEN AS CLOSE TO HIM AS ANY LIVING MAN OVER THIS PERIOD OF TIME – I HAVE NEVER HEARD HIM, EVEN IN OUR PRIVATE CONVERSATION, UTTER ONE WORD OF PESSIMISM.

HE SEES NO DIFFICULTIES AND RECOGNIZES NO POSSIBILITY OF DEFEAT. IN OTHER WORDS, HE GOES ON THE THEORY THAT AS LONG AS A MAN KEEPS ON FIGHTING HE IS NOT LICKED, BECAUSE THE FIGHT IS NOT OVER.

When Dr. Norris spoke to over 6,000 business men in the beautiful ball room of the Texas Hotel, Fort Worth, at a luncheon given in his honor, October 1939.

## Traitors On The Inside

Of course, in building a work of world-wide interest and receiving more than fourteen thousand new members in Temple Church, it was inevitable that there would be many eddies, sometimes traitors, as our Lord had.

On one occasion, when a man whom we had trusted and who was the teacher of a large class at that time – he was shrewd enough to cover up his tracks and build a little nest for himself – in fact, build the class away from the church – when he pulled off a little eddy or revolt, I called up Dr. Norris by long distance in Fort Worth and instead of his being disturbed, without a second's hesitation, he said, "The finest thing that could happen to the Temple Baptist Church!"

I wasn't quite ready to see it fully at that time, but it wasn't long before his judgment was vindicated and that proved to be the remaking of that class, and truly a great thing had happened to the Temple Baptist Church.

One of Dr. Norris' slogans is that a "whirling grindstone throws off muddy water."

Hon. Winston Churchill – picture given to Dr. Norris in an interview with Churchill when he was Prime Minister, September, 1941

### Visit To The Prime Minister

In his contacts with men abroad, heads of governments, perhaps the most outstanding example was when he was the guest of Prime Minister Winston Churchill for a period of forty-five minutes and when he left after the interview, Mr. Churchill said, "Before you return to America, please call me again."

Of course, these great contacts have been used by him solely and wholly for one purpose and that is for the work that he represents. He has never profited by these contacts himself, but his work has, and I am in the position to testify firsthand of the wonderful blessings it has brought to our work.

But the most notable and profitable contact of men in high authority was when Dr. Norris made three trips to Washington to see his personal friend, Secretary of State Cordell Hull, and secured the release from a Japanese prison of our missionaries, Dr. and Mrs. Fred Donnelson, Lois Donnelson (now Mrs. Bill Logan), and Oscar Wells, wife and baby.

There had been only one relief ship before this bringing Americans home from Japanese prisons. And but for the intervention of Dr. Norris and the several trips to Washington, which he made at his own expense and time, they would have remained and might have died as others died who remain in this awful prison.

The father of Mrs. Oscar Wells, Dr. Lee S. Huizenga, died in this same prison of starvation.

Even after he secured the release of Mrs. Donnelson and Lois and the Wells family Dr. Fred Donnelson was not on the list. When Dr. Norris received this information, a long list from the Secretary of State, he jumped on a plane one morning at four o'clock and went to see Secretary of State Cordell Hull and made the plea that he intervene with the Japanese command at Shanghai, but intervention had to be made through the Swiss Embassy through the Swiss Government, and in the last nick of time Fred Donnelson was released.

Nobody asked Dr. Norris to do this but he did it as a matter of love.

Of course, such contacts as no other minister that I know of has been able to make, would inevitably provoke a certain amount of jealousy. He says there are three ways to earn the jealousy, especially of preachers – first, having more; second, doing more; third, knowing more.

It seems that Dr. Norris has been guilty of these three things at some time or another.

He has been assailed and attacked perhaps as no minister since the days of the Apostle Paul.

I was present through the ill-fated radio hate-fest for eight nights in 1926, when the denominational leaders went on the radio for eight nights for the kill, and I sat by his side from then on through every conflict and in answer to every mean thing that has ever been said, published or circulated about him, his one word is, "May God pity and forgive."

And, incidentally, it has been rather peculiar that every man who has schemed to destroy his work has fulfilled the promise of God – "No weapon that is formed against thee shall prosper; and every tongue that shall rise against thee in judgment thou shalt condemn. This is the heritage of the servants of the Lord, and their righteousness is of me, saith the Lord."

20,000 hear Dr. Norris on his return from one his trips around the world, Oct. 1, 1939

# Dr. Norris' Letter To President Truman

Fort Worth, Texas<br>
Oct. 2, 1947

Hon. Harry S. Truman
President United States
Washington, D. C.

Dear Mr. President:

Mr. Matthew J. Connelly wired me New York October 1st and suggested that I write you certain matters of my trip to Palestine. First, I want to thank you for your very kind personal letter of August 5th, which was of invaluable assistance in all my travels.

I have given extensive study to the Jewish Palestinian question. The issue is whether we will take the authority of the Bible of our mothers or the Koran with the sword and flame.

In that whole controversy the big issue is who owns the land, who has the title to that land f If that question is settled there is no other question.

The Lord God Almighty in Genesis the 17th chapter, specifically states that the title to Palestine is given not to Ishmael, the ancestor of the Arabs, but to Isaac and his seed for ever.

"And God said, Sarah thy wife shall bear thee a son indeed; and thou shalt call his name Isaac: and I will establish my covenant with him for an everlasting covenant, and with his seed after him." (Gen. 17:19)

This covenant was confirmed to Isaac – Genesis 26:3 –

"Sojourn in this land, and I will be with thee, and will bless thee; for unto thee, and unto thy seed, I will give all these countries, and I will perform the oath which I sware unto Abraham thy father."

This covenant was also confirmed to Jacob – Genesis 28:13:

"And, behold, the Lord stood before it, and said, I am the Lord God of Abraham thy father, and the God of Isaac: the land whereon thou liest, to thee will I give it, and to thy seed."

The covenant was likewise confirmed to Moses in Deuteronomy 30:3-5.

"That then the Lord thy God will turn thy captivity, and have compassion upon thee, and will return and gather thee from all the nations whither the Lord thy God hath scattered thee.

"If any of thine be driven out unto the outmost parts of heaven, from thence will the Lord thy God gather thee, and from thence will he fetch them.

"And the Lord thy God will bring thee into the land which thy fathers possessed, and thou shalt possess it; and he will do thee good, and multiply thee above thy fathers."

David specifically states the title to that land is to the Jews and the descendants of Jacob; Psalm 105:9-12:

"Which covenant he made with Abraham, and his oath unto Isaac;

"And confirmed the same unto Jacob for a law, and to Israel for an everlasting covenant.

"Saying, Unto thee will I give the land of Canaan, the lot of your inheritance:

"When they were but a few men in number; yea, very few, and strangers in it."

Thirteen hundred years ago the Arabs were usurpers, Mohammet with fire and sword, and they were robbers of property that belongs to the Jews.

A second and very important authority in addition to Scriptural authority, Great Britain was given mandate over Palestine for the purpose of Jewish immigration into that land and for making it a national home.

This mandate was confirmed by the United States Government and by the 57 Nations of the League of Nations.

The tragedy and the cause of all the present trouble is that Neville Chamberlain, Prime Minister, put on a two-fold appeasement in 1939.

First, with Hitler, and that brought on World War II.

Second, with the Arabs, who were the allies of Hitler.

Chamberlain violated the international law giving that land as a national home for Jews in 1939, and said only 70,000 Jews would be permitted to go; for the next five years, and after that none except by the consent of the Arabs. But the mandate made no such restrictions.

Therefore the present Jewish immigration into Palestine is not "illegal"; it's legal,

Based on the mandate given to Great Britain over Palestine, and confirmed by the United States Government and confirmed % the League of Nations, the Jews invested six hundred and fifty million dollars in Palestine, built cities, public works, and the curse of God Almighty is on every hand that violates this most solemn agreement – the mandate three times over confirmed.

Now, Mr. President, it certainly is a matter that should cause us to stop and think that the Arab leaders from the Grand Mufti on down were allies of Hitler, and it ill becomes them to come now into court with their hands dripping with the blood of the Jews—six million of them murdered by Hitler.

I interviewed many Arab leaders, and without question I found that the whole crowd are for Stalin, just like they formerly were for Hitler.

While this country was fighting Hitler, thirty thousand young Jews from Palestine volunteered and went to the battle front and not a single Arab regiment.

If the Arabs and Jews in Palestine were left alone they would get along and settle their troubles.

Russia is doing everything at her command to foment the trouble.

The time has come, and long past, when the United States should keep its promise and take a firm stand for law and order in that land that has given the world its Bible and Saviour.

Yours very sincerely,

JFN ;r

J. FRANK NORRIS

THE WHITE HOUSE
WASHINGTON

October 7, 1947

Dear Dr. Norris;

I am most grateful for your thoughtful letter of October second. I deeply appreciate having the benefit of this expression of your views because I know that you have given long and extensive study to the Jewish Palestinian question.

Very sincerely yours,

Harry Truman

Reverend J. Frank Norris,
First Baptist Church,
4th and Throckmorton Streets,
Fort Worth, Texas.

President Truman asked for an opinion of Dr. Norris on the Palestine situation, and upon receipt of the information the President sent the above personal letter.

Upon Dr. Norris' return from his fifth tour of Europe and Palestine he spoke to a great crowd at LaGrave baseball park in Fort Worth, October 5th, 1947. Because of the huge crescent shape of LaGrave baseball park and because of the immense crowd, it was impossible to take a panoramic view in one picture. Only several shots could be taken and while some of these may overlap, yet the photographer was unable to take the entire crowd and several sections did not show.

Another angle of the Crowd at LaGrave Field.

Two Views Student Body Bible Baptist Seminary – in order to give the fill student body, it was inevitable that they would overlap but the great hall was filled with only students and faculty.

Made in the USA
Lexington, KY
24 September 2015